SEXUAL HARASSMENT

A Reference Handbook

Second Edition

Other Titles in ABC-CLIO's
CONTEMPORARY
WORLD ISSUES
Series

Books in the Contemporary World Issues series address vital issues in today's society such as terrorism, sexual harassment, homelessness, AIDS, gambling, animal rights, and air pollution. Written by professional writers, scholars, and nonacademic experts, these books are authoritative, clearly written, up-to-date, and objective. They provide a good starting point for research by high school and college students, scholars, and general readers, as well as by legislators, businesspeople, activists, and others.

Each book, carefully organized and easy to use, contains an overview of the subject; a detailed chronology; biographical sketches; facts and data and/or documents and other primary-source material; a directory of organizations and agencies; annotated lists of print and nonprint resources; a glossary; and an index.

Readers of books in the Contemporary World Issues series will find the information they need in order to better understand the social, political, environmental, and economic issues facing the world today.

SEXUAL HARASSMENT

A Reference Handbook

Second Edition

Lynne Eisaguirre

CONTEMPORARY WORLD ISSUES

ABC-CLIO

Santa Barbara, California
Denver, Colorado
Oxford, England

Library of Congress Cataloging-in-Publication Data

Eisaguirre, Lynne, 1951–
  Sexual harassment : reference handbook / Lynne Eisaguirre. — 2nd ed.
    p. cm.—(Contemporary world issues)
  Includes bibliographical references and index.
  ISBN 0-87436-971-1 (alk. paper)
  1. Sex discrimination—Law and legislation—United States. 2. Sex discrimination—United States. I. Title. II. Series.
KF4758.E36 1997
342.73'0878—dc21   97-35489
                                                              CIP

02 01 00 99 98   10 9 8 7 6 5 4 3

ABC-CLIO, Inc.
130 Cremona Drive, P.O. Box 1911
Santa Barbara, California 93116-1911

This book is printed on acid-free paper ⊚ .

Manufactured in the United States of America

342.73
E13

For Elizabeth and Nicholas:
May they live in a world without walls.

Contents

4 Facts and Statistics, 81

Preface

The purpose of this book is to provide access to the available information, as well as the full range of thought, on sexual harassment in employment and education. It is not intended to promote any particular view, except the view that all commentators should be heard and considered. Historical and factual background information is offered, along with resources for further exploration into the legal, social, psychological, and political aspects of sexual harassment. Because this work gathers together a wide array of information not available in any other single source, it may prove helpful to many different people—students, researchers, writers, journalists, historians, and activists, as well as individuals who are interested in clarifying their own thoughts and feelings about sexual harassment. In this fast-changing and evolving field, however, be aware that any single source mentioned may be out-of-date by the time you read this book.

A particular attempt has been made to include writers and activists who question the whole idea of the imposition of legal or social penalties for what is called sexual harassment. Such voices are few and have been difficult to identify, because there is a lack of expression of what seems to be an increasingly unpopular viewpoint.

Organization

Like other titles in the Contemporary World Issues series, this book is meant to serve as a complete resource and a guide to further research. Chapter 2 sets the historical context with a chronology that includes significant legislation, court decisions, trends, political events, and other relevant occurrences. This chronology is necessarily limited, as the term *sexual harassment* did not even come into the lexicon until the 1970s. Chapter 3 contains biographical sketches of some key persons in the field, including activists, lawyers, politicians, commentators, and others. Chapter 4 offers factual information about sexual harassment, including laws and policies, statistics, relevant studies, and a summary of important cases. Chapter 5 is an annotated directory of organizations, including activist groups, research organizations, educational organizations, legal defense funds, political lobbying groups, and support services. Chapter 6 is an annotated bibliography of print resources, such as bibliographies, anthologies, books and monographs, and loose-leaf services. Chapter 7 is an annotated listing of nonprint resources, including films and videocassettes. A glossary of important terms, a note on how to read legal citations (following the Preface), and an index complete the volume.

About the Language Used in This Book

Because the vast majority of sexual harassment claims are brought by women against men, this book uses feminine pronouns in places where use of the words *he or she* seems awkward or incorrect. This is not meant to deny that women sometimes sexually harass men or that same-sex harassment occurs but is simply an attempt to make the text easier to read.

In addition, much of the information about sexual harassment focuses on legal decisions. To avoid continually interrupting the text with complex discussions, many legal terms are used without explanation. Consult the glossary for any legal terms that are unfamiliar to you.

How To Read Case and Statute Citations

A case may be reported by several different reporting services, which are generally found in law libraries. If a case is decided by the United States Supreme Court, it will be found first in a loose-leaf service entitled *U.S. Law Week* (U.S.L.W.) and then, later, in either the *United States Reports* (U.S.) or the *Supreme Court Reporter* (S. Ct.). If it is a federal case decided by a court other than the U.S. Supreme Court (either a federal district or federal appeals court), you can find the case soon after it has been decided in *U.S. Law Week* and then in either the *Federal Reporter, Second Series* (F.2d) or the *Federal Supplement* (F. Supp.).

Most state courts print their own official state reports. In addition, all published state court decisions are included in the West Reporter System. The West Company has divided the country into seven regions. A particular state's court decisions will be reported in the reporter for the region to which that state has been assigned. The abbreviations for these reporters are as follows:

- A. and A.2d: The *Atlantic Reporter (First and Second Series)*, which includes decisions from Connecticut, Delaware, the District of Columbia,

Maine, Maryland, New Hampshire, New Jersey, Pennsylvania, Rhode Island, and Vermont.

- N.E. and N.E.2d: *Northeastern Reporter (First and Second Series)*, which includes decisions from Illinois, Indiana, Massachusetts, New York (except for decisions from New York appellate courts, which are published in a separate volume, *New York Supplement* [N.Y.S.]), and Ohio.
- N.W. and N.W.2d: *Northwestern Reporter (First and Second Series)*, which includes decisions from Iowa, Michigan, Minnesota, Nebraska, North Dakota, South Dakota, and Wisconsin.
- P. and P.2d: *Pacific Reporter (First and Second Series)*, which includes decisions from Alaska, Arizona, California (except California appellate decisions, which are published in a separate volume, the *California Reporter* [Cal. Rptr.]), Colorado, Hawaii, Idaho, Kansas, Montana, Nevada, New Mexico, Oklahoma, Oregon, Utah, Washington, and Wyoming.
- S.E. and S.E.2d: *Southeastern Reporter (First and Second Series)*, which includes decisions from Georgia, North Carolina, South Carolina, Virginia, and West Virginia.
- So. and So.2d: *Southern Reporter (First and Second Series)*, which includes decisions from Alabama, Florida, Louisiana, and Mississippi.
- S.W. and S.W.2d: *Southwestern Reporter (First and Second Series)*, which includes decisions from Arkansas, Kentucky, Missouri, Tennessee, and Texas.

A case citation provides the names of the people, schools, government agencies, or companies on each side of a case (the plaintiff[s] and defendants[s]); the volume of the reporter in which the case can be found; the page number on which the case begins; and the year in which the case was decided. For example:

Ellison v. Brady, 924 F.2d 872 (9th Cir. 1991)

Ellison and Brady are the names of the parties involved in the case. Ellison is the plaintiff and Brady is the defendant. The case is reported in volume 924 of the *Federal Reporter, Second Series,* beginning on page 872. The Ninth Circuit (a federal court of appeals) decided the case in 1991.

Introduction 1

The Current Controversy

Since the first edition of *Sexual Harassment: A Reference Handbook* was published in 1993, I have spoken to hundreds of groups and organizations about the subject of sexual harassment; trained thousands of employees, managers, and executives; and consulted with dozens of corporate executive officers (CEOs), administrators, and organizations about specific complaints or investigations. Each month during the past four years, I have expected the furor and headlines over sexual harassment to diminish, yet each morning's newspaper seems to bring some new outcry, scandal, investigation, or complaint about the issue.

Haven't we educated the entire country on this issue? I keep wondering. *Aren't we ready to move on to some other topic?*

Apparently not. As this book goes to press, the United States Supreme Court has just decided that the sitting president of the United States, Bill Clinton, will be required to respond to a sexual harassment lawsuit brought by Paula Jones, a former employee of the state of Arkansas. One of the highest ranking officers in the army, Sergeant Major of the Army Gene McKinney, recently appointed to an army panel charged with combating sexual harassment, has himself been accused of sexual harassment by Sergeant Major Brenda Hoster, his former press aide. Two of the four women finally admitted to the previously all-male Citadel in Charleston, South Carolina, after a fight for admission that rose all the way to the Supreme Court, have resigned, claiming severe and repeated sexual harassment. And in response to news reports, a national debate has erupted over whether grade school children should be disciplined for sexual harassment when they kiss a playmate on the schoolyard.

What accounts for the continuing attention to this issue? Is it, as Molly Yard, the former head of the National Organization for Women, concluded after the Clarence Thomas confirmation hearings, that "men just don't get it"? Or is it, as some commentators complain, that women are either lying about the issue or hypersensitive? Perhaps, as critics of the legal system claim, too many people are lawsuit happy and use the court system as a kind of legalized blackmail, forcing large organizations to pay money for dubious claims rather than risk public exposure of the lawsuit or the unpredictability of a jury trial.

Although this book takes no position on the answers to these questions, it will allow readers to find the resources, people, and facts to determine their own conclusions. What is clear is that since the first edition of this book was published, the national preoccupation with sexual harassment has continued. Courts, juries, attorneys, activists, researchers, and lawmakers have kept up the debate to define and redress the issue of sexual harassment. Major events and milestones have punctuated the discourse, including the resolution of the 1991 U.S. Navy Tailhook scandal; the resignation of Senator Robert Packwood; the unanimous Supreme Court *Harris v. Forklift* decision, which affirmed that a recipient of sexual harassment need not prove severe psychological injury to sue for damages; and the $7.1 million in damages a jury awarded against the world's largest law firm, Baker and McKenzie.

The Continuing Clarence Thomas/ Anita Hill Controversy

The shock waves from the 1991 Clarence Thomas confirmation hearings also continued to reverberate. When I speak to groups about this issue, I am still asked—six years later—whom I believe and what I think happened. I never answer those questions, since I was not present during the investigation or during the alleged incidents. Yet I do acknowledge that the hearings sparked the enduring national "teach-in" on sexual harassment and have served as a prime example of how *not* to conduct an investigation.

Other authors have expressed their own opinions about why this historical event still fuels arguments. Celia Morris, author of *Bearing Witness: Sexual Harassment and Beyond—Everywoman's Story*, writes,

> The hearings were that important because Americans had sat before their television sets transfixed by a spectacle unprecedented in our history—yet at the same time, by a scene that felt painfully familiar: an obscure woman publicly accusing a powerful man of verbal sexual abuse and intimidation, and in response, a jury of even more powerful men abusing her once again. (Morris 1994, p. 5)

The hearings have spawned new books on the subject, including the best-selling *The Real Anita Hill* by David Brock, a writer for the *American Spectator,* who claimed that evidence exists to support the view that Anita Hill lied or was confused about the entire issue. Senator John Danforth issued his own proclamation and a defense of his role in the hearings as a friend and supporter of Thomas in *Resurrection: The Confirmation of Clarence Thomas.* Two writers for the *Wall Street Journal,* Jane Mayer and Jill Abramson, weighed in with *Strange Justice: The Selling of Clarence Thomas,* asserting that credible evidence and witnesses existed but were not offered during the hearings to prove that Anita Hill was telling the truth. And Hill, who had long resisted the idea of writing a book, finally realized that her life would never be the same and signed a reported million-dollar contract to write two books on the issue, one from a policy perspective and the other more personal. Both are scheduled for publication in 1997.

The Controversy for Women: Speak Out or Remain Silent?

More women are starting to speak up about sexual harassment. In the years between 1985 and 1990, the number of sexual harassment complaints filed with the Equal Employment Opportunity Commission (EEOC) went from 4,953 to 5,557. Since 1989, the number of sexual harassment charges has increased 112 percent each year. As a result of charges resolved by the EEOC in 1993, 1,546 complainants won $25.2 million in benefits from their employers (Center for Women in Government 1994). Yet researchers report that 80 to 90 percent of sexual harassment cases go unreported, mainly became women fear reprisals or disbelief.

Public cases continue to prove that some women's fears of retaliation are well-founded. The original 1981 U.S. Merit Systems study found that the majority of victims who responded assertively believed doing so "made things better." But in reanalyzing these data, researchers found that "assertive responding was associated with more negative outcomes of every type—psychological, work related, and health related" (Koss et al. 1994, p. 135).

The Tailhook scandal, in which 83 women were assaulted or molested at a U.S. Navy convention in 1991, and subsequent events, including a top admiral's manipulation of the investigation to shield his own involvement in the incidents, provide an example of the reprisals women may face when they speak out. Lieutenant Paula Coughlin, who had been present at Tailhook and who was instrumental in pressing for subsequent investigations, resigned because of continued harassment over the scandal. Upon resigning, Coughlin stated in a public letter, "The physical attack on me by the naval aviators at the 1991 Tailhook convention and the covert attacks on me that followed have stripped me of my ability to serve" (*New York Times*, February 11, 1994, Section A, p. 24, column 4).

Recent studies have continued to show that at any given time at least 15 percent of working women have been harassed within the past year, and 40 to 60 percent of American women suffer harassment at some point in their careers. Yet a *Working Woman* survey has discovered that only 21 percent of women feel justice is done in harassment cases. Sixty percent report that such charges are either ignored or the harassers are insufficiently punished—and 55 percent say most harassers get off scot-free. A 1993 *Washington Post* poll of women working on Capitol Hill found that half of the respondents had either been harassed or knew of someone who had and that one-third of the harassment cases involved wrongdoing on the part of a representative or a senator. Two-thirds of those surveyed would not come forward to complain because of fear of reprisals. What is especially significant about these figures is that this survey was conducted after the Hill/Thomas, Tailhook, and Packwood incidents.

Courtroom Controversies

At least in the legal system, as more sexual harassment cases have wound their way through the courts, a national shift in consciousness has occurred around the issue of sexual harassment. Significantly, the *Harris v. Forklift* decision was unanimous, swift, and brief—a rare example of harmony in a usually divided Supreme Court. The decision supported the view that an employee need not be forced to resign or to "have a nervous breakdown," as Justice O'Connor wrote, for harassment to be taken seriously. The $7.1 million awarded by a mostly male jury in the sexual harassment case filed against Baker and McKenzie (later reduced by the judge to $3.5 million and now on appeal) sent a clear message to employers that they cannot ignore claims against a successful owner of a firm and that they are responsible for creating a safe, nondiscriminatory workplace free from sexual harassment.

At the same time, other legal issues in the area of sexual harassment remain murky. The 1991 "reasonable woman" standard, created by some federal courts to allow for the perspectives and experiences of women, for example, was not clarified by the *Harris* decision and continues to be tested by lower courts, with varying results. Although the standard may have sensitized the judicial system to the experiences of women—especially in ambiguous situations—some researchers and lawmakers have noted that it may not be as efficacious as had been hoped. On a theoretical level, academicians such as Barbara Gutek and Jolynn Childers began to examine whether the "reasonable woman" standard may in fact reify old stereotypes of gender difference and hurt those women who seek justice within the courts.

Recently, many mental-health professionals have started to examine the professional standards and ethical concerns of sexual harassment. They have focused on defining sexual harassment as a stressful, psychologically damaging experience with long-lasting effects. Although previous studies have overwhelmingly demonstrated a perceptual gap between men and women as to what constitutes sexual harassment, some researchers such as Barbara Gutek, Beth Dietz-Uhler, and Audrey Murrell, among others, have found that the public outcry may have had some impact on men's understanding of what constitutes sexual harassment.

Many workplaces and schools now have sexual harassment policies and procedures. For instance, 73 percent of the lawyers who responded to a survey conducted by the *National Law Journal* said their firms had adopted detailed sexual harassment policies, almost double the 38 percent in a survey four years earlier (Slade 1994).

Unfortunately, many workplace policies may be inadequate or too formalized or may have been implemented unartfully, thereby creating an atmosphere of mistrust between men and women. At the beginning of training sessions I have conducted, many male managers have asserted that they intend to solve the problem of sexual harassment by simply not hiring women, not traveling with women, and not being alone with women. Clearly, such solutions only lead to new forms of discrimination.

With each step forward, there has been a corresponding backlash. The rise in the number of court cases has triggered a legal trend as employers seek to minimize their liability through aggressive tactics that attack female complainants' credibility. Many women, such as Lieutenant Paula Coughlin, who have been public whistle-blowers, assert that retaliation is alive and well. The media has sensationalized the issue by characterizing public pressure for the adoption of sexual harassment policies as witch-hunting by hypersensitive women. At times, media reports have clearly sacrificed facts for sensational headlines, as in the case of numerous public reports of grade school teachers disciplining students over kissing incidents. Television and print sources ignored the fact that such discipline usually occurred when students and their parents complained about repeated behavior, not just after one playful kiss.

New Schoolroom and College Controversies

Despite the public surprise and media skepticism about sexual harassment in schools, the situation has been documented by two recent major studies. In a 1993 *Seventeen* magazine poll of 4,200 girls ages 9 to 19, 89 percent reported having experienced harassment such as pinching or grabbing, with 39 percent of respondents experiencing harassment at school on a daily basis. A survey commissioned by the American Association of University Women (AAUW) in 1993 showed that most at-school harassment occurs in grades six through nine, peaking in seventh grade. That survey, the "Hostile Hallways" poll of eighth to eleventh graders conducted by Lou Harris and Associates, also found that 85 percent of girls and 76 percent of boys reported experiencing harassment at school. Most said harassment came from fellow students, but 25 percent of the girls said they had been harassed by a teacher or another school employee.

Sexual harassment of girls by boys includes everything from obscene graffiti, jokes, and taunts to "bra-snapping" or "skirt-flipping days," from groping and pinching to assembling lists of "sluts" or "dogs." Although they are aware of much of this harassment, many teachers and administrators consider it normal behavior for boys and do little to stop it. As a result, many girls feel helpless and fearful: 33 percent of girls responding to the Harris poll said they did not want to come to school after being harassed, and 39 percent reported feeling afraid in school.

Following the media publicity and commentary skeptical of the high percentage of students who had experienced harassment—much of it critical of the AAUW report—researchers Eleanor Linn and colleagues (1996) reexamined the AAUW data, filtering out those incidents that did not fall within the stricter sexual harassment definitions. They found that the numbers were still almost as high as those in the AAUW report.

The girls involved in actual court cases tell stories that may silence many critics who think the issue of sexual harassment in schools is exaggerated. In the first agency complaint pursued by a grade school girl in 1993, six-year-old Cheltzie Hentz of Eden Prairie, Minnesota, had grown tired of feeling afraid of the boys who had been taunting her with sexual obscenities on the school bus. She and her parents had complained repeatedly to the school, but the school refused to respond and the sexual taunting and teasing continued. Cheltzie filed and won a Title IX claim with the U.S. Education Department Office of Civil Rights against her school district for failing to protect her from student-to-student, or "peer," harassment, the first such reported decision.

Similarly, Katy Lyle, a Duluth, Minnesota, high school sophomore and honor student who had never had a boyfriend, was shocked to learn that a stall in the boys' restroom was covered with sexual graffiti about her, including such expressions as "Katie Lyle is a slut. Katie Lyle sucked my d--- after she sucked my dog's d---. Here's Katie Lyle's number." Katy and her parents repeatedly complained to the school. At first the principal told Katy to ignore the incident, claiming "boys will be boys." When her parents continued to complain, the school said this was a building maintenance issue and that the school had no money to repaint until the next year. Rumors swirled around the school, and during her long daily bus ride Katy was harassed by boys who repeated the graffiti. Katy's telephone rang repeatedly; callers would hang up when a family member answered. Katy became depressed, and her grades slipped. It took a formal complaint filed with the Minnesota Department of Human Rights to force the school to finally paint the walls.

Recent news reports have included accounts of the rape of a 13-year-old girl on a crowded school bus in Fort Worth, Texas; the sexual assault of numerous girls ages 10 to 16 by competing members of a Los Angeles gang, the Spur Posse; the abuse of a retarded 17-year-old girl in Glen Ridge, New Jersey, by 12 boys armed with bars and brooms; and attacks against girls at public pools in New York City, where boys formed "whirlpools" to surround and molest girls.

Proponents of educating grade school children about sexual harassment cite these severe and dramatic incidents to show why apparent overreactions by grade schools to recent well-publicized (and satirized) playground "kissing" incidents deserve more attention than we might believe at first. For one thing, assert experts such as Wellesley College's Nan Stein, we teach grade school kids about appropriate behavior; this should be no different. We may not want to use the term *sexual harassment,* Stein urges, but ignoring the issue allows it to escalate in a society in which sexual violence against young women has become increasingly common. And as one exasperated, anonymous dad asked in one news report, "How old does a little girl have to be before no means no?"

Academic researchers have also continued to document sexual harassment in colleges and universities. Yet attempts to regulate verbal sexual harassment have been met by an enraged outcry from professors and some students, who claim that First Amendment rights are especially precious and should prevail in university settings. In one well-publicized case, University of New Hampshire professor Donald Silva sued and won the right to be reinstated as a professor. The university had suspended him after charges that he used sexual examples in his class lectures. University officials, who were leery of lawsuits, hardly knew which way to turn.

In spite of these challenges, advocates continue to press for policies to prevent the sexual harassment of college women. Numerous studies by management consultant Freada Klein have found that 40 percent of undergraduate women and 28 percent of female graduate students have been harassed. Other recent surveys have placed the figures for undergraduates at 30 percent to 89 percent and for graduate students at 35 percent to 60 percent. (As noted in Chapter 4, differences in survey results may be large because of the way sexual harassment is defined, the respondents polled, or the way the survey questions are phrased.) Meanwhile, 11 percent of all (male and female) university staff and 14 percent of all faculty say they have been harassed by their peers or superiors. Perhaps more interesting, 26 percent of male faculty members say they have had voluntary sexual contact with students, whereas 48 percent of female faculty members say they have been harassed by students. As in other settings, most victims of campus harassment do not report it. Even if they confront their harassers in private, as surveys report 70 percent of those harassed do, both student and faculty victims of campus harassment may suffer permanent damage to their academic careers.

Some other researchers claim that military academies such as West Point, Annapolis, and the Citadel offer female students an even more controversial environment. A 1992 Air Force Academy study showed that 78 percent of female cadets and 52 percent of male cadets heard sexist and demeaning comments about women on a daily basis. In 1993, a study of all of the academies showed that 80 percent of female cadets had either experienced or heard about sexists comments within the past year.

In February 1994, the U.S. General Accounting Office (GAO) released a statement on harassment at U.S. military academies. Although few incidents are reported, the survey showed that nearly all women and virtually no men experience harassment—especially verbal—and subsequent stress. According to the GAO, fully one-half to three-quarters of all academy women encounter one or more of the following forms of harassment at least once a month: comments, jokes, or name calling; suggestive posters, graffiti, or pictures; obscene gestures or catcalls; sexually explicit letters or messages; exclusion by male cadets; sexual horseplay or hijinks; pressure for dates; or unwanted sexual advances. Even though all of the academies have instituted prevention and investigation procedures, most female cadets are afraid to go through the formal grievance channels and choose to deal with harassment informally. The GAO noted that none of the academies systematically evaluated or tracked the results of their sexual harassment policies in attempts to seek improvement.

The resignations of two of the four women admitted in 1996 to the previously all-male South Carolina military academy the Citadel created yet another imbroglio. The women alleged that they were sexually assaulted, that their clothes were set on fire, and that their mouths were washed out with cleanser. The women asserted that they had never asked for special treatment, yet as Kim Messer, age 18, stated, that was precisely what she got: "Special treatment by way of criminal assaults, sadistic illegal hazing, and disgusting incidents of sexual harassment." All of this, the women claim, was tolerated by the Citadel top brass.

The Military Controversy

Chastened by the Tailhook scandal and pressured by Congress, the Pentagon has recognized the need to correct the persistent problem of sexual harassment in the military. The U.S. Armed Services Committee—prodded by its then-chair, Patricia Schroeder, former congressional representative from Colorado—called for action by the leaders of the various service branches to end sex discrimination much as the military had successfully reduced racial discrimination after World War II. In particular, the U.S. Navy established a stricter harassment policy in the wake of Tailhook, including a more extensive training program and accountability for officers and their subordinates. The navy's effort includes a toll-free sexual harassment advice and counseling hot line and a "green-light, yellow-light, red-light" poster that defines acceptable, questionable, and objectionable behavior. When the poster was publicized, many commentators and cartoonists enjoyed dreaming up creative scenarios involving colored lights.

Despite all of these efforts, the navy has continued to make headlines. In 1993, for example, San Diego–based naval aviators targeted Pat Schroeder, an outspoken critic of military harassment, with obscene T-shirts and banners. More recently, the army has been rocked by a series of charges and investigations leading all the way to the top enlisted officers. The constant barrage of charges against all branches of the service and the service academies has led some commentators to suggest that the effort to integrate women into the service should be declared a failure and should be abandoned. In response, *Time* magazine columnist Barbara Ehrenrich has issued the following rejoinder:

We may have to concede at last that the experiment with a sexually integrated military has failed. Some no doubt saw the end coming when their American G.I.s shamed their nation by raping a Japanese schoolgirl in 1995. Others, more prescient, must have realized years ago that in the modern age of "peace-keeping," a military that runs on testosterone is about as useful as a platoon armed with maces and pikes. So enough of this indiscriminate mixing of the genders; any realist will conclude, it's time to shift to an all-female military. (Ehrenrich 1996)

The Government Agency Controversy

Women who work for other government agencies have also made news. In December 1994, the Central Intelligence Agency (CIA) settled a complex and controversial sex discrimination case brought by Janine M. Brookner, its former station chief in Jamaica. One of the first women to reach the upper echelons of the agency, Brookner had worked there for 24 years with a sterling record as an officer in the prestigious covert operations directorate. While heading the CIA's Jamaica office, she disciplined some subordinates for misconduct and reported one agent to her superiors for repeatedly beating his wife. These same agents then accused Brookner of drinking heavily, dressing suggestively, and harassing them sexually. The CIA inspector general conducted an investigation without interviewing Brookner or her allies and issued a report that referred to Brookner as a promiscuous alcoholic. On his recommendation, Brookner was denied a promotion to the post of Prague station chief and was assigned to a desk job at CIA headquarters in Langley, Virginia.

In response, Brookner filed a discrimination suit in 1995, asserting that the covert operations directorate had "a pervasive atmosphere of machismo and sexual discrimination receptive to accepting malicious and sexist allegations against women." Scores of female agents within the directorate concurred and threatened to file a class-action sex discrimination lawsuit. During the pretrial investigation of the Brookner case, several high-ranking government officials testified to her good character and impeccable professionalism. The CIA concluded that the accusations against Brookner were dubious and decided to settle her suit. Although it denied any wrongdoing, the agency paid her $410,000 and opened settlement negotiations with the agents who had threatened to make the class-action claim. As of this writing, the result of those negotiations has not been publicly announced.

The Corporate Controversy

Corporate America has fared no better than other sectors in its efforts to respond to the rising tide of sexual harassment claims. The jury in the Baker and McKenzie case mentioned earlier seemed to be swayed toward awarding a record amount by evidence that the firm had minimized repeated complaints. Rena Weeks, who had brought the suit, alleged that Martin Greenstein, a senior partner in the international firm, had repeatedly grabbed her and made sexual remarks to her. At the trial, several other women confirmed that the firm had failed to discipline Greenstein, even though numerous women had complained about him as early as 1987. He had been transferred from Chicago to Palo Alto, California, after one reprimand and was sent to sensitivity training in response to Weeks's charges. Weeks, however, was transferred after complaining and resigned from the firm two months later. The jury ordered the firm to pay Weeks $50,000 for emotional distress and $6.9 million in punitive damages, twice the amount she had requested. In addition, Greenstein was ordered to pay Weeks $225,000.

In April 1996, Mitsubishi Motor Manufacturing of America was slapped with a lawsuit by the EEOC, thereby unleashing the largest sexual harassment case in history. The suit alleged widespread sexual harassment in which hundreds of women were subjected to sexual innuendo and unwanted "grabbing, groping, and touching." As many as 500 plaintiffs could be eligible for $300,000 each in punitive damages, costing the company a possible $150 million.

In attempts to salvage its reputation while continuing to deny liability, Mitsubishi hired former Secretary of Labor Lyn Martin to address the internal problem. In February 1997, Martin released the results of her nine-month study and called on Mitsubishi to embrace her 34-point "model workplace plan," which she argued would help to prevent harassment and would resolve future accusations. The suggested points included better management training, mandatory workshops for all employees, and a revamping of the company's human resource department. On the surface, Martin's report appears to support the plaintiffs' case.

Mitsubishi may be seeking to avoid Wal-Mart's 1995 fate when a federal jury in Missouri found that the company should pay more than $50 million to a former employee who accused her supervisor of sexual harassment. The plaintiff alleged that Wal-Mart failed to respond to her repeated complaints and refused to enforce its own written policy. Wal-Mart declared itself "shocked" by the verdict and has appealed.

These large jury awards have sparked a predictable corporate backlash. Under federal law, damage awards in sexual harassment cases are capped based on the size of the company being sued. For cases preceding under state civil tort laws, however, no such caps exist, and most large jury awards have been the result of such decisions on punitive damages. Punitive damages are, by law, meant to reflect the worth of the defendant and are to be set at an amount that will punish the defendant; they do not reflect the actual damages to the plaintiff. Current proposals for legal reform in Congress and in many states would place limits on the amounts of these recoverable damages.

The Frontiers of the Controversy

In spite of these challenges, advocates continue to push the boundaries of sexual harassment. A March 1993 *Harvard Law Review* article described and provided a theoretical legal foundation for the problem of "street harassment"—catcalls and sexual remarks made by strangers in public. A 1987 *Wisconsin Law Review* article, as well as the Rutgers School of Law Women's Rights Litigation Clinic, addressed the issue of "housing harassment" in which landlords, building supervisors, and others harass female tenants. The first arrest in history of a male student at the University of Michigan in 1995 for going on-line with graphic descriptions of raping, torturing, and murdering a female classmate made news, and an article in the *New Republic* described the problem, noting that "harassment of women is so common that women often pretend to be men to avoid sexually suggestive e-mail" (Chapman 1995, p. 13). The problem of harassment over this new medium forces many chatters to disguise their female identity when on-line.

As these new types of sexual harassment show, the controversy over sexual harassment will not soon be resolved.

The Background of the Controversy over Sexual Harassment

Anthropologist Margaret Mead launched one of the earliest and most direct volleys in the debate over the issue of sexual harassment. Writing for *Redbook,* she argued that "it isn't more laws that we need now, but new taboos." In 1978, at a time when nearly half of all adult women were working, Mead contended that we need a taboo, saying clearly and unequivocally, "You don't make passes at or sleep with the people you work with" (Mead 1978).

Mead defined *taboos* as internalized prohibitions directed against behavior that "is unthinkable and which affirms what we hold most precious in our human relations." It has always been "the basic taboos—the deeply and intensely felt prohibitions against 'unthinkable' behavior—that keep the social system in balance." Although earlier ancient taboos governed relations between men and women in the home, there were no comparable taboos governing relations between men and women on the job. According to Mead, we are in a period of transition that requires the development of "decent sex mores in the whole working world." Citing recent developments in coeducational dormitories, she noted that an informal taboo has developed: a prohibition against serious dating among those who live in the same dormitory. Such taboos, she submitted, are now necessary at work.

Some critics, however, find this view prudish and unrealistic. They argue that many people today expect to meet and marry someone from work (Farrell 1993). In our modern society, workers move frequently and have severed many traditional family ties that fostered age-old ways of meeting and matchmaking. Work may be their major social contact; for many people, work is the only chance to find and court a suitable mate. Now that sexual harassment is also clearly a form of illegal sex discrimination in education, critics complain that even meeting someone in school or college may be a problem, since acceptable social interactions have become more complex.

Where natural courting runs into problems may be in the different expectations men and women bring to the workplace or to school. Out of the plethora of studies that have been conducted on this subject, one of the most interesting is that by Barbara Gutek. In *Sex and the Workplace* (1985), which summarizes studies conducted in the early 1980s, Gutek found that little is known about workers' attitudes about sexual overtures at work. There are even relatively few myths or stereotypes relevant to this issue, she contends. The stereotype that women go to college to find husbands was prevalent in the past, but the view that women seek jobs for the purpose of finding husbands is less common.

Perhaps the most common relevant stereotype is the idea that some women are willing to use their sexuality to advance their careers and thus gain an unfair advantage over men who are competing for the same job. Some people in Gutek's studies expressed this concern, although she found virtually no evidence that women benefit in this way. Nevertheless, this belief may lead some people to attribute any advancement by women to their willingness to "put out." These stereotypes assume that women encourage and welcome sexual advances from men.

Yet these stereotypes are about women only. Comparable statements about men—that they "sleep" their way to the top or get jobs to find wives—are rare. Although some people believe that women use their sexuality as a resource at work, apparently few believe men do. Although she observed that none of these stereotypes has been studied empirically, Gutek did find a "giant gender gap" concerning people's attitudes and reactions to overtures from the opposite sex.

Sixty-seven percent of the men in Gutek's survey said they would be flattered by a proposition made by a woman at work, but only 17 percent of the women said they would be flattered by a proposition from a man. Whereas most women (62.8 percent) said sexual advances are insulting to them, only a minority of men (15 percent) felt this way.

What makes this finding so astounding, Gutek observed, is that neither men nor women are aware of this gender gap. Both sexes are aware that men are flattered if a woman propositions them, especially if she is attractive. What is surprising, however, is that both men and women also report that women are complimented and flattered by advances from a man, especially an attractive man. Although both sexes assume that men are complimented more than women, they still report that they believe women are similarly complimented.

It is perhaps understandable that men believe women are complimented—after all, men are. Why should women not be complimented, too? If, for various reasons, women do not directly tell men that they are angered, insulted, or disgusted by male advances, it is possible to understand how men who are not sensitive to women's responses might assume that women are complimented. Harder to explain is how women who report that they personally are insulted believe other women are flattered and complimented by male advances.

One possible explanation is that women, along with men, hold the general belief that being attractive to men is extremely important to women and that overtures and advances are an indication of that attractiveness. This is a variation on the common theme that women take jobs in male-dominated fields because they are looking for sex or for husbands. Work is simply one of those areas in which a woman's attractiveness can be "validated" by comments, overtures, and advances from men.

Why, then, are individual women insulted? Perhaps because those advances frequently have job-related consequences (such as a lighter or heavier workload, longer or shorter hours) and because women want their work, not their physical attractiveness, to be noticed and evaluated. In other words, in the workplace indications of women's sexual desirability are less important than indications of their worth as employees.

Nevertheless, women somehow separate their own reactions from their views of other women's reactions. An individual victim may feel that she did nothing to encourage an advance and may be concerned that if she does not act flattered, her circumstances at work will suffer; yet, according to Gutek's findings, she apparently assumes that other women who receive advances must have welcomed or even encouraged them.

Men's and women's responses to other questions in Gutek's survey support this theory. For example, both sexes generally reported that both men and women, but especially women, dress to be attractive at work (Gutek 1985). In addition, a majority of both sexes agreed with the statement that if a man or woman was propositioned at work, he or she could have done something to prevent it. In general, both men and women in the Gutek survey tended to blame or place responsibility on the recipient rather than to attribute advances to some outside societal force like sex-role expectations. The responses of women to this whole issue appear to illustrate a classic case of a group endorsing a stereotype about itself. Gutek concluded that both men and women are apparently misinformed about women's reactions to sexual advances by men at work.

There is another, more compelling reason women are insulted by sexual overtures whereas men are complimented by them. For women, overtures more frequently lead to unpleasant and negative job or educational consequences, whereas there are few such results for men (Gutek 1985).

The cluster of attitudes held by both sexes, at least in the early 1980s, was not consistent with the existence of widespread sexual harassment. The belief that both sexes could prevent overtures, overtly or covertly encourage propositions, and dress to be sexually attractive supports the idea that any social-sexual encounters must have been welcome rather than harassing. These attitudes help to explain both why sexual harassment was overlooked in the past and why so much documentation was necessary before people would believe that the problem really did exist.

Major studies have shown widely disparate results—anywhere from 15 to 88 percent—with regard to the amount of sexual harassment perceived to be occurring in the workplace. Much of this discrepancy can be tied to the lack of a definition of *harassment;* many studies have not been careful to ask questions based on the legal definition but have instead simply asked people for their own opinions, leaving the definition up to the individual. Furthermore, answers varied depending upon whether people responded voluntarily or were surveyed randomly.

What is clear is that the nomination hearings of Clarence Thomas during October 1991 and the Civil Rights Act of 1991 served as wake-up calls to women and employers. Millions of Americans sat glued to their television sets for several days while the Senate Judiciary Committee struggled to determine if the sexual harassment charges of Anita Hill, a law professor from Oklahoma, against Thomas, the Supreme Court nominee, were true. Through these hearings, the nation participated in a giant teach-in on the law and social theory of sexual harassment. The Equal Employment Opportunity Commission reported a surge in formal sexual harassment complaints following the Thomas hearings. Formal complaints increased 70 percent over the previous year; informal inquiries were up 150 percent in the nine months following the hearings (Solomon 1992). The intense television coverage of the Thomas hearings dramatically increased awareness of what sexual harassment is and also of the rights of victims. According to two ABC News polls, conducted before and after the hearings, the percentage of women reporting that they had been sexually harassed more than doubled.

Another action in that same year—the enactment of the Civil Rights Act of 1991—changed the law to allow up to $300,000 in compensatory and punitive damages, in addition to the preexisting remedies of reinstatement, back pay, and injunctive relief. The act also now allows jury trials in sexual harassment cases. Because juries may be more likely than judges to decide against employers and award plaintiffs substantial monetary settlements, lawyers are now much more actively pursuing harassment cases in an attempt to gain compensation for the victims. Employers can be found liable for sexual harassment even though they prohibited such conduct and were unaware that it was happening. Both the dramatic Thomas hearings and the new Civil Rights Act led to a growing national debate on the entire issue of sexual harassment.

Several other stories in the news in 1992 also contributed to the rise in public awareness. At the Tailhook convention, a group of women (some of them U.S. Navy officers) accused navy fliers of sexual harassment and assault during a drunken convention party, which led to an investigation of sexual harassment in the navy and the resignation of several high-ranking officers. Three U.S. senators were accused of sexual harassment by current or former staffers. The United States Supreme Court jumped into the fray in 1992 by deciding a case concerning sexual harassment in schools, thus settling a decade of legal debate over whether the schools themselves can be liable for monetary damages for sexual harassment by employees or students. In the 1990s, suddenly, sexual harassment was no longer an issue confined to the interest of feminist scholars or social scientists. Employers, educators, workers, and students were all forced to decide what they thought about the issue.

To date, feminists, courts, legal theorists, and management have had different responses to this problem. There has been no organized opposition to the movement to make sexual harassment illegal, perhaps because private employers have been quick to realize that sexual harassment directly affects their profitability in terms of lost productivity and morale, as well as legal fees and damage awards if a complaint is filed. A study of Fortune 500 companies estimated that sexual harassment costs each company over $7 million per year in worker turnover and decreased productivity (Klein 1988).

The public sector may have been slower to recognize the problem. Some writers noted that the most serious, pervasive complaints have come from public institutions (Paul et al. 1991). Perhaps, these writers speculate, workers with the relative security of a government paycheck can afford to take time off for such unprofessional behavior and, because of civil service protections, face fewer management sanctions if they do.

Since the late 1970s in the United States, the impact of sexuality at work and at school has become the concern of four different groups, each approaching the issue from a different point of view—including a feminist perspective, a legal perspective, a management perspective, and the male response. Oddly absent is any organized perspective of men—the group charged in 90 to 95 percent of cases with perpetrating sexual harassment. These points of view are neither independent nor mutually exclusive. For example, some men are feminists, many feminists are managers, and some lawyers are managers.

The feminist perspective argues that fundamental social changes are necessary to eliminate sexual harassment. The legal and managerial perspectives tend to seek solutions through less sweeping changes in the workplace, such as establishing regulations about personnel behavior or sanctions for misusing power. Each perspective is presented in this text in its strongest form; not all feminists, lawyers, or managers would agree with the views exactly as they are outlined here. It is difficult to address the issue in a way that satisfies all four groups. Understanding the divergent perspectives is important because the way the problem is framed drives the proposed solutions.

The Feminist Perspective

The feminist viewpoint sees sexual harassment as an expected consequence of sexism in society. It is both a cause and an effect. Sexual harassment exists because women are considered the inferior sex. Men can and do exploit women, without sanctions, in the workplace, in school, and outside these institutions.

One of the ways gender stereotypes are maintained is by emphasizing sex-role expectations. Being a sex object is part of the female sex role. Sexual harassment is a reminder to women of their status as sex objects—even at work or at school. Feminists contend that even when women behave in a seductive manner at work or at school or are willing to exchange sexual favors for promotions or grades, they do so because they are rewarded more for that behavior than for professional or academic competence.

Because sexual harassment is an outgrowth of society's gender expectations, its occurrence in organizations may be viewed as normal or expected by nonfeminists. At the very least, handling sexual harassment may be viewed by nonfeminists as a woman's responsibility. If a woman wishes to venture into the world of work or into educational institutions dominated by men, she should expect sexual overtures from men and be able to handle them. The general attitude of managers who responded to a survey sent to readers of the *Harvard Business Review* was that women should be able to handle whatever comes their way (Collins and Blodgett 1981). Feminists, therefore, contend that sexual harassment is difficult to treat because it is not always viewed as a problem. Accordingly, they are committed to documenting the existence of harassment and exposing it as a form of male domination over women.

Because the feminist perspective sees sexual harassment as an outgrowth of sexism in society, commentators who hold this viewpoint have had relatively little to say about workplaces or educational institutions themselves. The workplace or school is just another sphere of male domination and another arena—like marriage—where men can exert their power over women.

The Legal Perspective

Still in the process of development, the legal perspective on sexual harassment currently parallels the legal approach to sex discrimination. The United States Supreme Court has determined that sexual harassment is a form of sex discrimination in the workplace and in school and is, therefore, illegal; yet many other legal questions—such as whether the victim's perspective should be that of the reasonable man or the reasonable woman—remain. In determining whether sexual harassment has occurred, courts will focus on the *effects* rather than the *intent* of harassment. Sexual harassment impacts an employee's or a student's performance, mental and physical health, and job or school satisfaction. One type of sexual harassment occurs when submission to sexual requests serves as a basis for employment or educational decisions, such as employee selection, grades, graduation, performance appraisal, merit increases, promotions, or tenure. Sexual harassment also occurs when the workplace or educational institution is so permeated with sexual behavior or innuendos that the environment is hostile or intimidating. Any particular behavior is considered harassment when it leads to negative consequences for the worker or student or puts members of that worker's or student's group—in most cases, women—at a disadvantage relative to other groups, usually men.

Although the legal perspective recognizes that society influences sexual harassment, it focuses on behavior in the work and educational environments rather than on broader social changes. Thus, in the law's view, complying with the legal requirements simply necessitates some changes in regulations and actions in the workplace or schools. Employers and educators must attempt to create an environment free of harassment through written policies and training and must respond promptly and vigorously to complaints of sexual harassment.

The Management Perspective

The management perspective—either in the workplace or in educational institutions—comes in two variants, one old and the other relatively new (Gutek 1985). The older view does not take the existence of sexual harassment very seriously: sexual interactions are seen as personal matters that occasionally get out of hand. For example, perhaps a woman cannot handle the office "Don Juan," or perhaps he becomes too aggressive with one too many female employees. This point of view also tends to see an allegation of sexual harassment as an outgrowth of a lovers' quarrel or the result of misunderstandings or misperceptions. A woman may be insulted by a remark that a man meant as a compliment. Women's complaints of sexual harassment arise from their own inability to handle men who are too friendly, their own sensitivity or prudishness about sexuality, or their own retaliatory anger over a rejection by the man they have accused.

From this point of view, protecting the reputation of the senior employee—almost always a man—from false charges that could damage his career may be the organization's primary concern. Allegations of harassment are usually handled informally because they are viewed as personal matters. The accuser may be transferred or fired; sometimes the harasser may be moved or fired. Because the organization is primarily concerned with keeping the services of the more valuable of the two employees, the high-status person usually stays. Thus, even when the accuser is acknowledged to have a legitimate case, she or he may be transferred or asked to leave.

The second, newer management point of view takes sexual harassment more seriously. Harassment is viewed as an interpersonal problem but one that is also the organization's business, as it leads to decreased morale and productivity. Sexual harassment is viewed as an expression of personal preferences in a damaging way, when a person misuses the power associated with his or her organizational position. As such, it is unproductive and unprofessional behavior.

An organization that maintains this perspective may use classes, seminars, and written statements to emphasize that harassing behavior is unprofessional and will not be tolerated. The organization may also establish an office to formally handle cases of sexual harassment, to provide counseling to the harasser and to the harassed, or to discipline offenders.

The Male Response

Although women sometimes sexually harass men, and there is some evidence of same-sex harassment, 90 to 95 percent of all sexual harassment claims are brought by women against men. Despite this, men in the workplace and educational institutions are curiously unorganized and silent, as a group, in the face of the recent barrage of charges. Men have not banded together to protest the imposition of liability for sexual harassment of women by men. A few individual voices have been raised, however, to question whether the charges are fair and whether the sanctions are appropriate or necessary; some individuals have revealed a fear of false charges (Farrell 1993; Paul et al. 1991). Yet beyond some sporadic grumbling about wasting time on sexual harassment training classes at work or school, most men have remained mute.

Another question left open for future resolution is the issue of backlash. Will the increasing number of sexual harassment claims, more intensive training, and a growing male fear of false charges make men in power more reluctant to hire, teach, travel with, or promote women? Virtually no discussion of this issue has yet emerged in the literature or the case law.

Today, what is clear is that sexual harassment is illegal—and the legal definition is expanding. More and more companies and schools are creating sexual harassment policies and training programs. Whether this trend will continue remains uncertain. The number of claims and the continued prevalence of office and school romances indicate that we are still a long way from Mead's suggestion of a new taboo against sex at work or at school.

References

Brock, David, *The Real Anita Hill* (New York: Free Press, 1993).

Center for Women in Government, "Cost of Sexual Harassment to Employers up Sharply," *Women in Public Service* no. 4 (Spring 1994): 38–39.

Chapman, Gary, "The Flamers: The Internet and Decline of Public Discourse," *The New Republic* 186, no. 4 (April 10, 1995): 13–15.

Collins, Eliza G.C., and Timothy B. Blodgett, "Sexual Harassment: Some See It . . . Some Won't," *Harvard Business Review* 59, no. 2 (March–April 1981): 76–96.

Ehrenrich, Barbara, "Essay," *Time* (December 2, 1996).

Farrell, Warren, *The Myth of Male Power* (New York: Simon and Schuster, 1993).

Gutek, Barbara A., *Sex and the Workplace* (San Francisco: Jossey-Bass, 1985).

Hoffman, Lisa (Scripps Howard News Service), "Sex Harassment Last Straw for Career Soldier," *Rocky Mountain News* (February 16, 1997), p. 3A, col. 1.

Klein, Freada, *The 1988 Working Woman Sexual Harassment Survey Executive Report* (Cambridge, MA: Klein Associates, 1988).

Koss, Mary P., Lisa A. Goodman, Angela Browne, Louise F. Fitzgerald, Gwendolyn Puryear Keita, and Nancy Felipe Russo, *No Safe Haven: Male Violence against Women at Home, at Work, and in the Community* (Washington, DC: American Psychological Association, 1994).

Linn, Eleanor, Valerie Lee, Robert Croninger, and Xinglei Chen, "The Culture of Sexual Harassment in Secondary Schools," *American Education Research Journal* 33, no. 2 (Summer 1996): 383–417.

Mayer, Jane, and Jill Abramson, *Strange Justice: The Selling of Clarence Thomas* (Boston: Houghton Mifflin, 1994).

Mead, Margaret, "A Proposal: We Need Taboos on Sex at Work," *Redbook* (April 1978): 31–33, 38.

Morris, Celia, *Bearing Witness: Sexual Harassment and Beyond—Everywoman's Story* (Boston: Little, Brown, 1994).

Paul, Ellen Frankel, Lloyd R. Cohen, Linda C. Majka, Alan Kors, Jean Bethke Elshtain, and Nicholas Davidson, "Sexual Harassment or Harassment of Sexuality?" *Society* 28, no. 4 (May–June 1991): 4–39.

Sandroff, Ronni, "Sexual Harassment: The Inside Story," *Working Woman* (June 1992): 47–51.

Slade, Margot, "Law Firms Begin Reigning in Sex-Harassing Partners," *New York Times* (February 25, 1994), p. 19A, column 2.

Solomon, Alisa, "One Year After Anita Hill . . . Has America's Crash Course in Preventing Sexual Harassment Made a Difference?" *Glamour* (November 1992): 238–311.

Thompson, Mark, "Sergeants at Odds," *Time* (February 17, 1997): 46.

Zimmerman, Jean, *Tailspin: Women at War in the Wake of Tailhook* (New York: Doubleday, 1995).

Chronology 2

A few important cases and legislative developments have substantially changed the legal complexion of sexual harassment, often wiping out all of the decisions and developments that came before. When one is doing research on sexual harassment, some of the older resources may provide interesting historical perspectives, but check the following dates to be sure the information offered on specific points has not become obsolete.

Pre-Twentieth Century

Although the term *sexual harassment* did not come into the lexicon until the 1970s, the problem is ancient. As far back as Genesis 39, the master's wife "casts her eyes upon" the servant Joseph and demands that he "lie with" her as an implied condition of his employment. Joseph refuses, somehow leaving his clothes behind in his rush to flee from his amorous employer. In retaliation, the wife uses the garments as evidence that Joseph tried to attack her, and the master shows his wrath by throwing the innocent Joseph into prison.

Until the late twentieth century, victims of sexual harassment in employment or educational settings had no recourse unless the attack rose to the level of an assault and battery. To prevail in such a case, a victim usually had to allege that she had been beaten, seriously molested, or raped. As early as 1875, however, in *Croaker v. Chicago and Northwestern Railway*, 36 Wis. 657 (1875), a court awarded a woman $1,000 in damages in an assault and battery claim for both mental suffering and "being wronged" when a male train conductor thrust his soiled hand into the muff she wore to keep her hands warm and then kissed her several times.

Early Twentieth Century

Despite the 1875 *Croaker* case, most early courts remained leery of sexual harassment claims. As summarized by Petrocelli and Repa (1992), "When evaluating evidence of outrageous and sometimes brutal attacks by a male co-worker, court opinions would quaintly ponder for pages whether a man had 'put his hands upon a woman with a view to violate her person.'"

Women factory workers in the early 1900s, wherever they worked, were sexually harassed by male workers, foremen, and bosses. In fact, learning to tolerate this abuse was one of the first lessons on the job. Male supervisors or employers commonly demanded sexual favors from female workers in exchange for a job, a raise, or a promotion (Hymowitz and Weissman 1978).

Mid- to Late Twentieth Century

1934   A group of female servants publishes a notice in the *New York Weekly Journal* that announces, "We think it reasonable we should not be beat by our mistresses' husbands, they being too strong and perhaps may do tender women mischief" (Clark 1991).

1964   In July, Congress considers the Civil Rights Act, which would outlaw discrimination in employment and create the Equal Employment Opportunity Commission. Ironically, as it is originally introduced in Congress, the act only prohibits discrimination in employment based on race, color, religion, or national origin. Discrimination based on gender is attached to the bill at the last moment, when conservative southern opponents introduce an amendment prohibiting discrimination on the basis of sex; they assume that adding sexual equality is so preposterous that the amendment will scuttle the entire bill. Although the very idea of prohibiting sex-based discrimination engenders mirth on the floor of Congress and in the editorial pages of major newspapers, the Johnson administration wants the Civil Rights Act passed so badly that it decides not to oppose the amendment. Although some members laughingly argue that men can now sue to become Playboy bunnies, the virtually all-male Congress passes the bill.

1974   Lin Farley, a 29-year-old women's movement activist who teaches an experimental course on women and work at Cornell University, discovers that many of her students were the targets of unwelcome advances during their summer jobs. All had been so affected that they had been forced to leave those jobs.

Around the same time, Carmita Woods, a 44-year-old administrative assistant, leaves her job with a Cornell physician to escape his sexual overtures and files for unemployment compensation. Farley and two Cornell colleagues, Susan Meyer and Karen Sauvigné, find a lawyer for Wood and invent a name for her claim: *sexual harassment*.

1975–   In the mid-1970s, several early sexual harassment cases
1978   begin to wend their way through the courts. All of the first women to file suits claiming sexual harassment—Paulette Barnes, Jane Corne, Geneva DeVane, Margaret Miller, and Adrienne Tomkins—lose at the lower court level. In the earliest decided case, a Washington, D.C., federal judge rejects the argument that sexual harassment constitutes a cause of action under Title VII of the Civil Rights Act, holding that "the substance of plaintiff's complaint was that she was discriminated against not because she was a woman but because she refused to engage in a sexual affair with her supervisor." *Barnes v. Train (Costle)*, 13 Fair Empl. Prac. Cas. (BNA) 123, 124 (D.D.C. 1974).

In *Corne v. Bausch and Lomb*, 390 F. Supp. 161 (D. Ariz. 1975) and *Miller v. Bank of America*, 418 F. Supp. 233 (N.D.

1975–
1978
cont.

Cal. 1976), the courts determine that sexual harassment is not sex discrimination because the acts complained of are not sufficiently tied to the workplace. In Corne's case, the sexual advances are seen as "a personal proclivity, peculiarity, or mannerism"; in Miller's case, the "isolated misconduct" is not considered attributable to employer "policy." In *Corne*, the court quoted *Barnes* to find again that the behavior is not "based on sex" within its legal meaning: "The substance of plaintiff's complaint is that she was discriminated against, not because she was a woman, but because she refused to engage in a sexual affair with her supervisor."

1975

In May, the Cornell group holds a "speakout" in a community center in Ithaca, New York. A questionnaire reveals that a large number of the women present have been victims of the newly identified problem, sexual harassment (Brownmiller and Alexander 1992).

Eleanor Holmes Norton, then chair of the New York City Commission on Human Rights, holds hearings on women and work. Lin Farley arrives to testify, half expecting to be laughed out of the hearing room. "The titillation value of sexual harassment was always obvious," Farley recalls (Brownmiller and Alexander 1992), but Norton takes the issue seriously. Reporter Enid Nemy covers the Human Rights Commission hearings for the *New York Times.* Her story, "Women Begin To Speak Out against Sexual Harassment at Work," may be the first on the topic in a major publication. It appears on August 19, 1975, and is syndicated nationally. Thousands of responses pour in from women around the country.

Around 1975, Sauvigné and Meyer set up the Working Women's Institute in New York City to serve as a clearinghouse for inquiries, to develop a data bank with an eye toward public policy, and to assist women in finding legal counsel and tracking important cases.

Carmita Woods loses her case; the unemployment insurance appeals board rules that her reasons for quitting were personal.

1976   As in *Corne* and *Miller,* the lower court in *Tomkins v. Public Service Electric and Gas Co.,* 422 F. Supp. 553 (D.N.J. 1976), considers sexual harassment neither employment related nor sex based but a personal injury properly pursued in state court as a tort. The *Tomkins* court holds that a firing for a complaint about sexual harassment is not discriminatory.

In April, a Washington, D.C., judge—not the one who decided *Barnes*—becomes the first to recognize sexual harassment as a form of sex discrimination in allowing a lawsuit by a black public information specialist in the Department of Justice. The employee claimed her supervisor harassed her and then fired her after she refused to have sex with him. This is the first case to find sexual harassment to be treatment "based on sex" within the meaning of Title VII, although it leaves the employment relatedness of the incidents to be determined at trial. *Williams v. Saxbe,* 413 F. Supp. 654 (D.D.C. 1976).

1977–   By 1977, three of the early cases rise to the appellate level,
1979   and the results are different from those in the lower courts. All three appellate courts rule that a harassed woman has a right, under Title VII of the Civil Rights Act, to sue the corporate entity that employed her. *Barnes v. Costle (Train),* 561 F.2d 983 (D.C. Cir. 1977); *Miller v. Bank of America,* 600 F.2d 211 (9th Cir. 1979); *Tomkins v. Public Service Electric and Gas,* 568 F.2d 1044 (3d Cir. 1977). *Tomkins* contains the clearest statement that the courts will no longer view harassment as a personal problem but as sex discrimination. In *Barnes,* the Court of Appeals for the District of Columbia holds that making sexual compliance a "job retention condition" is sex-based differentiation under the circumstances, because it imposes an employment requirement upon a woman that would not be imposed upon a man.

Also in the late 1970s, Freada Klein and a group of feminists form a Boston-area advocacy group called the Alliance against Sexual Coercion. Soon, the term *sexual coercion* is abandoned and the term *sexual harassment* dominates the movement. Several leading women's magazines run stories on the issue in the late 1970s, including a

1977–
1979
cont.
survey by *Redbook* in 1976 and a *Ms.* speakout and cover story in 1977. Even anthropologist Margaret Mead leaps into the fray with a 1978 article in *Redbook* entitled "A Proposal: We Need Taboos on Sex at Work."

1977
The first student brings a claim of sexual harassment under Title IX of the 1972 Education Act Amendments. Ronnie Alexander, a female undergraduate at Yale University, claims her professor offered her an A in his course in exchange for sex and told her that if she refused she would receive a C. In *Alexander v. Yale*, 459 F. Supp. 1 (D. Conn. 1977), Alexander asks that the grade be removed from her record. Four other students and a faculty member join in the suit. The district court holds that sexual harassment may constitute sex discrimination under Title IX, stating,

> It is perfectly reasonable to maintain that academic advancement conditioned upon submission to sexual demands constitutes sex discrimination in education, just as questions of job retention or promotion tied to sexual demands from supervisors have become increasingly recognized as potential violations of Title VII's ban against sex discrimination in employment.

1978
Lin Farley's groundbreaking book, *Sexual Shakedown: The Sexual Harassment of Women on the Job,* is published by McGraw-Hill after being rejected by 27 other publishers. "I thought my book would change the workplace," Farley said. "It is now out of print" (Brownmiller and Alexander 1992).

1979
Following close behind Farley, Catharine MacKinnon, a young lawyer who followed the early cases while a student at Yale Law School, publishes *Sexual Harassment of Working Women*, a book that provides the first legal theoretical analysis of the issue.

Without much publicity, the courts continue to broaden the definition and scope of unlawful harassment. As the number of women in the workplace grows, new cases go beyond the situation of bosses suggesting sex in exchange for jobs. A court decision in Minnesota establishes that co-worker harassment also poisons the workplace and is illegal; a New York court holds that a receptionist should not be required to wear revealing clothes that bring her unwanted attention.

A clerk-typist named Karen Nussbaum starts to organize women office workers through a national network she calls 9 to 5. Jane Fonda—an old friend from the antiwar movement—visits Nussbaum's headquarters in Cleveland with the idea of making a movie about underpaid and harassed secretaries.

1980   Ronnie Alexander's suit is ultimately dismissed, because she has graduated from Yale and thereby mooted the issue. The university, however, establishes a sexual harassment grievance procedure for dealing with complaints, and the *Alexander* case stands for the proposition that sexual harassment is illegal in education as well as employment.

The movie *9 to 5,* starring Jane Fonda, Lily Tomlin, and Dolly Parton, is produced by Fonda's IPC Films. Parton plays a secretary dodging the advances of an amorous boss. The movie, which is a commercial success, uses comedy to fuel the public consciousness about the issue of sexual harassment in employment.

On November 10, in the last days of the Carter administration, Eleanor Holmes Norton, the chair of the EEOC, issues a set of federal guidelines on sexual harassment in a single-page memorandum. The guidelines were published earlier, in the spring, and were subjected to public discussion and debate. The guidelines declare sexual activity as a condition of employment or promotion to be a violation of Title VII.

A federal district court allows a suit over an "atmosphere of discrimination." *Brown v. City of Guthrie,* 22 Fair Empl. Prac. Cas. (BNA) 1627 (W.D. Okla. 1980). Even though the female plaintiff cannot show a loss of tangible job benefits, she does establish that the harassment created a hostile, offensive, and unbearable work environment. *Brown* is the first court opinion to cite the 1980 EEOC guidelines, quoting

1980   Section A, that sexual harassment is a violation of Title VII
cont.   when "such conduct has the purpose or effect of substantially interfering with an individual's work performance
or creating an intimidating, hostile, or offensive work
environment."

1981   Following shortly after *Brown,* in *Bundy v. Jackson,* 641 F.2d
934 (D.C. Cir. 1981), another circuit court rules on the basis
of an atmosphere of discrimination and also cites the
EEOC guidelines. This court holds that the phrase "terms
and conditions of employment" protected by Title VII
means more than tangible compensation and benefits.

The Merit Systems Protection Board releases the results of
a random survey of 20,100 federal employees, which
reveals that 42 percent of the government's female workers experienced an incident of sexual harassment in the
previous year. This is the first survey to use a reliable
methodology.

In July, homosexual advances at work are found to be
within the purview of the Civil Rights Act. *Wright v.
Methodist Youth Services, Inc.,* 551 F. Supp. 307 (N.D. Ill.
1981).

1982–   During this two-year period, two federal circuit courts of
1983   appeal adopt their own standards for sexual harassment
cases, identifying two kinds of sexual harassment: (1)
harassment in which a supervisor demands sexual con-
siderations in exchange for job benefits ("quid pro quo")
and (2) harassment that creates an offensive environment
("condition of work" or "hostile work environment"
harassment). *Henson v. City of Dundee,* 682 F.2d 897 (11th
Cir. 1982); *Katz v. Dole,* 709 F.2d 251 (4th Cir. 1983). The
Henson court establishes four elements a plaintiff must
prove to establish a case of quid pro quo sexual harassment: (1) he or she belongs to a protected group (that is, is
male or female); (2) he or she was subjected to unwelcome
sexual harassment; (3) the harassment complained of was
based on sex; and (4) the employee's reaction to the
harassment complained of affected tangible aspects of the
employee's compensation, terms, conditions, or privileges of employment. The *Henson* case also reverses the

lower court's holding that the plaintiff must show some tangible job detriment in addition to the hostile work environment created by sexual harassment. The *Katz* court lists the same four elements as required for quid pro quo sexual harassment but adds the requirement that the employer knew, or should have known, of the harassment in question and failed to take prompt remedial action.

In September 1982, a federal judge in Wisconsin upholds a verdict in favor of a male social services worker who claimed he was sexually harassed by his female supervisor. *Huebschen v. Health and Social Services Department,* 547 F. Supp. 1168 (D. Wis. 1982).

1986　　In June, the U.S. Supreme Court decides its first sexual harassment case and issues a historic ruling that harassment is sex discrimination and is illegal under Title VII of the Civil Rights Act, even if the victim suffers no economic loss. *Meritor Savings Bank v. Vinson,* 477 U.S. 57 (1986). Hired by the bank as a teller trainee, on the basis of her abilities Mechelle Vinson advanced to the position of assistant branch manager before her ultimate termination for excessive use of sick leave. About a year later, Vinson sued the bank and Sidney Taylor, her supervisor, alleging hostile environment sexual harassment. Vinson claimed that during her four years at the bank she had sex with Taylor 40 or 50 times. He allegedly also followed her into the ladies' room, fondled her in front of co-workers, and raped her several times. Although the bank had an antidiscrimination policy and a stated complaint procedure, Vinson did not use the internal process, claiming that she feared reprisals. In their defense, Taylor and the bank alleged that the ongoing relationship was entirely voluntary and that no liability should attach because there was no notice to the employer. Despite the length of the relationship and the lack of notice, the Supreme Court allows Vinson's hostile environment claim in a landmark decision with far-reaching implications for employers.

The Court holds that "the language of Title VII is not limited to 'economic' or 'tangible' discrimination and the phrase 'terms, conditions, or privileges' of employment in the law indicates a congressional intent to 'strike at

1986
cont.
the entire spectrum of disparate treatment of men and women,'" including harassment that creates a hostile work environment. Quoting *Henson,* the Court finds that

> Sexual harassment which creates a hostile or offensive environment for members of one sex is every bit the arbitrary barrier to sexual equality at the workplace that racial harassment is to racial equality. Surely, a requirement that a man or woman run a gauntlet of sexual abuse in return for the privilege of being allowed to work and make a living can be as demeaning and disconcerting as the harshest of racial epithets.

The Supreme Court's important holdings are:

- Sexual harassment is a form of sex discrimination that is illegal under Title VII of the 1964 Civil Rights Act.
- Sexual harassment is illegal even if the victim suffers only a hostile work environment and not the loss of economic or tangible job benefits.
- Employers are not automatically liable for sexual harassment by their supervisors.
- Lack of knowledge of the harassment does not automatically relieve the employer of liability for a supervisor's harassment.
- The complainant's consent to the behavior does not relieve the employer of liability. The issue is not the "voluntariness" of the complainant's participation but whether her conduct indicates that the behavior was unwelcome.
- The complainant's behavior, such as provocative speech and dress, may be considered in determining whether the complainant found particular sexual advances unwelcome.

1988
One of the first cases of "paramour preference," *Broderick v. Ruder,* 685 F. Supp. 1269 (D.D.C. 1988), is decided by a judge in Washington, D.C. The plaintiff, a staff attorney at the Securities and Exchange Commission, alleges that several supervisors were involved in sexual relationships with secretaries and a staff attorney and rewarded them with promotions, cash, and other job benefits. Broderick also alleges

isolated instances of harassment directed at her. (In one, a drunken supervisor untied her top and kissed her at an office party.) The court finds that a hostile environment was created, even though all of the relationships were entirely consensual. The court emphasizes that the sexual activity in the office was widespread and that it formed the basis for decisions on the terms and conditions of employment. When the plaintiff made it clear that she would not participate, the quality of her work assignments changed.

1990   In March, the EEOC issues new guidelines on how to define and prevent sexual harassment, updating the guidelines it issued in 1980. This new publication reflects agency and court decisions since the first guidelines were issued.

A number of studies and surveys are conducted and their results published. In September, the Pentagon releases the largest military survey ever on sexual harassment, which shows that of 20,000 military respondents worldwide, 64 percent of the women and 17 percent of the men reported that they have been sexually harassed.

In business, estimates continue to run from 15 to 40 percent of women and 14 to 15 percent of men reporting that they have experienced sexual harassment. In education, 40 to 70 percent of female students report having experienced harassment, mostly from other students.

Women's groups and others push a bill through Congress that would allow an employee to sue for compensatory damages for personal injuries in a sexual harassment case. Under the previous law, damages were limited to lost wages. President George Bush vetoes the bill.

1991   In January, an appellate court in Florida rules that nude pinups in the workplace could lead to a "hostile work environment" and could constitute illegal sexual harassment. *Robinson v. Jacksonville Shipyards*, 760 F. Supp. 1486 (Fla. Dist. Ct. App. 1991). Robinson, a female shipyard welder, wins this first case to find that such pictures are sexual harassment in and of themselves; in other cases, courts had found that pornographic pictures merely contribute to an atmosphere of sexual harassment. In this

1991
cont.

case, the plaintiff claimed she had told her co-workers that their behavior was sexual harassment and that they had then subjected her to new ridicule. The *Robinson* court finds that the employer and two of its employees were directly liable for the harassment and rejects what it calls their "ostrich defense." (They claimed to be unaware of the victim's complaint.) The judge holds that the shipyard maintained a "boys' club" atmosphere with a constant "visual assault on the sensibilities of female workers." Some of the pictures posted on the walls in *Robinson* included close-ups of female genitals. The judge finds that the sexualized atmosphere of the shipyard had the effect of keeping women out of the workplace, and he orders the employer to institute a sexual harassment policy written by the National Organization for Women's Legal Defense and Education Fund, which brought this case to trial.

About a week after *Robinson*, an appellate court for California recognizes that, in considering what qualifies as sexual harassment, the behavior should be evaluated by the "reasonable woman standard," as opposed to the reasonable man standard that was formerly applied. *Ellison v. Brady*, 924 F.2d 872 (9th Cir. 1991). In *Ellison*, the employer's response to the harassment was to counsel the harasser, instructing him to leave the woman alone, and to transfer him to a different facility for four months. The court finds that the employer should have consulted the victim about the harasser's return to the office and should have taken some other kind of disciplinary action. With regard to the reasonable woman standard, the court finds:

- An understanding of the victim's perspective requires an analysis of the different perspectives of men and women.
- A female employee may state the basics of a case of hostile environment sexual harassment by alleging conduct a reasonable woman would consider sufficiently severe; however, the employer does not have to accommodate the idiosyncrasies of a hypersensitive employee.
- The reasonable woman standard is not static but will change over time as the views of reasonable women change.

- There can be unlawful sexual harassment even when harassers do not realize that their conduct creates a hostile working environment.

The facts upon which the court decided *Ellison* are significant, because many critics use this case to argue that the courts have gone too far in enforcing sexual harassment claims. Ellison was an Internal Revenue Service (IRS) agent who accepted an invitation to lunch with a fellow employee, Gray. A few months later, he asked her out again and she refused. Gray then started to write her love letters. Ellison testified that she was frightened by his attentions and filed a complaint with her employer, who then transferred Gray. Three months later, the IRS, without consulting Ellison, allowed Gray to return. When Ellison learned that Gray was returning to her workplace, she requested and received a transfer. She then filed suit. The trial judge dismisses the case, ruling that under the reasonable person standard Gray's actions were "isolated and genuinely trivial." The Ninth Circuit reverses and orders a trial, ruling that a hostile work environment must be judged from the perspective of the victim, in this case the "reasonable woman."

In October, law professor Anita Hill charges Supreme Court nominee Judge Clarence Thomas with sexually harassing her when she worked with him. At first, the United States Senate Judiciary Committee decides to ignore the charges and vote on the nomination. A delegation of congresswomen, led by Representative Pat Schroeder, marches into the Senate hearing from the House and demands a more thorough investigation. After receiving thousands of calls and letters from outraged constituents, the committee votes to hold hearings. The televised proceedings before the Judiciary Committee fuel a dramatic leap in public awareness about sexual harassment on the job. Despite the accusations, the all-male committee votes in favor of confirmation, as does the full Senate.

In one of the most quoted statements on the Hill/ Thomas controversy, Molly Yard, president of the National Organization for Women, in an October 10, 1991, plea to members to help finance campaigns of women who are running for Congress, writes:

1991
cont.

They just don't get it. Those men just don't understand how injurious, how demeaning, and how frightening sexual harassment really is. So it took a massive eruption of outrage from women across America—and across party lines—to shock those senators into delaying the vote on Thomas so that the charge could be investigated. (Petrocelli and Repa 1992, 1/24)

In the wake of the Thomas hearings, the issue of amending the Civil Rights Act is again brought before Congress. Although the Bush administration still opposes allowing employees to sue for damages, at the last minute, bowing to political pressure, it agrees to a compromise bill. An employee can now sue for compensatory damages in addition to lost wages, but a strict limit is placed on the total amount the employee can recover—$50,000 to $300,000, depending upon the number of employees in the company.

Women's groups and others point out that no other group is subject to such severe limits on the amount of damages that can be recovered in a personal injury action. Faced with the alternative of staying with the old law that would allow no compensatory damages, however, women activists reluctantly support the bill. The act passes and becomes part of the Civil Rights Act of 1991.

Several other federal courts follow *Ellison* and adopt the reasonable woman rule during 1991 and 1992.

1992 In February, the Supreme Court decides the first case relating to sexual harassment in schools. In *Franklin v. Gwinnett County Public Schools*, 112 S. Ct. 1028 (1992), a high school student alleges that she was sexually harassed by her sports coach and teacher. After the school became aware of the harassment, it conducted an investigation. The teacher resigned on the condition that all matters pending against him be dropped. Franklin's suit was dismissed by the court of appeals on the basis that Title IX (which prohibits sex discrimination in educational institutions that receive federal funds) does not authorize an award of money damages. The Supreme Court disagrees. It determines that Title IX allows compensatory damages to be awarded to the student, even though the school investigated the claim and the teacher resigned.

A group of at least 26 women, half of them U.S. Navy officers, claim they were sexually harassed at a party of navy pilots at the Tailhook convention in Las Vegas in late 1991. The navy conducts only a cursory investigation until one of the women, an admiral's aide, Lieutenant Paula Coughlin, continues to press the issue. Feeling the heat of congressional and media pressure in early 1992, the Pentagon and the House Armed Services Committee conduct in-depth investigations of the incident. In June of the same year, several high-ranking officers are forced to resign, including Navy Secretary Lawrence Garrett and Admiral John Snyder. The investigation of at least 69 other officers continues.

Three senators are accused of sexual harassment by current or former staff members or other women. Senator Bob Packwood, R-Oregon, issues an apology after the *Washington Post* publishes a story in late November 1992 stating that he had harassed as many as ten staffers and former staffers over the years. Packwood had been reelected to a new six-year term earlier that month, before the story broke. Also during 1992, Senator Daniel Inouye, R-Hawaii, is accused of molestation by his longtime hairstylist and several other women. Senator Brock Adams, D-Washington, does not seek reelection in 1992 after the daughter of a family friend accuses him of drugging and molesting her, and a newspaper publishes similar allegations by several other women. Congress is forced to investigate all three incidents.

1993   In April, the Pentagon releases its final report on the Tailhook scandal, directly implicating a total of 117 officers in the sexual harassment of 83 women and 7 men. Fifty-one others are cited for lying to investigators. Secretary of the Navy John H. Dalton appoints a Marine Corps lieutenant general and a navy vice admiral to take disciplinary action against the perpetrators. Only 7 officers are disciplined before the statute of limitations on their violations runs out in September. Naval aviators in San Diego distribute

1993
cont.
obscene T-shirts targeting Representative Pat Schroeder (D-Colorado), who pushed for investigations of sexual harassment charges in the military.

In July, the New Jersey Supreme Court issues a landmark ruling in *Lehmann v. Toys "R" Us, Inc.,* joining several other jurisdictions that have found that courts should use the reasonable woman standard when evaluating sexual harassment suits.

The Senate Ethics Committee subpoenas Senator Packwood's diaries in October. He refuses to produce them.

In November, the Supreme Court issues a short, unanimous ruling in *Harris v. Forklift Systems, Inc.,* holding that recipients of sexual harassment need not prove severe psychological harm under Title VII. It is enough, the Court finds, to show that the harassment affected the recipient's ability to do her job. Although the court uses the term *reasonable person* in the ruling, whether the court meant to reject the *reasonable woman* standard remains unclear.

As 1993 draws to a close, the Senate Ethics Committee persuades a federal district court to seize Packwood's diaries to prevent him from editing or destroying them.

1994
In February, the United States General Accounting Office issues a report on the prevalence of sexual harassment at military academies.

In an attempt to define acceptable and unacceptable behavior, in April the navy issues a directive on sexual harassment based on red, green, and yellow lights, encouraging enlisted men and women to use these shorthand commands to distinguish between welcome and unwelcome sexual attention.

In September, a San Francisco jury awards nearly $7 million in damages to Rena Weeks, a temporary secretary at the world's largest law firm, Baker and McKenzie. A judge later reduces the award to $3.5 million.

Also in September, Donald Silva, a professor at the University of New Hampshire, persuades a federal court to grant a preliminary injunction on First Amendment grounds to restore his job. Silva had been suspended by the university for using sexual examples in class lectures. In a complex 103-page decision, the court holds that the university failed to balance the professor's First Amendment rights against the rights of students to be free from harassment.

In December, the Central Intelligence Agency (CIA) agrees to pay $410,000 to Janine M. Brookner to avoid a trial. Brookner, a former Jamaica station chief, sued the agency for sex discrimination. The agency had blocked Brookner's career advancement after accepting charges of sexual harassment from subordinates whom she had disciplined. Brookner alleged that no appropriate investigation of the charges had taken place and that, in fact, the charges were a sham to force her out of the agency.

1995   In February, a male student at the University of Michigan is arrested after posting sexually violent e-mail messages concerning a female classmate.

A jury in Missouri rules on June 28 that Wal-Mart Corporation must pay more than $50 million to a former employee who accused her supervisor of sexually harassing her and the company of ignoring her complaints. A judge later (February 1997) reduces the award to $2 million.

In September, Packwood finally resigns from the Senate after the Ethics Committee finds him guilty of sexual harassment.

1996   In May, Paula Jones, a former Arkansas state employee, files suit against President Bill Clinton, alleging that he sexually harassed her while he was governor of Arkansas. Clinton's lawyers attempt to have the suit delayed until he is out of office, taking their arguments all the way to the United States Supreme Court. The year passes without a ruling from the High Court, although in 1997 the Court rules that the case may proceed while Clinton is still in office.

Alleged sexual harassment in grade schools is in the news, as several boys are disciplined for unwelcome kissing or

1996   touching, setting off a national debate about the appropri-
cont.   ateness of maintaining such policies at the grade school
        level.

        Allegations of sexual harassment break out in several U.S.
        Army bases, forcing resignations and investigations of
        numerous officers. The first allegations come from the
        Aberdeen training center in Maryland, where a score of
        recruits allege that they were assaulted or raped by a drill
        sergeant. The army sets up a hot line for sexual harass-
        ment complaints, and hundreds pour in. Brenda Hoster, a
        22-year army veteran and public information specialist,
        accuses her former boss, Sergeant Major of the Army
        Gene McKinney, of sexual harassment.
            In August, Hoster resigns, frustrated because the
        Army is ignoring her accusations. In November, Hoster
        goes public with her complaints after McKinney is named
        to a blue-ribbon panel investigating sexual harassment in
        the army; she files a 13-page federal court complaint. Two
        other female service members come forward to allege that
        McKinney also acted improperly toward them.

1997   In January, two of the four women admitted to the previ-
        ously all-male Charleston, South Carolina, military acad-
        emy the Citadel as a result of a U.S. Supreme Court order
        resign, claiming sexual harassment. They allege that they
        were sexually assaulted and that other cadets set their
        clothes on fire and washed their mouths out with cleanser.
        The women claim the top brass knew of the incidents and
        did nothing.

        In February, the army suspends McKinney from his duty
        of overseeing the 410,000 enlisted soldiers in the force.
        McKinney denies the sexual harassment accusations.

References

Brownmiller, Susan, and Dolores Alexander, "From Carmita Wood to
Anita Hill," *Ms.* (January–February 1992).

Clark, Charles S., "Sexual Harassment," *CCQ Researcher* 1, no. 13 (August
9, 1991): 539–545.

Hymowitz, C., and M. Weissman, *A History of Women in America* (New York: Bantam, 1978).

MacKinnon, Catharine A., *Sexual Harassment of Working Women* (New Haven, CT: Yale University Press, 1979).

Omilian, Susan M., *Sexual Harassment in Employment* (Wilmette, IL: Callaghan, 1987).

Petrocelli, William, and Barbara Kate Repa, *Sexual Harassment on the Job: What It Is and How To Stop It* (Berkeley: Nolo Press, 1992).

Webb, Susan L., *Step Forward: Sexual Harassment in the Workplace* (New York: Mastermedia, 1991).

Biographical Sketches

3

To list all of the people who have contributed to the debate on the issue of sexual harassment or related gender discussions would be impossible, because many people have written just a few important articles or given several speeches on the issue rather than making the subject of sexual harassment the focus of a career. This is particularly true of those who criticize the idea of making sexual harassment a legally actionable wrong. It has been difficult to identify representatives on all sides of the issue, as there is currently no organized opposition to either the legal or social movements to eliminate sexual harassment. Therefore, because an attempt is made in this book to present all points of view, some critics of sexual harassment laws and policies may be featured more prominently in these biographies than might appear warranted by their involvement in the issue. Conversely, some proponents of the movement to make sexual harassment illegal have necessarily been omitted. The list is not meant to be comprehensive but rather represents a sample of persons related to the issue. The list profiles some of the important writers, researchers, attorneys, politicians, lawsuit plaintiffs, political activists, and others who have figured in the issue.

Stephen F. Anderson (1947–)

Stephen Anderson began conducting training sessions on the issue of sexual harassment while serving in the U.S. Air Force in the 1970s, as a result of his volunteer work in a sexual assault clinic. Before that time, he had also worked as a trainer on the issue of race relations for the air force. In 1980, after reading Lin Farley's book *Sexual Shakedown*, he designed a training program on sexual harassment for private companies. In doing so, he became one of the first corporate and government trainers to focus exclusively on the issue. Over the past 18 years, he has developed a variety of training programs, manuals, videotapes, and other materials on the issue of sexual harassment. In his training programs and materials, Anderson has focused on what he calls "subtle sexual harassment," actions that may not rise to the level of a legal claim but that may, if allowed to expand in the workplace without question, lead to a hostile work environment lawsuit. Anderson's company has trained over 100,000 management personnel and other employees in 500 organizations and educational institutions. In addition to sexual harassment training, his company provides workshops in team building, working with irritating people, and other workplace issues. Anderson also serves as an expert witness in sexual harassment cases. He emphasizes that "in sexual harassment situations, it is the *impact[,] not the intent[,]* of the behavior that creates interpersonal conflicts and legal and financial liabilities" (quoted in *Intent vs. Impact* video; full source in Chapter 7). Anderson holds a bachelor's degree in psychology and a master's degree in personnel administration.

In 1992, Anderson reported that the issues women face were the same issues of subtle sexual harassment they confronted in 1980 when he first began conducting harassment training. Anderson has noticed a new form of sex discrimination developing, a new excuse to discriminate against women: Men claim they fear false sexual harassment claims and therefore refuse to work with women. He sees "a lot of backlash and distancing" when he conducts training in today's corporate environments.

Stephen A. Bokat (1946–)

As vice-president and general counsel of the U.S. Chamber of Commerce, Stephen Bokat has represented the business and management point of view on the issue of sexual harassment in amicus curiae (friend of the court) briefs before the United States Supreme Court and other federal courts, as well as serving as a speaker, panelist, and counselor to management on the issue. In the case in which the Supreme Court first addressed the issue of sexual harassment, *Meritor Savings Bank v. Vinson*, the Chamber of Commerce, under Bokat's direction, took the position that sexual advances without any loss or threatened loss of tangible job benefits did not state a case of sexual harassment under Title VII, that an employer should not be strictly liable under Title VII for a supervisor's advances when the employer neither knew nor reasonably could have known of the advances, that evidence relating to the plaintiff's behavior and dress should be admissible (a position adopted by the Court), and that the Court should establish guidelines for analysis of sexual harassment cases.

Bokat is frequently called to represent the management perspective on sexual harassment cases on educational panels or in media interviews. He also conducts training programs on sexual harassment. He believes most businesses are now receptive to training on the issue because sexual harassment "doesn't improve anyone's bottom line. It doesn't improve productivity, and it has no place in the workplace" (personal interview with the author). Bokat sees problems when employers are not informed about the law or when some people are overly sensitive. During the Clarence Thomas nomination hearings, he was interviewed on radio and television shows daily. The Chamber of Commerce supported Thomas's nomination.

As general counsel of the U.S. Chamber of Commerce, Bokat is in charge of the chamber's legal department. He also serves as executive vice-president of the National Chamber Litigation Center, a public-policy law firm associated with the U.S. Chamber of Commerce and established to represent business before the courts and federal regulatory agencies. He joined the chamber in June 1977 after serving as an appellate litigator for the Occupational Safety and Health division of the Solicitor's Office of the U.S. Labor Department. Earlier, he served as attorney adviser to both the chair of the Occupational Safety and Health Review Commission and a member of the National Labor Relations Board. A graduate of Adams State College, he received his law degree from the George Washington University Law School in 1972. Bokat is coeditor in chief of *Occupational Safety and Health Law* (1988), published by the Bureau of National Affairs.

Catherine A. Broderick (1953–)

Catherine Broderick was an attorney with the Securities and Exchange Commission (SEC) when she filed a lawsuit alleging that she was the subject of a hostile work environment because other women in her department were given promotions as a reward for engaging in sexual relationships and favors. (This case is discussed in Chapters 2 and 4.) The atmosphere, she has since reported, was "all ingrown and festering." Broderick sued only after she was threatened with termination for complaining about the environment in her office. The case garnered national media attention on the new claim of "paramour preference," and Broderick has been interviewed by a number of national radio and television programs. As a result of her legal victory, she was awarded a choice of jobs in the agency. She now works in the general counsel's office on appellate litigation, where she describes the work environment as "very professional."

Broderick has been employed by the SEC since 1979; currently, she serves as counsel to the assistant general counsel. Before that assignment, she was the senior attorney of corporation finance, where she supervised the staff review of antitakeover proposals in proxy statements. She also served as an attorney in the Division of Enforcement, where she worked on litigation and compliance. Before joining the Securities and Exchange Commission, she was in private practice in New York. Broderick has an LL.M. in securities from Georgetown University Law Center. She received her J.D. from the New York University School of Law, her M.A. in English from the same university, and a B.F.A. from Carnegie Mellon University in 1972.

Lloyd R. Cohen (1947–)

Lloyd Cohen is an associate professor of law at Chicago-Kent College of Law in Chicago. He has written and lectured widely on issues of ethics and law. Recently, he has been one of the few legal scholars to write and speak out as a critic of laws and regulations governing sexual harassment. Cohen's articles on this subject have appeared in the *New York Times, Society,* and *Academic Questions,* a publication of the National Association of Scholars. His basic thesis has been that the workplace is one of the central or primary places in our society where women and men can meet romantic partners. In his *New York Times* piece, entitled "Fear of Flirting," he argued that "at work they can flirt and in other ways get things rolling in a largely unthreatening environment. Should this be substantially limited by regulations, the lives of those affected will be diminished" (December 12, 1991, section 1, p. 29, col. 1). He has also been a critic of so-called harassment speech codes on campus—including those designed to prevent sexual harassment—because he fears they will lead to infringement of the First Amendment and interfere with the university's role as the "temple of thought, discourse, and intellectual dispute."

Cohen has taught at the University of Chicago Law School and the California Western School of Law. In addition to a law degree with honors from Emory University, he holds a Ph.D. in economics from SUNY-Binghamton. He graduated from Harpur College with a major in economics in 1968. Before Cohen started his career as a law professor, he served as special counsel to the vice-chair of the U.S. International Trade Commission.

Frances Krauskopf Conley (1940–)

Frances Conley, M.D., made national headlines in 1991 when she resigned as a professor of surgery (neurosurgery) at Stanford University School of Medicine, alleging that she could not work under the newly appointed chair of her department because he perpetrated sexual harassment against her and other women. Going public with her reasons for the resignation, in a press release Conley stated,

> I resigned my professorship because, under his stewardship, my professional work environment was truly hostile and because I wanted no part of an institution that proved incapable of recognizing that its actions were diametrically opposed to those beliefs it publicly articulated. Just because I had chosen to close my eyes to inappropriate behavior and remarks in my quest for success did not mean that I should continue to facilitate the career of one who is offensive and who, perhaps more importantly, would subject yet another generation of women and minorities to the same abuse.

As a result of Conley's resignation, the university commenced an investigation. Two days before the effective date of her resignation,

Conley rescinded it and returned to her faculty position, convinced that her presence might force the medical school to remedy the problem. The supervisor Conley had accused of sexism was ultimately asked to step down, as the investigators found that "it would not be in the interests of the school for him to continue in the position of acting chair." The doctor, Gerald Silverberg, agreed to participate in training and counseling programs focused on gender and sensitivity and also agreed to undergo a procedure to monitor his behavior. In a press release he apologized to "anyone I may have offended." Silverberg went on to state that "it was never my intention to demean or insult any women, but it is now clear to me that some things I said or did in jest or from affection were taken as signs of disrespect."

Frances Conley was educated in California public schools, attended Bryn Mawr College, received a B.A. in biology with distinction from Stanford, and went on to obtain both an M.D. degree and an M.S. in management from Stanford. A tenured faculty member at Stanford, she has been the recipient of many honors, is board certified in neurological surgery, and has published numerous writings in her field. She was the nation's fifth woman to be certified in neurosurgery. Now a frequent speaker on the issue of sexual harassment, Conley notes that after years of accepting sexual harassment in her male-dominated field, she "sinned twice" against the male status quo, "first by refusing to play the game anymore and refusing to keep silent and then by going public" with her reasons for dropping out.

Paula Anne Coughlin (1962?–)

Lieutenant Paula Anne Coughlin, a U.S. Navy aviator, made national headlines when she complained to her superiors about sexual harassment at a 1991 meeting of the Tailhook Association in Las Vegas. At that meeting, 26 women—half of them military officers—claimed they had been sexually assaulted while being pushed down a gauntlet of drunken naval aviators in a hotel hallway. Just days before Anita Hill testified in the Senate, Paula Coughlin filed her complaint with the navy. Later, when interviews with around 1,500 men at Tailhook turned up only 2 names of men on the gauntlet, she went public, "putting a name and a face to this." Her courage was instrumental in forcing the Pentagon to reopen the investigation. The final report blasted the navy for its handling of the scandal, concluding that the men in charge were worried more about covering the navy's tail than about uncovering Tailhook. The investigation eventually led to the resignation of Navy Secretary Lawrence Garrett and several other top navy officials. After the investigation, the Pentagon engaged in a new push to halt sexual harassment; the program includes a videotape on the subject that now accompanies training packets sent to every U.S. Navy command.

Coughlin, the daughter of a retired naval officer, has stated about the incident, "I've been in the Navy almost eight years and I've worked my ass off to be one of the guys, to be the best Naval officer I can and prove that women can do whatever the job calls for. And what I got, I was treated like trash. I wasn't one of them." A graduate of Old Dominion University and a native of Virginia, Coughlin was commissioned in the United States Naval Reserves and began her service in the Hampton Roads Naval Reserve Officers Training Corps unit in 1984. Lieutenant Coughlin worked as an aide to the commander in the Naval Air Test Center and has flown more than ten different models of aircraft. Designated an unrestricted aviator in 1987, Lieutenant Coughlin has been awarded one Navy Commendation Medal, two Navy Achievement Medals, three Meritorious Unit Commendations, the Armed Services Defense Medal, and two sea service ribbons. In a letter dated February 7, 1994, Coughlin resigned from the Navy, stating:

> I feel continued service would be detrimental to my physical, mental, and emotional health. The physical attack on me by Naval aviators at the 1991 Tailhook convention, and the covert and overt attacks on me that followed, have stripped me of my ability to serve. The foundation on which I serve my country remains steadfast, but I am unable to continue serving effectively as a United States Naval officer or as a Naval aviator.

In a separate statement released through her attorney, Coughlin said, "My request to resign should not be viewed as a message to other women to refrain from reporting a physical assault."

Coughlin filed a lawsuit against the Las Vegas Hilton and the Tailhook Association when the navy investigation failed to find anyone responsible for her assault. The Tailhook Association settled before trial for an undisclosed amount. The Hilton tried the case aggressively, but the jury sided with Coughlin. After a lengthy trial, on October 28, 1994, it took the jury less than three hours to find the Hilton negligent for having allowed the convention to be held in its hotel when the company knew previous Tailhook conventions had caused problems and failed to provide adequate security. The jury awarded Coughlin $1.7 million in compensatory damages for the emotional distress she had suffered as a result of Tailhook. Later, the jury awarded $5 million in punitive damages as well.

Peggy Crull (1946–)

Peggy Crull served as both research director and executive director of the Working Women's Institute (WWI) from 1977 through 1985. WWI was probably the first institute devoted exclusively to combating sexual harassment in the workplace. As research director, Crull instituted some of the first studies ever conducted on the issue. When publicity about the institute started to reach women, Crull was "flooded with mail and phone calls" from sexual harassment victims who wanted to share their experiences. Crull realized that the letters represented a "gold mine" of original research material on a subject that had not been extensively documented. From those data, in 1987 she published the first study ever conducted on the incidence of sexual harassment in the workplace. She went on to direct research and write articles on the stress effects of sexual harassment, as well as to pursue original research on the issue of sexual harassment of women in blue-collar and other nontraditional jobs. She remembers that it was difficult to obtain funding for research on the issue in those early days because, unlike rape or other forms of physical assault against women, "sexual harassment was not a criminal offense."

Since the 1970s, Crull has continued to develop her expertise on the issue, testifying in sexual harassment cases and serving on the New York Governor's Task Force on Sexual Harassment. She was one of a number of women who sought to convince members of the Senate Judiciary Committee during the Thomas hearings to consider expert testimony on sexual harassment, especially on such issues as whether it is common for victims not to report the harassment at the time it occurs—a major issue in the Hill testimony. (The senators could not understand why Hill had waited ten years to come forward with her story.) Currently, Crull serves as the research director of the New York Commission on Human Rights; in that role, she has helped to organize hearings on harassment in the construction industry.

Warren Farrell (1943–)

Dr. Warren Farrell is the author of *The Liberated Man* (1974), *Why Men Are the Way They Are* (1986), and *The Myth of Male Power* (1993), the latter of which includes an entire chapter on the issue of sexual harassment. The second book was a national best-seller, won two national awards, and was published in more than 51 countries in eight languages. The *New York Post* called it "the most important book ever written about love, sex, and intimacy." Over a period of 20 years, Farrell has worked with hundreds of men's and women's groups on gender issues and relationships between the sexes. He is the only man to have been elected three times to the board of the National Organization for Women in New York City; he has also served on the boards of the National Organization for Changing Men and the National Congress for Men. The *Chicago Tribune* described Farrell as "the Gloria Steinem of Men's Liberation."

More recently, Farrell has been criticized by some women activists, because he began to write and speak out on the subject of men's liberation, challenging the feminist assumption that society's problems are caused by the power men have over women. He argues that male power is a myth, because most men have little control over their lives and are required in our society to support their families, work in dangerous occupations, and serve in the armed forces. On the issue of sexual harassment, especially in *The Myth of Male Power,* Farrell argues that many claims are the result of the mixed signals women send out in the workplace; many women expect to meet and even marry men they meet at work. He also argues that allowing such claims will lead to a new form of discrimination against women, as some men—leery of false claims of sexual harassment—will be reluctant to hire, travel with, or promote women into close working relationships. What is called sexual harassment, Farrell also argues, is the result of our society's expectations that men will take the lead in initiating sexual relationships.

A frequent commentator on gender issues on television and radio shows, Farrell has written for numerous magazines and professional journals. Although his Ph.D. was in political science, he has also taught at the college level in departments of psychology, sociology, sexual politics, and public administration at several universities, including the Schools of Medicine at the University of California and Georgetown University. Currently, Farrell conducts workshops across the country on men's roles and other gender issues. He stresses in these workshops that although women have valid complaints that they are "sex objects," men are treated as "success objects."

Barbara Gutek (1949?–)

Barbara Gutek is one of the pioneering researchers on the incidence of sexual harassment and other issues relating to sex in the workplace. Author of the widely read book *Sex and the Workplace,* published in 1985, Gutek conducted one of the first random-sample studies on the issue of sexual harassment. In that book, she reported that her studies revealed that sex at work is a problem for up to half of all workers and that "it is a mistake to assume that sex at work is simply a product of biological attractions between men and women and that none of it has work related consequences." Gutek has also consulted on or designed a number of other major studies. She has served as a faculty member at several universities in the schools of psychology, sociology, management, and business. She received her Ph.D. from the University of Michigan, specializing in organizational psychology. Currently a professor of management and policy at the California Institute of Technology, she has also taught at the University of Arizona, Claremont Graduate School, and a number of other institutions.

In addition to her work in the field of sex and work, Gutek has studied the issues of computer use and learning at work, women managers and entrepreneurs, and other workplace issues. The recipient of numerous fellowships, she has consulted with major corporations and government entities on sexual harassment and other workplace issues, as well as serving as an expert witness in cases involving equitable promotion systems, sexual harassment, and survey research methods. She is the author of many books and articles on the issues of women and work.

Anita Faye Hill (1956–)

The youngest of 13 children in a poor black farm family, Anita Hill graduated with honors from Oklahoma State University in 1977. In college she was a National Merit Scholar, a University Regents Scholar, and a member of the president's and dean's honor rolls. After receiving her law degree from Yale University, she worked in private practice at a large, prestigious Washington, D.C., law firm before working for Clarence Thomas in the Office of Civil Rights at the Department of Education. She then followed Thomas to the EEOC. After leaving the EEOC, Hill became a law professor at Oral Roberts University in Tulsa and then taught at the University of Oklahoma Law School, where she was awarded tenure after four years on the faculty.

Hill worked far from the public eye in all of these endeavors until her accusations in 1991 against then Supreme Court nominee Clarence Thomas. Her claim that Thomas had sexually harassed her when she worked with him ten years before his nomination stunned the Senate and the country. Despite her charges and the nationally televised hearings that mesmerized and divided the American people on the issue of sexual harassment, the Senate Judiciary Committee voted to confirm Thomas.

Since that time, Hill has received more than 40,000 letters and 1,000 speaking requests. Despite critics' predictions that she would use her notoriety for personal gain, she has not written a sensational book, sold her story for a television movie, or appeared on the talk-show circuit. After initially refusing many generous offers to write a book, Hill signed a contract to do so after the 1993 appearance of David Brock's book *The Real Anita Hill,* which raised many questions about her personal and professional life and her honesty. In May 1994, she signed a million-dollar book contract to write two books, one personal and the other more theoretical. The money allowed her to take a leave of absence from her teaching job, move to California to be closer to her sisters, and found the Institute for Social Change in Berkeley, California. The institute is dedicated to research on sexual harassment, gender, and other civil rights issues.

Although Hill tried to return to teaching and to live a private life, she found it impossible to do so. As she told Jane Mayer and Jill Abramson, the authors of *Strange Justice,* during an interview in 1993, "I had to make a decision . . . whether I could spend all of my energy trying to disengage myself, which didn't work, or try to make something positive of this dismal situation. Basically, that's what I have done."

Although she has turned down most speaking requests and nearly all media requests, when she does speak she avoids rehashing the charges against Thomas and instead discusses the history and effect of sexual harassment and discrimination. "Sexual harassment is used as a tool of exclusion," she tells her audiences. In a 1992 speech before the Women Judges Fund for Justice, she noted that

The nation's courts often misunderstand women victims. . . . One of the things that became quite evident last year during the hearings was the Senate did not grasp the seriousness of sexual harassment and the pervasiveness of it. And unfortunately, it was because of a lack of perspective.

Public opinion polls have shown an increase in the number of people who believe Hill's allegations about Thomas. A *Wall Street Journal*–NBC poll taken in September 1992 found that 44 percent of those surveyed believed Hill, up from 24 percent in 1991. Belief in Thomas's testimony had dropped from 47 percent to 34 percent during the same period.

Brenda Hoster (1958–)

Sergeant Major Brenda Hoster retired in August 1996 after 22 years in uniform because the army refused to address her sexual harassment complaint against Sergeant Major of the Army Gene McKinney. McKinney had served in one of the army's most revered posts and was supposed to be the role model and champion of the service's 410,000 enlisted men and women. Hoster filed a formal complaint after Army Secretary Togo West Jr. named McKinney to an army panel charged with combating sexual harassment and the army issued a video in which McKinney appears declaring war on sexual harassment.

Following allegations that drill sergeants had allegedly assaulted female trainees at Maryland's Aberdeen Proving Ground and other bases, Hoster came forward. Unlike most rookie soldiers at Aberdeen, Hoster was no raw recruit. A Bronze Star winner and former drill sergeant, she was one of the youngest sergeant majors in history. In May 1995, McKinney asked Hoster— even though he did not know her well—to be his public relations adviser. Hoster says that within weeks McKinney's "Jekyll and Hyde behavior"—personable and professional in public, enraged and profane in private—turned her life into "a living hell."

At a conference in Hawaii in April 1996, Hoster alleges that McKinney came to her hotel room at 11:30 one night clad in shorts and a T-shirt, ordered a male colleague out, and stated, "You know, you're just what I need right now." Hoster rebuffed his physical advances, reminding him that his wife was right down the hall. She asked him to leave, but he blocked the door and grabbed her. At one point, McKinney allegedly stated, "I could take you right here, right now." Hoster says she responded, "If you do such a stupid thing, you had better kill me, because if I live I will tell."

Hoster remained quiet about the incident for several weeks, pondering her options, and then complained to two male superiors and asked for reassignment. When two months had passed with no response to her request, she retired. Only in November, when McKinney was appointed to a blue-ribbon panel investigating sexual harassment in the army, did Hoster go public and file a lawsuit against her former boss and the army.

She says she is motivated now by a desire to fix the system and protect other women: "One thing I hope comes out of all this is that if it helps one woman now or in the future, then it's worth it" (*Rocky Mountain News*, February 16, 1997, pp. 3A, 70A).

Hoster was born in Port Clinton, Pennsylvania. She joined the army in 1974, served as a drill sergeant in South Carolina for three years, and then served in South Korea as a public affairs supervisor. Hoster reported for *Stars and Stripes* for more than three years, went to Hollywood as the army's technical adviser to the movie industry, and won a Bronze Star for her public affairs work in Saudi Arabia during Operation Desert Storm. In 1992, she became one of the youngest soldiers ever to be promoted to the rank of sergeant major.

Hoster now works as an office manager in a Santa Teresa, New Mexico, dentist's office. Since her public disclosure, two other female service members have come forward to allege that McKinney acted improperly toward them. The army has suspended McKinney from his duty while the allegations are investigated. He has denied the accusations.

Paula Corbin Jones (1967–)

Jones began work at the Arkansas Industrial Development Commission in March 1991; she left in May 1993. In 1993, Jones made public her charges that President Bill Clinton had sexually harassed her on May 8, 1991, at the Excelsior Hotel in Little Rock, Arkansas. At the time the alleged harassment took place, Clinton was the governor of Arkansas. Jones claims that while she was working at a state event in Little Rock, an Arkansas state trooper brought her to Clinton's hotel room at his request. When she refused his advances, Clinton allegedly told her to keep quiet about the incident and appeared to threaten her, telling her that her boss was his "good friend." In 1995, a federal court blocked her case from proceeding until Clinton leaves office because the president is immune from civil suits while in office, a procedural issue that was argued before the Supreme Court on January 13, 1997. Most legal commentators predicted that the Court would delay her suit until the president left office, but in mid-1997 the Court ruled that the suit could proceed during Clinton's tenure as president.

Meanwhile, Jones has produced two witnesses who assert that she told them about the incident the day it happened. Other friends and even relatives have expressed doubts about her story. She claims she finally came forward in 1993 to "clear her name" after an article about her had appeared in the *American Spectator*. Her original press conference on the issue was organized by various conservative groups, however, causing some commentators to express reservations about her claim. Jones initially agreed to spilt any book deals or movie rights with her first attorney, but she has recently claimed she will give all profits to charity. Although she has turned down offers from the tabloids, she did make $50,000 for endorsing the No Excuses brand of jeans, half of which went to her lawyers. President Clinton has denied her allegations, although he admits he cannot remember whether he met her.

Jones is now a housewife in Long Beach, California, where she lives with her husband and two sons.

Freada Klein (1952–)

Dr. Freada Klein has worked on issues of discrimination and diversity since the early 1970s. In 1976, she cofounded the Alliance against Sexual Coercion in Boston, one of the first organizations in the United States to offer comprehensive services, training, and consultation on the topic of sexual harassment to both the private and public sectors. She assisted in the formation of similar organizations in Connecticut, Ohio, and Canada. She is the author of a number of articles and coauthored the book *Fighting Sexual Harassment: An Advocacy Handbook*, one of the first manuals written about sexual harassment. The Alliance against Sexual Coercion was founded because Klein and three associates who had worked in rape crisis centers recognized that most women had complaints about what Klein decided to call "sexual coercion" in their workplaces—including requests for sex in return for jobs, as well as actual assaults.

More recently, Klein has consulted with dozens of organizations—including General Motors Corporation and Harvard University—to help them develop harassment policies, grievance procedures, and training programs. Her research on discrimination and her diversity surveys for corporations and universities included the first large, methodologically sound study on the issue for the Merit Systems Protection Board. She was also a consultant on the first major Defense Department study, the *Harvard Business Review/Redbook* study—a major study of managers in Fortune 500 companies and their attitudes on this subject—described in Chapter 4 (Collins and Blodgett 1981), and many others. She received a fellowship from the Social Science Research Council for her doctoral dissertation on sexual harassment. In 1988, Klein completed a survey of the Fortune 500 manufacturing and service firms for *Working Woman* magazine to determine the effectiveness of corporate efforts to address sexual harassment. Klein frequently speaks to professional associations and conferences and guest lectures in educational institutions on sexual harassment issues. She also serves as an expert witness in sexual harassment litigation. In 1991, Klein was invited to testify at hearings before the U.S. House of Representatives Labor and Education Committee on the proposed Civil Rights Bill of 1991, during which she provided data from the results of various surveys. During the Senate confirmation hearings on Clarence Thomas, Klein was asked to provide commentary on several television shows and was quoted extensively in press reports.

Formerly the director of organizational development for Lotus Development Corporation, Klein currently heads Klein Associates, Inc., in Cambridge, Massachusetts, an organizational development and human resource consulting firm. Klein holds a Ph.D. in social policy and research from Brandeis University, where she concentrated on employment policy. She received her B.A. in criminology with highest honors from the University of California at Berkeley.

Judith Ellen Kurtz (1948–)

As the managing attorney for Equal Rights Advocates, Inc. (ERA), a nonprofit legal and educational corporation whose purpose is to end sex discrimination, Kurtz has been involved in a number of important legal cases involving sexual harassment and other kinds of discrimination against women. She also contributed to the plaintiff's Supreme Court brief in *Meritor Savings Bank v.*

Vinson. ERA continues to bring important test cases concerning the issue of sexual harassment, including a consent decree entered against the City of San Francisco Police Department in May 1988.

After her graduation from Hastings College of Law, Kurtz began her career in private practice, specializing in domestic relations and criminal law. She has worked as an attorney with Equal Rights Advocates since 1978 and was promoted to managing attorney in 1986. In addition to sponsoring complex litigation, ERA provides advice and counseling for employees and employers, along with public education and community outreach. As the senior staff attorney, Kurtz oversees the litigation as well as the counseling and educational activities of the staff. The office has a hot line for sex discrimination cases; Kurtz reports that sexual harassment complaints still account for more calls than any other category of discrimination complaint.

A frequent speaker throughout the United States on the issue of sex discrimination, Kurtz has also served as an instructor at San Francisco State University, where she taught a course on women and the law. She is a graduate of the State University of New York at Buffalo and coauthor of *Bargaining for Equality,* a guide to legal and collective bargaining solutions for workplace problems that particularly affect women.

John Leo (1935–)

John Leo is the widely read "On Society" columnist for *U.S. News and World Report.* His column is syndicated nationally by Universal Press. In that position he has written numerous columns addressing sexual harassment, rape, sexual discrimination, and other gender issues. With regard to the issue of sexual harassment, he has taken what he calls a "yes, but" position. Although he admits that the issue is an important one that can cause serious harm to victims and their careers, he has argued that some programs, authors, and judges have gone too far. He has criticized campus programs that address sexual harassment and other gender issues as examples of a new wave of "political correctness on campus," a movement he finds threatening to academic freedom and free speech. In his column he has also criticized the reasonable woman standard articulated in some recent cases as placing sexual harassment "in the same category as violations of college speech and behavior codes, which often turn on the feelings of the aggrieved rather than any objective and definable offense. . . . If feelings are trumps, how do we know when sexism and harassment end and hypersensitivity begins?" He has written that "the reasonable-woman standard is insulting to women because it shrinks what ought to be a universal standard of fairness into a merely tribal one." Leo has also been critical of the feminist perspective on rape, arguing that it is not an act of bias against women.

Before joining *U.S. News* in September 1988, Leo covered the social sciences and intellectual trends for *Time* magazine and the *New York Times*. He also reported on religion for the *Times* and wrote essays and humor columns. Leo is a former associate editor of *Commonweal* magazine, the former book editor of the sociology magazine *Society,* and a former deputy administrator of New York City's Environmental Protection Administration. He launched the "Press Clips" column in the *Village Voice* and is the author of a book of humor, *How the Russians Invented Baseball and Other Essays of Enlightenment* (1989). He earned a degree in philosophy and history with honors from the University of Toronto in 1957.

Judith L. Lichtman (1940–)

Judith Lichtman is president of the Women's Legal Defense Fund, an organization whose mission is to assert women's legal rights. Since the 1970s, she has been involved in crafting legal arguments and influencing public policy on sexual harassment and other discrimination issues. She was one of the attorneys involved in one of the first federal cases to consider the issue of sexual harassment, *Barnes v. Costle (Train).* She also appeared as an advocate before the EEOC to convince that agency to promulgate its first guidelines on the issue of sexual harassment and successfully lobbied Congress on the 1991 Civil Rights Act to expand the damage provisions relating to sexual harassment. She testified against Clarence Thomas's nomination to the Supreme Court.

Prior to assuming her position as president of the Women's Legal Defense Fund in 1988, Lichtman served as executive director of the fund. Before that, she was the legal adviser to the Commonwealth of Puerto Rico, a consultant and senior attorney at the U.S. Commission on Civil Rights, a staff assistant at the Urban Coalition, and an instructor in the history and political science departments at Jackson State College.

A longtime civil rights activist, Lichtman has served on the Glass Ceiling Commission for the Labor Department under Lyn

Martin, been co-chair of the Leadership Conference on Civil Rights, and acted as a member of many other groups. She was a founding member of the Women's Law and Public Policy Fellowship Program and of the Alliance for Justice, as well as serving on the Advisory Committee of the American Civil Liberties Union (ACLU) Women's Rights Project. She has won a variety of public service and legal awards, including the Association of Trial Lawyers of America Humanitarian Award, the American Bar Association Silver Gavel Award, and many others. Lichtman was named one of the 100 most powerful women in Washington in 1989 by *Washingtonian* magazine and one of America's 100 most important women by *Ladies Home Journal* in 1988.

She has published widely on the issue of sex discrimination. She recalls that she went to law school because, "for me, being a lawyer meant having a license to be an activist." A tireless advocate of women's rights, she asserts, "I define a feminist as somebody who believes in the equality of all people and has a commitment to equal justice, somebody who has a vision of everyone being able to be economically independent and treated fairly."

Katy Lyle (1972–)

In 1987, Katy Lyle, a student at Central High School in Duluth, Minnesota, learned obscene remarks about her had been scrawled on the walls of the boys' restroom, such as "Katie Lyle is a slut. Katie Lyle sucked my d--- after she sucked my dog's d---. Here's Katie Lyle's number." Two walls were covered with obscenities about her; the boys called them "the Katie stall."

An honor student and self-proclaimed "band nerd" who loved music and played the piano and the saxophone, Katy had never had a real boyfriend or even dated. She and her parents asked the principal repeatedly—16 times—to have the offending graffiti removed. Although the school continually promised to remove the graffiti, it was still there 18 months later at the start of Katy's senior year. The school offered many excuses, among them that "graffiti was considered a building maintenance problem" and that the school had funds to paint only every two years. Tired of seeing his sister crying all the time, Katy's older brother took a bucket of cleaning fluid into the boys' bathroom and washed off the paint, but the scratches in the wall remained.

After she complained, Katy was greeted on the school bus each day with such "delightful" remarks as "Are you as good as they say?" and "Katy, will you do me?" The Lyles lived some distance from town. Katy would try to laugh off the comments during the hour-and-15-minute bus ride, but she would burst out in sobs by the time she arrived home. She brought a bottle of Scrubbing Bubbles to school but never used it for fear she would get into trouble if she went into the boys' bathroom.

The Lyle family's telephone rang constantly. When a family member answered, the callers would hang up. Katy's father, Jim Lyle, stated that he would find his daughter rolled up in a fetal position every morning, crying and refusing to go to school. Katy went to three different counselors and to the principal, asking that the comments be stopped.

The bathroom walls were finally repainted after Katy and her parents filed a complaint with the Minnesota Department of Human Rights. In 1991, Katy won a $15,000 settlement from the school district just before her case was tried. Katy's case was the first in which a district actually paid to settle a peer harassment claim. Because of Katy, every school in Minnesota now has a sexual harassment policy.

Katy's case received extensive media coverage, including the front page of the *New York Times*; she also appeared on the *Phil Donahue Show* and the *Today Show*. In 1993, Katy's story was made into an ABC after-school special TV movie, *Boys Will Be Boys*, which is currently shown in many schools.

Katy graduated from the University of Minnesota and teaches elementary school music in a Duluth suburb.

Mary Jo McGrath (1952–)

A practicing attorney for 20 years, McGrath has practiced education law and represented school districts for 16 years. She is a nationally recognized expert on sexual harassment in schools, teacher termination litigation, and employee supervision, evaluation, and discipline. She designed the copyrighted *McGrath Template: Legally Fit Principled Management* to help schools work their way through the thorny issues of employee communication, performance, and evaluation. She also serves as an expert consultant to California governor Pete Wilson on the reformation of teacher tenure laws.

McGrath founded a training and development company in Santa Barbara, California, that specializes in providing legally based and principled workshops and video training systems to schools, groups, and private organizations; the company has trained over 35,000 school executives. She has also created a three-part sexual harassment video training system entitled *Sexual Harassment: Minimize the Risk,* deemed the "best on the subject" by many education professionals. McGrath offers the most extensive training available on how to investigate claims of sexual harassment at three different levels.

McGrath was one of the first experts to emphasize that schools must conduct their own independent investigations of teacher-to-student sexual harassment, even if they have reported the incidents to the police as required by child protection laws. Concerning the current controversy about sexual harassment in grade schools and the "kiss heard around the world," she stated in a personal interview with the author in February 1997 that critics of addressing the issue in schools "feed the eagerness that exists to minimize the issue. We don't allow first graders to use racial epithets," and she wondered, "what's the difference?"

McGrath graduated from the Loyola School of Law and the University of California, Los Angeles.

Catharine A. MacKinnon (1946–)

Catharine MacKinnon is a central figure in feminist legal thought and the author of the pioneering work, *The Sexual Harassment of Working Women* (1979). As such, she has been a frequent target of critics such as columnist John Leo, who lambasted her "pinched view" of sexuality as eroticized male power. MacKinnon was the first to articulate in a comprehensive book the argument that sexual harassment is sex discrimination and a violation of Title VII. She is also the author of numerous articles in scholarly journals on feminist theory, pornography, and the law in women's lives.

MacKinnon has participated as an expert witness and with expert briefs in major sexual harassment and women's rights cases, including *Thoreson v. Penthouse,* a case in which she argued that punitive damages should be available for sexual harassment in cases involving women and pornography. She also assisted with the case of *Alexander v. Yale,* arguing that sexual harassment in education violates Title IX. MacKinnon has served on various legal committees, testified before the U.S. Senate on the Pornography Victims Protection Act, written ordinances against pornography, and given extensive public lectures, workshops, speeches, media appearances, and interviews on the issues of sexual equality and the law. During the Clarence Thomas hearings, she provided extensive commentary on one of the major television networks. After the hearings, she fielded two to three speech requests per day. MacKinnon now focuses her efforts on pornography issues rather than sexual harassment. Pornography, she believes, will be a much more difficult battle for women, because businesses make money on pornography whereas "sexual harassment costs business."

A tenured professor of law at the University of Michigan, MacKinnon has also been a visiting professor of law at Yale Law School, Harvard Law School, Stanford University, the Chicago Law School, and several others. In addition, she has served as a visiting scholar at the Institute for Research on Women and Gender at Stanford University. She has authored nine law course casebooks on such subjects as sex equality, feminism and socialism, sexuality and legality, and pornography. She received her J.D. from Yale Law School in 1977 and her Ph.D. in political science from Yale in 1987. Her undergraduate degree was from Smith College. Among her academic honors are the Smith Medal from Smith College, the Honorary Doctor of Laws from Haverford College, and the Doctor of Humane Letters from Reed College.

Eleanor Holmes Norton (1937–)

Representative Eleanor Holmes Norton, a fourth-generation Washingtonian, is currently serving her fourth term as the Washington, D.C., representative to Congress. Previously, she was chair of the Equal Employment Opportunity Commission under President Jimmy Carter, the only woman to hold that position. Under her direction, in 1980 the commission drafted the first guidelines on sexual harassment, which affirmed that sexual harassment was unlawful discrimination because of sex. As a member of Congress, Norton has also urged the House and the Senate to endorse a sexual harassment policy based on these guidelines. She has signed the policy and mandated its terms in her congressional office. She spoke out from the floor of the House on Anita Hill's charges against Clarence Thomas, stating,

> I feel obligated because I am a black woman who cannot help but share some of the lonely pain Professor Anita Hill has courageously chosen to bear. . . . I cannot know where the truth lies, but I cannot imagine

why Professor Hill would have chosen to invent a story she knew would submit her to public torment.

Norton was one of several congresswomen who demanded that the Senate investigate Hill's charges. She has spoken and written about the controversy, most notably in *Ms.* magazine.

In addition to her service at the EEOC, Norton served as chair of the New York City Commission on Human Rights, where she held what may have been the first public hearings on the issue of sexual harassment in the late 1970s, and as a tenured professor of law at Georgetown University. A nationally recognized commentator, writer, civil rights and women's rights leader, and the recipient of 50 honorary degrees, Norton has been named one of the 100 most important women in America by *Ladies Home Journal* and one of the most powerful women in Washington by *Washingtonian* magazine.

Norton received her B.A. from Antioch College and then simultaneously earned a master's degree in American studies from Yale Graduate School and a law degree from Yale Law School. She has served on the boards of three Fortune 500 companies and the board of the Rockefeller Foundation, as well as on the board of governors of the D.C. Bar Association and as a trustee of many professional, civic, and civil rights organizations.

Robert Packwood (1932–)

Robert Packwood was born in Portland, Oregon, the great-grandson of William H. Packwood, a pioneer and a member of the 1857 Oregon Constitutional Convention. After receiving his B.A. from Willamette University and his J.D. from New York University, Packwood clerked for the chief justice of the Oregon Supreme Court, practiced law in Portland, and won election to the Oregon legislature. He was elected to the United States Senate in 1968, the youngest senator at that time, and was reelected four times. During the course of his career, he served on a variety of Senate committees, chairing the Communications Subcommittee—which handled telecommunications issues—and the Senate Finance Committee and serving on the Senate Commerce, Science, and Transportation Committee.

In the wake of the Hill-Thomas hearings, more than 20 women who had worked with Packwood between 1969 and 1992 charged him with sexual harassment. Packwood, a well-known proponent of women's rights, admitted varying degrees of guilt but fell short of accepting responsibility. The Senate initially declined to remove Packwood from office but launched an investigation into the charges against him. During the investigation, Packwood revealed that he had kept detailed diaries of his Senate career. He fought the subpoenas from the committee that sought to obtain the diaries, but a federal court finally ordered him to turn them over to the committee. Packwood resigned in 1995 after the results of the investigation—which found many of the allegations had merit—were made public. He is now president of his own consulting firm, Sunrise Research, Inc.

Michele A. Paludi (1954–)

Dr. Michele Paludi was one of the first, and remains one of the foremost, researchers on academic and workplace sexual harassment. She is the editor of *Ivory Power: Sexual Harassment on Campus* (1990) and *Sexual Harassment on College Campuses: Abusing the Ivory Power* (1996) and coauthor of *Academic and Workplace Harassment: A Resource Manual* (1991) and *Workplace Sexual Harassment* (1991). *Ivory Power* was selected the Outstanding Book on Human Rights by the Gustavus Myers Center for Human Rights. For five years, Paludi facilitated a research laboratory on sexual harassment located at Hunter College, where she was a full professor of psychology.

Her most recent research focuses on the academic sexual harassment of women of color. She has gained national media attention for her work on the psychological impact of sexual harassment and is host of the City University of New York and Schenectady, New York, television program *Gender Matters.* Currently, Paludi offers education and training in issues related to sexual harassment and gender to private corporations, governments, and educational institutions. She has received several awards for her research, including the 1992 Progress in Equity Award from the New York State chapter of the American Association of University Women. Paludi is the author of numerous scholarly papers on sexual harassment and has presented her findings at several professional conventions, including those of the American Psychological Association.

Paludi takes a feminist stance in her work. In *Ivory Power*, for example, she wrote that "sexual harassment, like rape, incest, and battering, represents male expressions of power and dominance over women." She emphasized that "sexual harassment is not simply an annoyance or flirtation. It can mean the difference between passing a college course and failing one, between being given a raise or being fired." Her research has focused on exploding myths such as the idea that the victim invited the harassment or that only attractive women are harassed.

Mary P. Rowe (1936–)

When Mary Rowe started working as a special assistant to the president of the Massachusetts Institute of Technology (MIT) in 1973, she began to notice a surprising trend: About one-fifth of the problems students brought to her involved some aspect of sex bias or other gender issues. She began to meet with groups of students and eventually developed a training program that related to these issues. Her early work with those students led to her becoming a nationally recognized expert in the field of sexual harassment problems and training. Currently, she serves as an MIT ombudsman, with a designation as an impartial counselor and informal complaint handler. Anyone in the MIT community can contact her for any reason, and members are encouraged to do so by MIT's complaint policy and by booklets called "Tell Someone," which are prepared for students and employees.

Rowe believes MIT is the first major employer in the United States to have "named" harassment as a problem and to have developed procedures to deal with concerns. She authored *Stopping Sexual Harassment: A Guide to Options and Resources at MIT* (1991), which has served as a guide for other employers. As a result of her role in developing the MIT sexual harassment program, she is also involved in consulting, teaching, conducting research, and writing for other organizations on the issue; she also serves as a consultant to other ombudsman programs. She is the author of numerous articles on such issues as the role of women and work, child care, and the role of corporate ombudsmen. Rowe is past president of the Corporate Ombudsman Association. She believes that with the increasing diversity in the U.S. workforce, lawmakers and corporate decision makers will need to prevent and deal with sexual and racial harassment. A corporate ombudsman, she finds, can help to resolve such complaints. Rowe holds a Ph.D. in economics from Columbia University and a B.A. in history (international relations) from Swarthmore College.

Karen Lee Sauvigné (1948–)

Karen Sauvigné was cofounder and executive director, from 1976 to 1983, of the Working Women's Institute (WWI), the pioneering organization that may have been the first to focus on sexual harassment in employment. The institute was established in 1975 to bring national attention to the widespread, but theretofore unspoken, problem of sexual harassment in employment. Sauvigné designed and implemented the institute's program of research and public education on sexual harassment and other equal employment issues. A recognized authority on sexual harassment, she has appeared on television, testified before congressional hearings, conducted workshops, and served as a policy consultant for government agencies, corporations, labor unions, educational institutions, and community groups. She has written articles and delivered speeches on sexual harassment in various publications and before various groups, including a presentation at the U.N. Decade for Women Forum in Nairobi, Kenya.

Sauvigné now serves as the associate director of continuing legal education, training, and consultation at City University of New York (CUNY) Law School at Queens College. Before assuming that position, she was the director of development at the law school. She has also served on the faculty and as a research director in the Human Affairs Program at Cornell University. Early in her career, she worked as the field coordinator for the CUNY College for Human Services and was assistant national director of the Civil Rights Research Council.

Sauvigné has received a number of awards, including the *Mlle* Award from *Mademoiselle* magazine for outstanding achievement and the Susan B. Anthony Award from the National Organization for Women. She was designated one of "Eighty Women To Watch in the Eighties" by *Ms.* magazine. She has served on the boards of the New York University Public Interest Law Foundation, the Institute for Women and Work of the New York State School of Industrial and Labor Relations at Cornell, and the Asian American Legal Defense and Education Fund. She holds a master's degree in comparative history from Rutgers University.

Phyllis Schlafly (1924–)

Born Phyllis MacAlpin Stewart in 1924 in St. Louis, Missouri, Phyllis Schlafly has been a leader in various conservative movements for more than 30 years. Considered a major force behind the defeat of the Equal Rights Amendment in many states, she is president and founder of a conservative organization called the Eagle Forum. Her *Phyllis Schlafly Report* has been published monthly for more than 25 years. She is a lawyer, author of 13 books, syndicated columnist, and radio commentator who is heard on 270 stations; her weekly live radio program on education is heard on 45 stations.

Schlafly has testified before more than 50 congressional and state legislative committees, advocating her conservative agenda on such topics as the Equal Rights Amendment, treaties, nuclear weaponry, education, child care, comparable worth, parental leave, and federal spending. One of her books, *A Choice Not an Echo* (1964), is one of the ten best-selling conservative books of all-time. Schlafly is a Phi Beta Kappa graduate of Washington University and of Washington University Law School. She received a master's degree in political science from Harvard University. Schlafly is the mother of six children and lives in Alton, Illinois.

On the issue of sexual harassment, Schlafly led an unsuccessful effort to repeal the EEOC guidelines during the Reagan administration, testifying at 1981 Labor Commission hearings that "sexual harassment is not a problem for the virtuous woman, except in the rarest of cases. When a woman walks across the room, she speaks with a universal body language that most men intuitively understand." In a November 1991 *Phyllis Schlafly Report* entitled *Feminism Falls on Its Face,* she wrote that "the confirmation of Clarence Thomas was a personal victory for an honorable man who was the victim of a savage eleventh-hour ambush by feminists in special-interest groups and in the media." Claiming the hearings were the result of a conspiracy between feminist and liberal politicians who would have used any tactic to defeat Clarence Thomas, Schlafly went on to write that "unscrupulous feminists and liberals will conspire to use false charges of sexual harassment to destroy a man who stands in their way." Schlafly doubted that a law school graduate could be a victim of sexual harassment, observing that the "very nature of being a lawyer is to thrive in a hostile environment. A lawyer complaining about this is like a doctor complaining about working in a 'bloody environment.'"

Patricia S. Schroeder (1940–)

Patricia Scott Schroeder, a Democrat, represented the First Congressional District of Colorado, which includes most of the city and county of Denver, for ten terms. Schroeder was elected in 1972 and was reelected nine times, winning 64 percent of the votes in 1990 and an even higher percentage in 1992. Schroeder was dean of the Colorado Congressional Delegation, as well as the most senior woman in Congress. She served in the House leadership as Democratic whip beginning in 1978 and was appointed deputy whip in 1987. In 1987, Schroeder explored a bid for the presidency. She was rated one of the six most respected women in America in a 1988 Gallup poll.

On the issue of sexual harassment, in fall 1991 Schroeder made headlines when a picture of her marching a group of female representatives from the House to the Senate was published in newspapers around the United States. She was instrumental in galvanizing the group to force the Senate Judiciary Committee to hold public hearings on Professor Anita Hill's claim that she had been harassed by Clarence Thomas. In addition, she persuaded the House to hold hearings in 1992 on the question of sexual harassment in the U.S. Navy after the Tailhook incident, and she helped to force the navy to conduct a more thorough investigation of the episode. As a result, a naval group displayed a lewd picture of her at one of its meetings; with typical Schroeder wit, the representative displayed the image during the House hearings, using the incident as evidence of the need for sexual harassment policies and training in the military. A former member of the House Armed Services Committee, Schroeder has long been an advocate of women in the military, working to prevent all kinds of sex discrimination in that institution.

Throughout her congressional tenure, Schroeder made women's rights issues, family issues, women's health issues, and defense burden sharing her top priorities. She was the leading House sponsor of the Family and Medical Leave Act, which gives workers a right to a job-guaranteed unpaid leave for family emergencies such as birth, adoption, or serious illness. Schroeder played a major role in the passage of the Voting Rights Act extension and the Civil Rights Act of 1984 and was a sponsor of the Civil Rights Act of 1991. In 1989, she introduced legislation to increase the federal commitment to birth control and infertility research, which was incorporated in the Women's Health Equity Act. She was a House sponsor of the Freedom of Choice Act, a bill that would put into federal law the principles of *Roe v. Wade*, thereby securing a woman's right to choose to terminate her pregnancy.

Schroeder was born in Portland, Oregon. She attended grade school in Texas, junior high in Ohio, and high school in Iowa. She graduated magna cum laude from the University of Minnesota, where she was a member of Phi Beta Kappa. Schroeder received her J.D. from Harvard Law School in 1964. Prior to her election to Congress, Schroeder practiced law and lectured at Denver colleges.

Schroeder resigned from Congress in 1996. Since that time she has taught public policy classes at Princeton and was recently elected president and chief executive officer of the Association of American Publishers.

Joseph M. Sellers (1953–)

Joseph Sellers was one of the lead attorneys for the plaintiff, Mechelle Vinson, in the Supreme Court case that established that sexual harassment did indeed violate Title VII of the Civil Rights Act. He has also served as counsel in a number of other important sexual harassment cases, including *Delgado v. Leeman,* a case that established important precedent on gender-based harassment and hostile work environment. In an area of the law in which many cases are settled before trial, Sellers estimates that he has actually litigated 10 to 12 sexual harassment cases and receives around a thousand requests to litigate EEOC-related claims each year.

Currently, Sellers is the director of the Equal Employment Opportunity Program of the Washington Lawyers' Committee for Civil Rights under Law. In this capacity, he has litigated dozens of civil rights cases on behalf of several thousand plaintiffs before various federal and state courts and administrative agencies. The claims in these cases have alleged discrimination on grounds ranging from race and color to sexual harassment to disability and family responsibility. In addition, he oversees the operation of an equal employment opportunity (EEO) Intake Program through the Washington Lawyers' Committee.

Sellers has also served as legal counsel to two civil rights testing programs. In the first, he assisted in the development of a professional program to test the delivery of taxi service in the District of Columbia and later served as counsel to plaintiffs in the only litigation that challenged the discriminatory practices of taxi companies. In the second, he assisted in the development of the first Equal Employment Testing Program and acted as counsel to the plaintiffs in the first EEO cases filed in the courts based on EEO testing evidence. Sellers has testified on a number of occasions before committees of the United States Congress regarding various civil rights matters. He chaired a two-year study of the federal EEO complaints processing system, the results of which were presented to the Subcommittee on Employment and Housing of the House Government Operations Committee. He has also lectured on various equal employment and other civil rights subjects, ranging from the design of affirmative action programs and how to manage a diverse workforce to the evaluation and litigation of various types of civil rights claims.

Sellers is a graduate of Brown University and Case Western Reserve School of Law, where he served as research editor of the *Law Review.* He has been active in political campaigns and has practiced law privately.

Anne E. Simon (1950–)

Anne Simon tried *Alexander v. Yale* (1977), one of the pivotal cases on sexual harassment that established the legal precedent that sexual harassment in universities is a violation of Title IX of the Civil Rights Act. Simon stated that she expected follow-up cases and was "astounded that universities all gave in right away." As a result of *Alexander,* most colleges and universities now have policies against sexual harassment.

Simon served as a staff attorney for the National Organization for Women (NOW) Legal Defense and Education Fund, where she counseled women on sexual harassment and other employment issues. A magna cum laude graduate of Radcliffe College, she received her J.D. degree from Yale Law School in 1976. She has written on sexual harassment and other women's rights issues, including the chapter on sexual harassment in the 1985 book *EveryWoman's Legal Guide* (along with P. L. Crocker). She currently serves as chief administrative law judge for the Massachusetts Department of Environmental Protection. She has also worked as a staff attorney for the Center for Constitutional Rights in New York City, where she focused on civil rights, international human rights, and public education. She taught at the New York University School of Law, where she conducted a seminar on women and the law. Early in her career, she had a general practice with the New Haven Law Collective, where she focused on sex and race discrimination, family law, nonprofit corporations, housing, and consumer law.

Arlen Specter (1930–)

Senator Arlen Specter, a two-term Republican moderate and former prosecutor, made an indelible impression on the public consciousness when he grilled Anita Hill as the designated Republican questioner during the Clarence Thomas confirmation hearings. Viewed by many observers as an unnecessarily relentless and probing examiner, Specter's role in the drama was ironic, since before that time he had been viewed as a lifelong advocate of civil rights, a man sensitive to many women's issues, and a pro-choice Republican. His role in the Judiciary Committee hearing debates earned him a close reelection contest against Lynn Yeakel, a political unknown who, because of the hearings, came out of nowhere to oppose Specter at the Democratic convention. Yeakel told a national television audience, "I can no longer stand by after this senator humiliated American women with his shameless performance last fall." During a five-way Democratic primary, without the party endorsement, Yeakel aired a television ad that ignored her primary opponents and instead aimed directly at Specter. In the ad, Specter's voice asked Hill a question, then Yeakel's voice asked voters, "Did this make you as angry as it made me?" Evidently it did. Yeakel shot from 1 percent in state polls in March 1992 to a decisive primary win in April, but she lost narrowly to Specter in November of that year.

A former district attorney, Specter has shown agility in questioning two conservative Supreme Court nominees. In 1987, right after he was reelected to the Senate, he angered Pennsylvania right-wingers by blocking Reagan nominee Robert H. Bork. Then in 1991, he eagerly supported Bush nominee Clarence Thomas, pleasing the political right before seeking reelection that year. "I call them as I see them," Specter stated.

Specter has run for office nine times during the past four decades, losing almost as often as winning. He failed in bids for Philadelphia mayor, for a third term as district attorney, for the Republican nomination to the Senate, and for the Republican nomination for governor of Pennsylvania. Then in 1980, he won the Senate race; he was reelected in 1986 and 1992.

Arlen Specter was born to immigrant parents in Wichita, Kansas, and grew up in the small town of Russell. After graduating Phi Beta Kappa from the University of Pennsylvania in 1951, he served in the Air Force Office of Special Investigations for two years during the Korean War. He attended Yale Law School, where he was editor of the *Yale Law Journal*. Specter began his public service career as assistant district attorney of Philadelphia, obtaining the first national conviction of labor racketeers. He quickly attained a reputation as a tough and effective prosecutor, which led to an appointment in 1964 as assistant counsel to the Warren

Commission to investigate the assassination of President John F. Kennedy. He is credited with playing a major role in the investigation and with developing the single-bullet theory. In Congress, he serves as the ranking Republican member of the Veterans Affairs Committee; the Appropriations Committee's Subcommittee on Labor, Health, and Human Services; the Education Committee; and the Judiciary Committee's Subcommittee on the Constitution.

Nan D. Stein (1947–)

Nan Stein was the first researcher in the United States to define and survey student-to-student sexual harassment in high schools and grade schools. Her pioneering curriculum and resource guide for schools, *Who's Hurt and Who's Liable: Sexual Harassment in Massachusetts Schools*, first published in 1979, has been used nationally as a model for a sexual harassment curriculum. She has been widely published in academic and educational journals, as well as in the popular press, including *U.S.A. Today.* She is coauthor of another classroom guide, *Flirting or Hurting*, a teaching guide for grades 6–12, and she helped to script and produce a video with the same name that won the Gracie Allen Award of the American Women in Film and Television Association in 1997. She has focused on the sexual harassment of students at the elementary and secondary levels.

Currently, Stein is project director and senior researcher for the Center for Research on Women at Wellesley College, where she is at work on a national research project on sexual harassment and child sexual abuse in schools. In cooperation with *Seventeen* magazine and the NOW Legal Defense Fund's Project on Equal Education Rights, Stein designed the first nationwide survey of sexual harassment and teens. The survey questionnaire was published in *Seventeen* in September 1992, and the results were published in 1993. Stein reported that letters arrived by the hundreds every day in response to the magazine's poll; "Open," "Urgent," and "Please Read" were scribbled on many of the envelopes.

Stein became interested in the subject of sexual harassment and teens in the late 1970s when she worked alongside a group of high school students at the Massachusetts Department of Education. At the time, she thought the problem of sexual harassment took place only when someone in power bothered someone of lesser authority. In watching boys work with girls in her office, however, she realized that the boys were constantly recounting sexual conquests, cornering the girls, or telling sexual jokes. The girls "were getting very disturbed by this." After talking with the students, Stein was told such activity "goes on all the time." This discovery led to Stein's career of studying, writing, and speaking about the issue. Sexual harassment in schools, Stein believes, is a serious problem because it can escalate into assault and battery—a phenomenon she sees increasing. She has discussed the subject on national television and consulted with schools around the United States.

Stein holds a B.A. in history from the University of Wisconsin, an M.A.T. from Antioch College Graduate School of Education, and a doctorate in education from Harvard University.

Nadine Taub (1943–)

Nadine Taub is a professor at Rutgers School of Law and is the director of the Women's Rights Litigation Clinic, an influential program that has been responsible for litigating a number of important women's rights cases. Taub was the lead attorney in one of the first cases to establish that Title VII provides a case of action for sexual harassment, *Tompkins v. Public Service Electric and Gas Co.* (1977). When the decision on the law was issued, Taub negotiated a highly favorable settlement that included a substantial monetary award, attorneys' fees, a change in the company's policy, the institution of grievance procedures, and a company-conducted information program concerning laws against discrimination. She has also worked on such significant sexual harassment cases as *Keil v. Toys "R" Us* (1988) (hostile environment) and *Thoreson v. Penthouse* (1989) and on the appeal in *Yale v. Alexander* (1977), all discussed in Chapter 4. She is one of the authors of *Sex Discrimination Law: Cases and Materials* (1993; the second edition of a casebook first published in 1974). Taub has also written a number of articles on discrimination and reproductive rights issues, including sexual harassment.

A frequent lecturer on sexual harassment, discrimination, and other women's rights issues, Taub emphasizes that "it's important to recognize that litigation may not always be the most appropriate way to address the problem." She recommends that women organize in groups to fight sexual harassment and that they confront their employers when incidences of harassment occur. Having worked closely with women who have brought sexual harassment claims, she recognizes their ambivalence about collecting damage awards. These women sometimes feel that "to bring the case is to say, I'm worth money for sex." Currently, Taub and her center are investigating the new area of sexual harassment in housing.

Clarence Thomas (1948–)

Clarence Thomas was nominated by President George Bush as associate justice of the United States Supreme Court and took the oath of office on October 23, 1991. Prior to his service on the high court, he had served on the U.S. Court of Appeals for the District of Columbia Circuit since March 12, 1990. His confirmation hearings before the Senate Judiciary Committee in October 1991 fueled a national debate on the issue of sexual harassment when Anita Hill, a professor at the University of Oklahoma School of Law, charged that he had sexually harassed her when she worked for him at the Equal Employment Opportunity Commission and the Department of Education.

Thomas was born in Pinpoint, Georgia, to a teenage mother in a house with dirt floors, no plumbing or electricity, and newspapers for wallpaper. In accepting Bush's nomination to the Supreme Court, he recalled that "as a child, I could not dare dream that I would ever see the Supreme Court—not to mention be nominated to it." Raised as a Catholic, Thomas attended Conception Seminary and Holy Cross College, from which he graduated cum laude in 1971. After receiving his degree from Yale Law School in 1974, Thomas served as assistant attorney general of Missouri, practiced privately for a brief time, and worked as a legislative assistant to Senator John C. Danforth of Missouri before being appointed assistant secretary for civil rights with the U.S. Department of Education. He served as chair of the U.S. Equal Employment Opportunity Commission from 1982 through 1990 before being appointed by President Bush to the D.C. Circuit Court.

Professor Anita Hill's charges against Thomas resulted in extensive televised hearings before an all-male Senate Judiciary Committee. Thomas totally denied the charges, stating that he had "been racking my brains and eating my insides trying to think of what I may have said or done to Anita Hill to lead her to allege that I was interested in her in more than a professional way" and claiming that he was the victim of a "high-tech lynching." Thomas declared indignantly that the hearings were "not American; this is Kafkaesque." At one low point, he stated that "no job is worth what I have been through." Despite several days of hearings on the issue, Thomas was confirmed by the committee and later by the full Senate. Millions of Americans watched the televised proceedings, however, and read the extensive press coverage. The debate introduced many for the first time to the issue of sexual harassment.

Karen (K. C.) Wagner (1951–)

K. C. Wagner was the counseling, program, and executive director of the Working Women's Institute from 1980 through 1987, where she helped to coordinate a brief bank and conducted research. The institute may have been the first organization in the country to focus on the issue of sexual harassment. In commenting on the history of the drive to raise awareness about the issue, Wagner emphasized that it was a diverse, "grassroots movement."

Currently, she is a counselor, corporate trainer, and consultant specializing in the prevention of sexual harassment and gender bias in employment and academia. Wagner has addressed these issues as they relate to traditional and nontraditional work environments for women in over 150 corporations, unions, nonprofit and public service organizations, and academic institutions. Wagner provided testimony as an expert on sexual harassment in two significant cases, *Broderick v. Securities and Exchange Commission* (1988) and *Robinson v. Jacksonville Shipyards* (1991). She has also appeared on numerous television shows as an expert on the issue of sexual harassment and has been interviewed on the subject by many national newspapers and magazines. Wagner coauthored a study entitled "Results of a Survey on Gender Bias and Sexual Harassment in the Federal Aviation Administration Eastern Region" and has written other articles on gender issues. She is currently on the EEO Studies Staff at Cornell University's New York State School of Industrial and Labor Relations. She holds a master's of social work degree from Hunter College School of Social Work and graduated cum laude from the University of Pennsylvania.

Susan L. Webb (1948–)

Webb is president of Pacific Resource Development Group, Inc., a Seattle-based consulting firm specializing in human relations issues and offering consulting and training in the area of sexual harassment. She is the editor of the *Webb Report,* the only national newsletter on the subject of sexual harassment. She has written three books, including the recent *Step Forward: Sexual Harassment in the Workplace.* Webb is interviewed frequently on television, for magazines, and on radio about the issue of sexual harassment and also provides expert witness testimony on sexual harassment and conducts investigations of sexual harassment complaints.

Webb reports that the first sexual harassment workshop she conducted was for 30 men in the Street and Sewer Maintenance Division of a public works department in 1981. They called it "the good ol' boy department." Five years later, she conducted another workshop for a similar group. When she went to the front of the training room, she found that one of the men had taped a tampon, colored with red ink so it appeared bloody, to the overhead projector. When she asked him why, "he said he'd heard that I was a bitch." Since that time, she has seen the interest in sexual harassment training "run the gamut, from high interest to outright hostility to support and understanding." Yet, she reports,

> The problem that bothers me the most is that in all these workshops, whether in 1981 or 1991, the same questions keep coming up over and over. The lack of knowledge and understanding . . . is appalling and sometimes discouraging to anyone who works in the field. There is so much more work to do even to make a dent in the problem.

Webb received her bachelor's degree in economics and a master's degree in human relations from the University of Oklahoma.

References

Collins, Eliza G. C., and Timothy B. Blodgett, "Sexual Harassment: Some See It . . . Some Won't," *Harvard Business Review* 59, no. 2 (March–April 1981): 76–95.

Hoffman, Lisa (Scripps Howard News Service), "Sex Harassment Last Straw for Career Soldier," *Rocky Mountain News,* February 16, 1997, p. 3A, col. 1.

Mayer, Jane, and Jill Abramson, *Strange Justice: The Selling of Clarence Thomas* (Boston: Houghton-Mifflin Company, 1994).

Phelps, Timothy M., and Helen Winternity, *Capital Games* (New York: Hyperion, 1992).

Thompson, Mark, "Sergeants at Odds," *Time* (February 17, 1997): 46.

Zimmerman, Jean, *Tailspin: Women at War in the Wake of Tailhook* (New York: Doubleday, 1995).

Facts and Statistics

4

This chapter provides general facts and statistics relating to sexual harassment so readers can evaluate what they see and hear about sexual harassment from other sources. Because the laws and the entire issue of sexual harassment are still relatively new and evolving, these facts and statistics are necessarily limited. The information given is as factual as possible, but in this rapidly changing field the reader should be aware that even this information may soon be outdated. The significance or meaning of any particular fact or statistic will vary depending upon the individual point of view. Because the presentation of facts is necessarily brief, suggestions for further reading are included where appropriate. This chapter consists of an overview of the law, including statutes and important cases; future trends in sexual harassment law; and statistics and surveys relating to sexual harassment.

Overview of the Laws on Sexual Harassment in Employment

Three categories of laws cover sexual harassment in the workplace: (1) the United States

Civil Rights Act, administered by the United States Equal Employment Opportunity Commission (EEOC); (2) state fair employment practices (FEP) statutes; and (3) common law tort principles. Each is considered separately in this section.

The Civil Rights Act and the EEOC

Title VII of the Civil Rights Act prohibits discrimination on the basis of sex. Sexual harassment has been found by the courts to be a form of sex discrimination in employment under this law. The law applies to most employers in the United States if they have 15 or more employees. The EEOC administers this federal statute.

The EEOC is charged with the responsibility of investigating employee harassment and discrimination complaints. The agency has subpoena power to compel the employer and others to turn over evidence. Generally, the EEOC negotiates with the employer in a process called *conciliation* to protect the harassed employee's rights. If negotiation fails, the agency has the power to file suit. Because of the number of claims and the limited resources of the agency, however, in most cases the EEOC issues a "right-to-sue" letter to the employee, allowing her to file a lawsuit to enforce her rights under the Civil Rights Act. Filing a claim with the EEOC is a necessary first step before the employee can start her own lawsuit.

The Civil Rights Act provides for five kinds of relief if an employee is successful in a suit:

1. *Reinstatement and promotion.* The court may order the company to rehire or promote the employee.
2. *Back pay and benefits.* The court may award any salary and benefits the employee lost because she was fired or forced to leave, demoted, or passed over for a promotion.
3. *Money damages.* The court may award money for any personal injuries the employee is able to prove, such as physical problems as the result of an actual assault or any stress-related problems. The amount awarded is limited to out-of-pocket losses, such as medical expenses and other damages, up to a limit—which varies depending upon the number of people employed—of between $50,000 and $300,000.
4. *Injunctive relief.* A court may direct the company to revise its polices to prevent harassment in the future, conduct

sexual harassment training, or provide any other relief the court deems appropriate.

5. *Attorney's fees.* A court may order the company to pay the employee's attorney's fees.

Legal Definitions of Sexual Harassment

Legal definitions of *sexual harassment* vary from state to state, but almost every state extends the minimum protection found in the regulations of the U.S. Equal Employment Opportunity Commission. EEOC definitions and standards are those used most often throughout the United States in defining sexual harassment.

The EEOC definition of *sexual harassment* is found in 29 Code of Federal Regulations (CFR) 1604.11(a):

> Harassment on the basis of sex is a violation of [the law]. Unwelcome sexual advances, requests for sexual favors, and other verbal or physical conduct of a sexual nature constitute sexual harassment when:
> 1. Submission to such conduct is made either explicitly or implicitly a term or condition of an individual's employment,
> 2. Submission to or rejection of such conduct by an individual is used as the basis for employment decisions affecting such individual, or
> 3. Such conduct has the purpose or effect of unreasonably interfering with an individual's work performance or creating an intimidating, hostile, or offensive working environment.

The EEOC regulations stress that most sexual harassment cases must be resolved by looking at all of the facts in context (29 CFR 1604.11(b)):

> In determining whether alleged conduct constitutes sexual harassment, the [EEOC] will look at the record as a whole and at the totality of the circumstances, such as the nature of the sexual advances and the context in which the alleged incidents occurred. The determination of the legality of a particular action will be made from the facts, on a case-by-case basis.

The terms *quid pro quo* and *hostile environment* are frequently used in the cases and literature about sexual harassment. These are the two major types of sexual harassment cases. *Quid pro quo* harassment occurs when an employee is confronted with sexual demands if she wants to keep her job or obtain a promotion. In other words, she has to do "this" to get "that." *Hostile environment* is used to describe other types of cases in which the threat is less direct. Such instances frequently involve sexually offensive conduct that pervades and poisons the workplace, making it difficult or unpleasant for an employee to do her job.

Although decisions vary, most government investigating agencies or courts consider four factors to determine whether sexual harassment has occurred:

1. Was the behavior sexual in nature?
2. Was the behavior unreasonable?
3. Was the behavior severe or pervasive in the workplace?
4. Was the behavior unwelcome?

Behavior of a Sexual Nature Behavior of a sexual nature that a court or the EEOC may determine to be sexual harassment includes:

1. Sexual advances, propositions, or attempts to obtain sexual favors from an employee.
2. Hostility toward women employees or a particular female employee. These types of situations range from pranks, threats, and intimidation to highly dangerous physical attacks.
3. Sexual or pornographic pictures, language, and jokes that permeate the workplace, creating an environment that is offensive. The sexual commentary and humor in such cases need not be directed at the particular employee, yet she may nevertheless find the atmosphere to be intimidating and offensive. Such an environment places her at a distinct disadvantage with respect to her male co-workers and is therefore discriminatory.

Because courts look closely at the kind of behavior to determine what is illegal sexual harassment, each type of sexual conduct is discussed in more detail.

Sexual Advances or Demands Unwelcome sexual advances and propositions are one of the most common forms of sexual harassment.

Whether a particular sexual advance constitutes illegal sexual harassment usually depends on who is making the advance.

Sexual advances from a supervisor or another person in authority will be scrutinized more closely than those of co-workers because of the strong possibility of intimidation. Supervisors are in positions of power in the workplace. It is usually presumed that the employer has knowledge of any sexual harassment committed by supervisors, so the employer is almost automatically responsible for its supervisors' actions—regardless of whether the employer had actual knowledge.

Sexual advances by supervisors frequently involve the classic sex-for-jobs situation. The EEOC regulations state that sexual advances under these circumstances are unlawful if they are "explicitly or implicitly a term or condition of an individual's employment." In other words, if a woman must put up with these demands as part of her job (regardless of whether she accedes to them), they may qualify as harassment.

In a supervisor-worker relationship, little conduct of a sexual nature is needed to support a finding of harassment. Even a relatively polite request for a date made by an employer or a supervisor can be the basis of a sexual harassment charge if future work assignments, promotions, or raises appear to depend on acceptance of the demand.

Sexual harassment can arise from unwanted sexual advances even if the person in authority makes a favorable employment decision on behalf of the employee. If a woman submits to an unwelcome sexual advance because of a promise from her supervisor, he is guilty of sexual harassment—regardless of whether he delivers on his promise. It is the act or threat of using sexual conduct as the basis for making employment decisions that constitutes the sexual harassment. The same rules apply to anyone with power over an employee who threatens to use such power to make an employment decision, even if the person in authority is not the employee's supervisor.

Unwelcome sexual advances or demands from a co-worker can also be the kind of conduct that gives rise to sexual harassment claims. Because these cases do not involve a supervisor or someone in a position of power, however, the threat to the woman employee is lessened. In these cases, the courts take a deeper look at all of the surrounding circumstances.

In addition, with a supervisor or someone in authority, the company is presumed to know what is going on and therefore is legally responsible for the situation. This presumption of knowledge does not apply to co-workers.

If the sexual solicitation comes from a co-worker and management is not involved, directly or indirectly, the focus is on the nature of the sexual advance. The emphasis is less on the "who" and more on the "how." Many facts are important in determining whether a co-worker has crossed the line from friendly flirting into the area of sexual harassment: the frequency of solicitations, the nature of propositions, the language used, the physical gestures, and the behavior of the co-worker. There is no hard-and-fast rule about how far is too far.

An employer can also be legally responsible for sexual harassment if it creates or allows a situation in which an employee will be sexually harassed by customers, salespersons, visitors, or even passersby. This can happen when the employer places an employee in a situation in which it knows or should know that unwelcome sexual advances are likely to occur. A company can, for example, require an employee to dress in sexy clothing, but it is then responsible if customers or passersby make sexual advances or remarks to her. A more serious situation occurs when the employer tries to force an employee to have sex with a client or someone else it wants to please.

A sexual harassment claim may also arise when sexual advances are made to two or more women with differing results. For example, if a supervisor denies a promotion to one employee because she will not sleep with him and gives the same promotion to another because she will, both women have experienced sexual harassment. The first employee would have a sexual harassment claim based upon the improper denial of her promotion by a person in authority in a sex-for-jobs situation. The second would also have a claim if the supervisor's sexual advances were unwelcome and she submitted only out of fear of losing the promotion.

In addition, if a supervisor has an affair mutually consented to with one of his employees and gives her promotions and raises in preference to other employees, this type of relationship (especially when combined with abusive behavior toward other employees) can be a form of sexual harassment. Such cases have come to be known as "paramour preference."

Hostility Related to Gender   Hostile acts related to an employee's gender are another type of suspect conduct of a sexual nature, even though they may not involve sexual overtures. This type of claim involves harassment *because* of a person's gender rather than sexual harassment as that term is sometimes understood.

Many cases of sexual harassment are based on outright animosity toward a particular female employee or toward women employees in general. Often the hostility surfaces when a pioneer enters a previously all-male occupation. Other times it comes from a scorned lover. Alternatively, a supervisor may be hostile toward a particular woman employee right from the start and may indulge his hostility in ways he would not think of doing if she were a man.

Some employers have tried to argue that sexual harassment is not involved if a co-worker treats a woman employee with hostility. Sexual harassment, they argue, requires some evidence of sexual overtures toward the female employee who registered the complaint. The courts have rejected this argument, finding instead that sexual harassment can exist without explicit sexual misconduct.

Plaintiffs have argued, and some courts have agreed, that hostile conduct is often a thinly disguised effort to force a woman employee out of the workforce. It is sometimes easier to analyze cases involving overt hostility as cases of sexual discrimination rather than sexual harassment. If a supervisor subjects his female employees to abuse because he would prefer to have men working for him, he is treating them differently than he treats his male employees and is, therefore, discriminating against women. Yet the conceptual difference between a sexual discrimination case and a sexual harassment case is not important, because both are subject to the same legal prohibitions. In fact, the laws against sexual harassment are largely derived from the laws against sexual discrimination.

Pornographic Material and Lewd Behavior Both the EEOC and the courts are beginning to recognize that pornographic material and lewd behavior in the workplace can create a hostile working environment or a "sexually poisoned" workplace for women. The offensiveness is not always directed at a specific individual but is often the result of the total effect of many offensive acts that may seem relatively mild when viewed in isolation. The main injurious result of this type of sexual conduct is a working environment that is hostile to working women as a group. The sexually poisoned workplace creates a situation in which discrimination against women flourishes. Plaintiffs have argued—often successfully— that lewd behavior is frequently sexist and woman hating, that it reveals discrimination on the job and a different standard of judging male and female employees.

Unreasonable Conduct The second legal factor in a sexual harassment case is unreasonableness. The law prohibits only *unreasonable* sexual conduct in the workplace. Many critics miss this requirement when they argue that trivial or unjust claims of sexual harassment will be allowed by the courts. Some harassing conduct is obviously unreasonable. If a supervisor makes sexual demands on an employee as a condition of getting a job or a raise, for example, this is clearly unreasonable under the legal standard. It is also always unreasonable for an employer to physically assault or attack women employees.

Reasonableness is more difficult to determine when the conduct may be ambiguous or subject to misinterpretation. Courts want to make sure the employee bringing the case is not complaining about conduct other people would find trivial. As the *EEOC Compliance Manual* (the handbook for personnel investigating harassment) states, the law should not "serve as a vehicle for vindicating the petty slights suffered by the hypersensitive."

Courts have traditionally used an objective test to determine if conduct is reasonable: Would a "reasonable person" find the subject behavior or occurrence offensive? Recently, however, courts have begun to recognize that men and women often perceive the same conduct differently. As one court submitted, "A male supervisor might believe, for example, that it is legitimate for him to tell a female subordinate that she has a 'great figure' or 'nice legs.' The female subordinate, however, may find such comments offensive." *Lipsett v. University of Puerto Rico,* 864 F.2d 881 (1st Cir. 1988). The *EEOC Compliance Manual* urges that the conduct be judged from the viewpoint of the woman employee: "The reasonable person standard should consider the victim's perspective and not stereotyped notions of acceptable behavior." Some courts have begun to agree. As one court noted:

> Many women share common concerns which men do not necessarily share. For example, because women are disproportionately victims of rape and sexual assault, women have a stronger incentive to be concerned with sexual behavior. Women who are victims of mild forms of sexual harassment may understandably worry whether a harasser's conduct is merely a prelude to violent sexual assault. Men, who are rarely victims of sexual assault, may view sexual conduct in a vacuum without a full appreciation of the social setting or the underlying threat of violence that a woman may perceive. *Ellison v. Brady,* 924 F.2d 872 (9th Cir. 1991).

This area of the law is still evolving. Ultimately, the Supreme Court may have to settle the debate over whether the standard should be that of a reasonable woman or of the traditional reasonable man.

Severe or Pervasive Behavior   The third factor to consider in evaluating sexual behavior is whether it is so severe or so pervasive throughout the workplace that it creates an intimidating, hostile, or offensive working environment. This requirement also guards against the possibility of trivial claims.

This factor is often assumed by the courts in certain types of cases. For example, if a co-worker physically assaults a woman employee, the situation is obviously severe.

EEOC Guidelines on Behavior   The *EEOC Compliance Manual* sets out guidelines for investigators to follow in determining whether any sexual behavior is severe or pervasive. According to the EEOC, investigators should consider:

- Whether the conduct was verbal, physical, or both
- How frequently the conduct was repeated
- Whether the conduct was hostile and obviously offensive
- Whether the alleged harasser was a co-worker or a supervisor
- Whether others joined in perpetuating the harassment
- Whether the harassment was directed at more than one individual

The *EEOC Compliance Manual* also outlines how conduct should be evaluated using these factors. According to the EEOC, unless there is a single, "quite severe" incident, the investigator should use a weighing process to determine whether the conduct gives rise to a sexual harassment claim. No weighing process is necessary in a quid pro quo situation, however, because the EEOC says "a single sexual advance may constitute harassment if it is linked to the granting or denial of employment benefits." Cases involving invasive touching or fondling are also usually considered severe, regardless of whether the incident involved a supervisor. In general, the EEOC considers physical actions to be much more serious than words, because "even a single unwelcome physical advance can seriously poison the victim's working environment." The *EEOC Compliance Manual* takes the position that "the more severe the harassment, the less the need to show a repetitive series of incidents. This is particularly true when the harassment is physical."

The Totality of the Circumstances   In the case of persistent sexual advances from co-workers or a sexually hostile workplace, courts will consider the totality of the working environment. No one fact may be decisive, but the sum total of all facts might be. According to one court, "A play cannot be understood on the basis of some of its scenes but only on its entire performance; similarly, a discrimination analysis must concentrate not on individual incidents but on the overall scenario." *Robinson v. Jacksonville Shipyards,* 760 F. Supp. 1486 (M.D. Fla. 1991).

Unwelcome Behavior   The EEOC regulations prohibit "unwelcome sexual advances, requests for sexual favors and other verbal or physical conduct of a sexual nature." The sexual conduct must actually be unwelcome and offensive to the employee bringing the complaint. In a quid pro quo situation, the supervisor or employer frequently claims the employee welcomed the sexual advances at the time and that the relationship was purely consensual. Likewise, in the case of the sexually hostile workplace, an employer often argues that the employee was a willing participant in the jokes and sexual banter. A court will look at several factors to determine whether the conduct was unwelcome.

For example, employers have argued that if a woman voluntarily submits to her employer's sexual advances she has consented to them. Courts have ruled, however, that a woman welcomed the sexual advance or conduct only if it can be shown that the act was something she wanted to do at the time. The best example of this situation is *Meritor Savings Bank v. Vinson,* 477 U.S. 57 (1986), in which the employee appeared to submit voluntarily to her boss's advances but later argued successfully that she had done so to keep her job.

In *Vinson,* the U.S. Supreme Court also found that a court can consider evidence of the employee's "sexually provocative speech or dress," along with other facts, in determining whether the employee truly welcomed any sexual advances. Many women activists have criticized this rule. It is virtually impossible to know what might be provocative speech or dress for any particular person; provocation is in the eye of the beholder.

Similarly, employers may argue that a woman welcomed the conduct because she failed to complain about it. Speaking out against harassment, however, is not always easy or possible; frequently, the employee is afraid of retaliation if she does so. A woman faced with harassing conduct in the workplace often adopts a coping strategy. Such behavior sometimes gives the appearance that she is a willing participant but in fact may only be her way of dealing with an unpleasant situation. These strategies may come back to haunt her when she files suit and the employer argues that she welcomed the conduct. An employee also does not forfeit her legal right to protection from sexual harassment if she was once romantically (and consensually) involved with a co-worker, but she has to make it clear to him that any further sexual advances are unwelcome.

Employers frequently argue that an employee has welcomed certain sexual advances or conduct because she willingly participated in some similar type of activity, citing instances in which the woman told a sexual joke as evidence that she must not object to the working environment. Yet mild jokes may escalate to hardcore pornography and dangerous threats that go well beyond the type of conduct she tolerated. By ignoring certain types of mild sexual conduct, a woman does not waive her right to challenge other, more serious forms of sexual harassment.

Even if a woman is hired to do a job that is based on sexual stereotypes, she does not give up her right to object to other forms of sexual conduct. The leading case on this point involved a woman hired as Pet of the Month by *Penthouse* magazine. Her job involved videotaped and personal appearances in highly sexualized settings. Even so, the magazine and its publisher were held liable for forcing her to have sex with business associates and others whom the publisher wanted to impress. *Thoreson v. Penthouse International, Ltd.*, 563 N.Y.S.2d 968 (N.Y. Sup. Ct. 1990).

A Special Note on the Sexual Harassment Law in Schools and Colleges

Sexual harassment in schools and colleges is illegal under the U.S. Civil Rights Act, Title IX of the Federal Education Amendments, which prohibits sexual discrimination in education. The courts have disagreed, however, on the issue of whether harassment by a teacher, professor, or administrator should be treated the same as student-to-student (or "peer") harassment. Title IX can be enforced through private litigation, the U.S. Education Department's Office of Civil Rights, or state departments of human rights. Under Title IX, educational institutions are required to maintain a grievance procedure that allows for prompt and equitable resolution of instances of sex discrimination. The definitions of *sexual harassment* used by the courts are usually the same as those under Title VII, as outlined earlier in this chapter. The courts and agencies will look to legal decisions in the area of sexual harassment in employment to decide a particular case involving harassment in education. The Office for Civil Rights, United States Department of Education—the agency responsible for administering and enforcing Title IX—has stated that "sexual harassment consists of verbal or physical conduct of a sexual nature, imposed on the basis of sex, by an employee or agent of a recipient that denies, limits, provides differently, or conditions the provision of aid, benefits, services, or treatment protected under Title IX."

On the issue of sexual harassment, the law under Title IX has not been considered as extensively by the courts as the law under Title VII. The first case to consider the issue was *Alexander v. Yale*, 631 F.2d 178 (2d Cir. 1980) *aff'g* 459 F. Supp. 1 (D. Conn. 1977), in which a federal district court ruled that in a university setting sexual harassment could constitute sex discrimination under Title IX. It was the first court to do so, but the court of appeals later dismissed the case, ruling that it was moot because Alexander had graduated and Yale University had adequately addressed Alexander's concern by setting up a sexual harassment grievance procedure.

It was not until 1992 that the U.S. Supreme Court finally considered the issue in *Franklin v. Gwinnett County Public Schools*, 503 U.S. 60 (1992). In that case, the Court ruled unanimously that sexual harassment in schools is a violation of Title IX and that students who suffer sexual harassment and other forms of sex discrimination can seek monetary damages from schools and school officials because of a violation of their civil rights.

Recent lower court cases have focused on the *degree of knowledge* schools have in deciding whether they should be liable. With regard to teacher, faculty, or administrator harassment of students, most courts have held that schools will be liable if they either knew or should have known about the harassment. See, for example, *Kinman v. Omaha Public School District*, 94 F.3d 463 (8th Cir. 1996). In the area of peer harassment, although the courts have been split on this issue, the trend seems to be that a school must have ignored repeated complaints by students or their parents before it will be held liable. In *Burrow by and through Burrow v. Postville Community School District*, 929 F. Supp. 1193 (N.D. Iowa 1996), for example, the court held that a student could bring an action because of the school district's failure to take action after repeated complaints of sexual harassment by peers. The law in this area is unclear, in part because most schools and universities have tended to settle these issues out of court rather than risk a large judgment at trial. Therefore, few written court decisions exist.

At the university level, the debate has centered on the issue of whether verbal sexual harassment is protected by the First Amendment. In one reported decision, *Silva v. University of New Hampshire*, 888 F. Supp. 293 (D.N.H. 1994), a case widely reported in the popular media, Donald Silva, who had been suspended for using examples of a sexual nature in his classroom lectures, sued and won the right to be reinstated as a university professor. Emphasizing the traditional importance of the First Amendment in university settings, the court found that universities must carefully balance the rights of students to be free from sexual harassment against the free speech rights of professors before disciplining them. In this case, the court found that the university had failed to carefully engage in that balancing analysis.

Several organizations of university professors have publicly opposed the institution of so-called speech codes and have written extensively in the popular press about the issue, attacking such codes as violating First Amendment principles.

The issues of peer harassment and of the First Amendment right to free speech—traditionally more protected in a university than in traditional workplace settings—will both eventually have to be clarified by the Supreme Court.

State Fair Employment Practices Statutes

In most states, victims of sexual harassment also have rights to sue under state fair employment practices statutes. Most state FEP laws prohibit sexual harassment in that state. A few states, such as Alabama and Arkansas, have no FEP statutes. In states with FEP laws, smaller companies that might not be covered under the 15-employee minimum provided in the federal Civil Rights Act are usually included.

Most states have adopted a definition of *sexual harassment* similar to that in the EEOC guidelines (see page 83). Usually, these same states also have agencies structured like the EEOC to investigate claims. The procedures and remedies offered to harassed employees under each state FEP law differ, especially as to whether an employee may recover monetary damages for personal injuries suffered as a result of the harassment. The following section includes a summary of each state's FEP laws. (Because state laws change frequently, the reader should research any particular law in a state's official statute reporter before relying on the information presented here.)

State Fair Employment Practices Laws

[This section is reprinted with permission from *Sexual Harassment on the Job* by attorneys William Petrocelli and Barbara Kate Repa, copyright

© 1995. Published by Nolo Press, Berkeley, CA. Available in bookstores, or by calling 1-800-992-6656, or at www.nolo.com.]

How To Use These Listings

The information here is divided into a number of categories.

Statute. The legal citation to your state FEP law, if there is one.

State agency. The name, address and phone number of the state organization responsible for administering and enforcing the FEP law. Only the main office is listed here. There may also be local offices that are more convenient. Call the state agency for information on how and where to file a claim.

Exclusions. Groups who are not entitled to the protections of the state FEP law.

Time limits. The time within which you must file a claim. Unless otherwise indicated, the time limit starts with the incident of harassment. So, for example, in Alaska, an employee would have 300 days from the date she was harassed to bring a claim with the Commission. If she tried to bring a claim after 300 days, she would not be allowed to do so. It is very important to keep on top of these limits. Call your state agency if you have questions about when to file. When in doubt, file early.

Exhaustion. Whether you must file a claim with your state agency before bringing a private lawsuit based on the state FEP law. The term is shorthand for "exhaustion of administrative remedies." Some states require you to follow all available administrative procedures before you can resort to a lawsuit. If there is a "yes" listed for your state, you must file a claim with the state agency as a prerequisite to a lawsuit. If there is a "no" listed, you are not required to file a claim before bringing a lawsuit. Some states follow a procedure like the EEOC. They require you to file a claim with the state agency, but they will give you permission to bring a private lawsuit—either through a right-to-sue letter or by some other method—after a certain number of days.

Monetary damages. The kinds of damages that can be awarded under the state FEP law. We specify here whether these damages are available from an administrative hearing, a private lawsuit, or both. Unless otherwise indicated, all states will award job-connected losses, such as back pay and lost benefits. In addition, some states award:

- compensatory damages, or money to compensate for personal injuries, pain and suffering, mental distress and humiliation, and
- punitive damages, or money to punish the harasser for particularly heinous behavior.

Administrative procedure. Some details about how your state agency works. Unless otherwise indicated, every agency will investigate your claim and make an attempt to reach a settlement between you and your employer. Some agencies will also hold an administrative hearing, like a court case. Many agencies provide an attorney to argue for your complaint at this hearing; others require that you hire your own attorney. Some states will also award attorney's fees.

Private lawsuit. The requirements for bringing a private lawsuit based on state law. Some states don't allow you to bring a lawsuit at all. Others require you to obtain a right-to-sue letter before bringing a lawsuit or impose other limitations.

Note: An asterisk (*) indicates that the state agency has not been designated by the EEOC. This means that there is no guarantee of the quality of the agency's work, and your claim will probably not be dual-filed automatically.

ALABAMA

No state FEP law.

ALASKA

Statute: Alaska Stats. §§18.80.010-300
State agency: Alaska State Commission for Human Rights
   800 A Street, Suite 202
   Anchorage, AK 99501
   (907) 276-7474
Exclusions: Domestic employment, social clubs and non-profit
   religious, fraternal, charitable or educational organizations
Time limits: 300 days
Exhaustion: No
Monetary damages: Compensatory damages can be awarded in a
   private lawsuit, but not by the administrative agency.
Administrative procedure: If you choose to bring your complaint to
   the Commission, an administrative hearing is available. The
   complaint will be represented by the Commission, but you can
   also hire your own attorney. Attorney's fees are available.
Private lawsuit: You can bring a lawsuit directly in state court. You
   must file this suit within two years.

ARIZONA

Statute: Arizona Rev. Stats. §41-1461 to 1465, 1481 to 1484
State agency: Arizona Civil Rights Division
   1275 West Washington Street
   Phoenix, AZ 85007
   (602) 542-5263
Exclusions: Employers of fewer than 15 employees, the United
   States, Native American tribes, bona-fide tax exempt private
   membership clubs, appointed staff of elected officials
Time limits: 180 days
Exhaustion: Yes. After 90 days, if the Division has not completed its
   administrative process, you can request a right-to-sue letter.
Monetary damages: No compensatory or punitive damages are
   available under state law.

Administrative procedure: The Division does not hold an administrative hearing. If, after investigation, the Division decides that there is reasonable cause to believe that harassment took place, the Division can bring an action on your behalf in state court against your employer, but it is not required to do so.

Private lawsuit: You can bring a private action only with a right-to-sue letter. If the Division decides not to bring a lawsuit itself, you can bring your own lawsuit starting 90 days after the complaint was originally filed. You can apply for a court-appointed attorney to represent you in this suit, or can petition the court for permission to begin the action without paying fees or court costs. Attorney's fees are available.

ARKANSAS
No state FEP law.

CALIFORNIA
Statute: Cal. Govt. Code §§12900 to 12996
State agency: California Dept. of Fair Employment and Housing
 2014 T Street, Suite 210
 Sacramento, CA 95814
 (916) 739-4621
Exclusions: Nonprofit religious groups
Time limits: One year
Exhaustion: Yes. If the Department has not completed its administrative process after 150 days, you can request a right-to-sue letter.
Monetary damages: Compensatory and punitive damages can be awarded in a private lawsuit, but the Department cannot award compensatory or punitive damages.
Administrative procedure: The Department will hold an administrative hearing. At this hearing, an attorney for the Department will represent the complaint.
Private lawsuit: You can bring a lawsuit for up to one year after receiving a right-to-sue letter.

COLORADO
Statute: Colorado Rev. Stats. §§24-34-301 to 406
State agency: Colorado Civil Rights Commission
 1560 Broadway Suite 1050
 Denver, CO 80202
 (303) 894-2997
Exclusions: Domestic employment, religious organizations not supported by public taxes
Time limits: 180 days
Exhaustion: Yes. If the complaint is dismissed after a finding of no probable cause, you can bring a private lawsuit within 90 days.

You can also bring a private lawsuit if there has been no administrative hearing 180 days after you filed your complaint, or 120 days after your employer was notified that it would have to respond to your complaint in a hearing.

Monetary damages: No compensatory or punitive damages can be awarded under state law.

Administrative procedure: The Commission will hold an administrative hearing. The complaint will be represented by an attorney for the Commission.

Private lawsuit: You can bring a private lawsuit only under the circumstances listed above, under Exhaustion.

CONNECTICUT

Statute: Conn. Gen. Stats. §46a-51 to 99

State agency: Connecticut Commission on Human Rights and Opportunities
90 Washington Street
Hartford, CT 06106
(203) 566-4895

Exclusions: Employers with fewer than three employees, domestic employment, those employed by their parent, spouse or child

Time limits: 180 days

Exhaustion: Yes. After 210 days, you can request a right-to-sue letter if the Commission has not completed its administrative process.

Monetary damages: Compensatory damages can be awarded both by the Commission and in private lawsuit. Punitive damages cannot be awarded under state law.

Administrative procedures: The Commission will hold an administrative hearing. The complaint will be represented by the Commission. You can hire your own attorney if you wish. Attorney's fees are not available from the Commission.

Private lawsuit: You can bring a lawsuit only with a right-to-sue letter.

DELAWARE

Statute: 19 Del. Code Ann. §§710 to 718

State agency: Delaware Department of Labor, Anti-Discrimination Section
820 North French Street, 6th Floor
State Office Building
Wilmington, DE 19801
(302) 571-3929

Exclusions: Employers with fewer than four employees, agricultural workers, domestic employees, those employed by their parent,

spouse or child, those who live with their employers as part of
their job

Time limits: 90 days

Exhaustion: Yes

Monetary damages: No compensatory or punitive damages can be
awarded under state law.

Administrative procedure: If the Department finds that there is cause
to believe harassment took place, there will be a hearing before
the Equal Opportunity Review Board. Once this Board issues a
ruling, the employer has 30 days to comply or appeal to the
state court. If the employer does not comply, the Department
will file an action in state court to enforce the ruling. You may
request an attorney from the Commission or hire your own
attorney, but no attorney's fees are available from the Board.

Private lawsuit: You cannot bring a private lawsuit.

DISTRICT OF COLUMBIA

Statute: D.C. Code §1-2501 to 2557

State agency: D.C. Office of Human Rights
  2000 14th Street, NW, 3d Floor
  Washington, DC 20009
  (202) 939-8740

Exclusions: Domestic employment in the employer's home, those
employed by their parent, spouse or child

Time limits: One year

Exhaustion: No

Monetary damages: Compensatory and punitive damages can be
awarded both by the Office and in a private lawsuit.

Administrative procedure: The Office will hold an administrative
hearing, called a fact-finding conference. You can hire an
attorney for this conference, but you are not required to have
one. If you do get an attorney, attorney's fees are available.

Private lawsuit: You can bring a lawsuit directly in district
court.

FLORIDA

Statute: Fla. Stats. Ann. §760.01 to .10

State agency: Florida Commission on Human Relations
  325 John Knox Road
  Building F, Suite 240
  Tallahassee, FL 32399
  (904) 488-7082

Exclusions: Employers with fewer than 15 employees

Time limits: 180 days

Exhaustion: Yes. After 180 days, you may withdraw your complaint
and bring a private lawsuit.

Monetary damages: No compensatory or punitive damages can be
awarded under state law.

Administrative procedure: The Commission will hold an informal hearing, at which attorneys are ordinarily not present. You may request a more formal hearing before the Department of Administrative Hearings; the Commission suggests that you hire an attorney for this hearing. Attorney's fees are available.

Private lawsuit: You can bring a lawsuit only after withdrawing your complaint from the Commission.

GEORGIA
Note: Only applies to employees of the state of Georgia

Statute: Code of Georgia Ann. §45-19-20 to 45

State agency: Georgia Office of Fair Employment Practices
156 Trinity Avenue, SW; Suite 208
Atlanta, GA 30303
(404) 656-1736

Exclusions: Employees of private employers, appointed staff of elected officials

Time limits: 180 days

Exhaustion: Yes

Monetary damages: No compensatory or punitive damages can be awarded under state law.

Administrative procedure: Only state employees are protected, and they are limited to this state remedy. All actions are confidential. The Office holds an administrative hearing, at which you will be represented by an appointed attorney.

Private lawsuit: You cannot bring a private lawsuit.

HAWAII
Statute: Hawaii Rev. Stats. §368-1 to 17, §378-1 to 9

State agency: Hawaii Civil Rights Commission
888 Mililani Street, 2d Floor
Honolulu, HI 96813
(808) 586-8655

Exclusions: The United States, domestic employment

Time limits: 180 days

Exhaustion: Unclear. You probably should file a complaint with the Commission first, to be safe.

Monetary damages: Both compensatory and punitive damages can be awarded by the Commission. The damages that can be awarded in a private lawsuit are unclear, as workers' compensation may severely limit any recovery in state court. You should talk to an attorney if you are planning to bring a lawsuit.

Administrative procedure: The Commission will hold an administrative hearing. If you choose to hire an attorney for this hearing, attorney's fees are available.

Private lawsuit: State law is unclear as to whether you can bring a private lawsuit directly.

IDAHO

Statute: Idaho Code Ann. §67-5901 to 5912

State agency: Idaho Human Rights Commission
450 West State Street
Boise, ID 83720
(208) 334-2873

Exclusions: Employers with fewer than five employees, private clubs not open to the public, domestic employment

Time limits: One year

Exhaustion: No

Monetary damages: No compensatory damages can be awarded under state law. Punitive damages of up to $1,000 can be awarded if you or the Commission brings a lawsuit on your behalf in state court.

Administrative procedure: The Commission has no administrative hearing. If there is cause to believe that sexual harassment has occurred, the Commission will bring a lawsuit on your behalf in state court. You may hire your own attorney, if you are bringing claims that do not fall within the state statute, such as a common law tort action. Attorney's fees are available.

Private lawsuit: You can bring a lawsuit directly in state court. You must file the suit within two years.

ILLINOIS

Statute: Ill. Ann. Stats., chapter 68, §§1-101 to 2-105, §7A-101 to 104, §8-101 to 105, §8A-101 to 104

State agency: Illinois Department of Human Rights
100 West Randolph Street, 10th Floor
Chicago, IL 60601
(312) 814-6245

Exclusions: Domestic employment, appointed staff of elected officials, nonprofit religious groups, administrative officers of state and municipal governments, evaluees or trainees in vocational rehabilitation facilities

Time limits: 180 days

Exhaustion: No

Monetary damages: Compensatory damages can be awarded both by the Commission and in a private lawsuit, but no punitive damages can be awarded under state law.

Administrative procedure: The Commission will hold an administrative hearing. You can hire an attorney for this hearing, and attorney's fees are available.

Private lawsuit: You can bring a lawsuit directly in state court.

INDIANA

Statute: Indiana Stats. Ann. §22-9-1-1 to 13, §22-9-4-1 to 6

State agency: Indiana Civil Rights Commission
32 East Washington Street, Suite 900

Indianapolis, IN 46204
(317) 232-2612

Exclusions: Employers with fewer than six employees, domestic employment, those employed by their parent, spouse or child, nonprofit fraternal or religious groups, clubs that are exclusively social

Time limits: 90 days, or 90 days from the end of a valid company or union grievance procedure

Exhaustion: Yes

Monetary damages: No compensatory or punitive damages can be awarded under state law.

Administrative procedure: The Commission will hold an administrative hearing. An attorney will be provided for you. No attorney's fees are available.

Private lawsuit: You cannot bring a private lawsuit.

IOWA

Statute: Iowa Code Ann. §601A.1 to .19

State agency: Iowa Civil Rights Commission
Grimes State Office Building
211 East Maple Street, 2d Floor
Des Moines, IA 50319
(515) 281-4121

Exclusions: Employers with fewer than four employees, domestic employment, employment for personal services

Time limits: 180 days

Exhaustion: Yes. After 60 days, you can request a right-to-sue letter. However, you can't get a right-to-sue letter if there has already been a finding of no probable cause, if a conciliation agreement has already been reached or if notice of the administrative hearing has already been issued.

Monetary damages: Compensatory damages can be awarded, both by the Commission and in a private lawsuit, but not punitive damages.

Administrative procedure: The Commission will hold an administrative hearing. The complaint will be presented by a Commission attorney. You can also hire your own attorney. Attorney's fees are available.

Private lawsuit: You can bring a lawsuit only with a right-to-sue letter.

KANSAS

Statute: Kan. Stats. Ann. §44-1001 to 1311

State agency: Kansas Commission on Human Rights
Landon State Office Building, Suite 851-S
900 S.W. Jackson Street
Topeka, KS 66612
(913) 296-3206

Exclusions: Employers with fewer than four employees, domestic employment, those employed by their parent, spouse or child, non-profit fraternal or social associations

Time limits: Six months

Exhaustion: Yes. After 30 days, you can request a right-to-sue letter.

Monetary damages: The Commission can award compensatory damages, but only up to $2,000. It is unclear whether compensatory or punitive damages can be awarded in a private lawsuit.

Administrative procedure: The Commission holds a public hearing if there is probable cause to believe discrimination has taken place. You will be provided with an attorney at this hearing.

Private lawsuit: You can bring a private suit only after receiving a right-to-sue letter.

KENTUCKY

Statute: Ky. Rev. Stats. §344.010 to .450

State agency: Kentucky Commission on Human Rights*
701 West Muhammed Ali Boulevard
P.O. Box 69
Louisville, KY 40201
(502) 588-4024

Exclusions: Employers with fewer than eight employees, domestic employment, those employed by their parent, spouse or child

Time limits: 180 days

Exhaustion: No

Monetary damages: Compensatory damages can be awarded both by the Commission and in a private lawsuit, but punitive damages cannot be awarded under state law.

Administrative procedure: If there is probable cause to believe that discrimination has occurred, there will be an administrative hearing. You can hire an attorney for this hearing, but the Commission will provide an attorney for you, if you wish. Attorney's fees are available, in the Commission's discretion.

Private lawsuit: You can file your own lawsuit directly.

LOUISIANA

Statute: La. Rev. Stat. Ann. §23-1006

State agency: None

Exclusions: Employers of fewer than 15 employees, religious organizations, non-profit corporations

Time limits: None indicated. If you are planning to bring a lawsuit, consult with an attorney about the appropriate statute of limitations.

Exhaustion: No, because there is no administrative procedure.

Monetary damages: Compensatory damages can be awarded in a private lawsuit.

Administrative procedure: None
Private lawsuit: You must bring a private lawsuit.

MAINE

Statute: Maine Rev. Stats. Ann., title V, §4551-4632
State agency: Maine Human Rights Commission
  Statehouse Station 51
  Augusta, ME 04333
  (207) 289-2326
Exclusions: Those employed by their parent, spouse or child
Time limits: Six months
Exhaustion: No. However, civil penal damages and attorney's
  fees are only available if you filed a complaint with the Commission that was dismissed after a finding that there were no
  reasonable grounds to believe that discrimination took place, or
  that could not be conciliated within 90 days of a reasonable
  grounds finding.
Monetary damages: Compensatory damages are available in state
  court. Punitive damages of $10,000 for the first violation, $25,000
  for the second violation and $50,000 for the third violation, can
  be awarded in a private lawsuit if you initially filed your
  complaint with the Commission, or if the Commission brings
  a lawsuit on your behalf.
Administrative procedure: There is no administrative hearing. After
  investigating and attempting to conciliate, the Commission will
  refer the case to its attorneys, who will bring a lawsuit on your
  behalf in state court. If the Commission cannot bring a lawsuit
  within a reasonable time, you will be given the right to sue.
  Attorney's fees are available.
Private lawsuit: The same remedies are available as through the
  administrative process if you initially filed a complaint with the
  Commission (see Exhaustion). If you did not bring a complaint,
  no attorney's fees or punitive damages are available.

MARYLAND

Statute: Ann. Code of Md. Article 49B, §1 to 39
State agency: Maryland Commission on Human Relations
  20 East Franklin Street
  Baltimore, MD 21202
  (301) 333-1715
Exclusions: Employers with fewer than 15 employees, bona-fide
  private membership clubs, appointed staff (not civil service) of
  elected officials
Time limits: Six months
Exhaustion: Yes
Monetary damages: No compensatory or punitive damages can be
  awarded under state law.

Administrative procedure: The Commission will hold an administrative hearing. You can hire an attorney if you wish, but no attorney's fees are available.

Private lawsuit: You cannot bring a private lawsuit.

MASSACHUSETTS

Statute: Ann. Laws of Mass. chapter 151B, §§l to 10

State agency: Massachusetts Commission Against Discrimination
One Ashburton Place, Room 601
Boston, MA 02108
(617) 727-3990

Exclusions: Employers of fewer than six employees, domestic employment, those employed by their parent, spouse or child, nonprofit clubs, associations or fraternal organizations

Time limits: Six months

Exhaustion: Yes. However, if you want to bring a private lawsuit, you may request a right-to-sue letter at any time. After 90 days, you can bring a private lawsuit even without a right-to-sue letter.

Monetary damages: Compensatory damages can be awarded by the Commission, and both compensatory and punitive damages can be awarded in a private lawsuit.

Administrative procedure: You can file your complaint anonymously if you wish. The Commission will hold an administrative hearing. An attorney will be provided by the Commission.

Private lawsuit: You can bring a lawsuit only after initially filing with the Commission.

MICHIGAN

Statute: Mich. Compiled Laws Ann. §37.2101 to .2804

State agency: Michigan Department of Civil Rights
Executive Plaza Building
1200 6th Street
Detroit, MI 48226
(313) 256-2615

Exclusions: Those employed by their parent, spouse or child

Time limits: 180 days

Exhaustion: No

Monetary damages: Compensatory damages can be awarded, both by the Department and in a private lawsuit. No punitive damages can be awarded under state law.

Administrative procedure: The Commission will hold a hearing. An attorney from the Commission will represent you, but you can also hire your own attorney if you wish. Attorney's fees are available.

Private lawsuit: You can bring a lawsuit directly in state court.

MINNESOTA

Statute: Minn. Stats. Ann. §363-01 to .15

State agency: Minnesota Department of Human Rights
　　Bremer Tower
　　Seventh Place and Minnesota Street
　　St. Paul, MN 55101
　　(612) 296-5665
Exclusions: Domestic employment, those employed by their parent,
　　spouse or child
Time limits: One year
Exhaustion: No. However, if you do file with the Commission,
　　you must wait 45 days before bringing a private lawsuit.
Monetary damages: Unlimited damages can be recovered for mental
　　suffering. In addition, you can recover up to three times the
　　amount of your actual damages, and up to $8,500 in punitive
　　damages. These damages can be awarded both by the Commis-
　　sion and in a private lawsuit.
Administrative procedure: The Commission will investigate and
　　attempt to conciliate and will often hold a fact-finding confer-
　　ence. After 180 days have passed since the complaint was filed,
　　you can request that the case be heard by the Department of
　　Administrative Hearings. The Commission will pay your costs,
　　but you must get your own attorney.
Private lawsuit: You can bring a lawsuit directly in state court.

MISSISSIPPI
Statute: Miss. Code Ann. §25-9-149
　　Although there is a state law prohibiting discrimination against state
employees, no damages, exclusions or other specifics are mentioned in
the statute.

MISSOURI
Statute: Vernon's Ann. Missouri Stats. §213-010 to .130
State agency: Missouri Commission on Human Rights
　　3315 West Truman Boulevard
　　P.O. Box 1129
　　Jefferson City, MO 65102
　　(314) 751-3325
Exclusions: Employers with fewer than six employees, religious
　　groups
Time limits: 180 days
Exhaustion: Yes. You can request a right-to-sue letter 180 days after
　　the harassment occurred if the Commission has not completed
　　its administrative process.
Monetary damages: Compensatory damages can be awarded, both
　　by the Commission and in a private lawsuit. Punitive damages
　　are available in a private lawsuit only.
Administrative procedure: The Commission will conduct an adminis-
　　trative hearing. At this hearing, the complaint will be presented

by the attorney general. You can join in the hearing and have your own attorney, if you wish. No attorney's fees are available.

Private lawsuit: You can bring a lawsuit only with a right-to-sue letter.

MONTANA

Statute: Montana Code Ann. §§49-1-101 to 49-2-601

State agency: Montana Human Rights Division
    Department of Labor and Industry
    Post Office Box 1728
    1236 6th Avenue
    Helena, MT 59624
    (406) 444-2884

Exclusions: Nonprofit fraternal, charitable or religious groups

Time limits: 180 days. However, if you are using a valid company or union grievance procedure, this time can be extended by the amount of time spent using the grievance procedure, up to an additional 120 days.

Exhaustion: Yes. You can get a right-to-sue letter if the Commission makes a finding that there is no reasonable cause to believe that discrimination has occurred.

Monetary damages: Compensatory damages can be awarded both by the Commission and in a private lawsuit. No punitive damages can be awarded under state law.

Administrative procedure: If there is a finding of reasonable cause, your claim will be certified for an administrative hearing. At this hearing, you can have an attorney. No attorney's fees are available from the Commission, but you can petition the state court for a rehearing solely on the issue of attorney's fees. Attorney's fees are routinely granted in this manner.

Private lawsuit: You can bring a lawsuit only after the Commission has made a finding of no reasonable cause.

NEBRASKA

Statute: Nebraska Rev. Stats. §48-1101 to 1126

State agency: Nebraska Equal Employment Opportunity
    Commission
    301 Centennial Mall South, 5th Floor
    P.O. Box 94934
    Lincoln, NE 68509
    (402) 471-2024

Exclusions: Employers with fewer than 15 employees, the United States, Indian tribes, religious organizations and private membership clubs, domestic employment, those employed by their parent, spouse or child

Time limits: 180 days

Exhaustion: Unclear. You should probably file your complaint with the Commission first, to be safe.

Monetary damages: No compensatory or punitive damages can be awarded under state law.

Administrative procedure: The Commission has no enforcement power. Thus, even if the Commission finds that you have been harassed, it cannot enforce an order unless your employer agrees. If your employer does not cooperate, you must sue your employer in state court.

Private lawsuit: See Exhaustion.

NEVADA

Statute: Nev. Rev. Stats. Ann. §613.310 to .430

State agency: Nevada Equal Rights Commission
    1515 East Tropicana, Suite 590
    Las Vegas, NV 89158
    (702) 486-7161

Exclusions: Employers with fewer than 15 employees, private membership clubs, the United States, Indian tribes

Time limits: 180 days

Exhaustion: Yes. If the Commission finds that there is probable cause to believe that you have been harassed, you can bring a private lawsuit.

Monetary damages: No compensatory or punitive damages are available under state law.

Administrative procedure: There is no administrative hearing, and the Commission has no enforcement power. After investigation and conciliation efforts, if the Commission finds that there is probable cause to believe that discrimination has occurred, it will advise you to go to the EEOC or to state court.

Private lawsuit: You may bring a lawsuit only after the Commission makes a finding of probable cause.

NEW HAMPSHIRE

Statute: N.H. Rev. Stats. Ann. §354-A:1 to A:14

State agency: New Hampshire Human Rights Commission
    163 Loudon Road
    Concord, NH 03301
    (603) 271-2767

Exclusions: Employers of fewer than six employees, fraternal, charitable or religious organizations, domestic employment, those employed by their parent, spouse or child

Time limits: 180 days

Exhaustion: No

Monetary damages: No compensatory or punitive damages can be awarded under state law.

Administrative procedure: The Commission will hold a hearing. The complaint will be presented by an attorney for the Commission, but you can have your own attorney if you wish. Attorney's fees are available.

Private lawsuit: You may bring a lawsuit directly in state court.

NEW JERSEY
Statute: N.J. Stats. Ann. §10:5-1 to 38.
State agency: New Jersey Division on Civil Rights
    31 Clinton Street
    Newark, NJ 07102
    (201) 648-2700
Exclusions: Domestic employment, those employed by their parent, spouse or child
Time limits: None indicated. Call the state agency for more information.
Exhaustion: No
Monetary damages: Compensatory and punitive damages can be awarded, both by the Division and in a private lawsuit, according to a recently enacted law. Check with the Division about how this law is being interpreted.
Administrative procedure: The Division will hold an administrative hearing. The complaint will be presented by an appointed attorney.
Private lawsuit: You may bring a lawsuit directly in state court. Attorney's fees are available.

NEW MEXICO
Statute: N.M. Stats. Ann. §28-1-1 to 15
State agency: New Mexico Human Rights Commission
    Aspen Plaza
    1596 Pacheco Street
    Santa Fe, NM 87502
    (505) 827-6838
Exclusions: Employers with fewer than four employees
Time limits: 180 days
Exhaustion: Yes. If the Commission has not settled the complaint or held a hearing within 180 days, you can request a letter of no determination, which will allow you to bring a private lawsuit.
Monetary damages: The Commission cannot award compensatory or punitive damages. State law is unclear as to whether compensatory damages can be awarded in a private lawsuit.
Administrative procedure: The Commission will hold an administrative hearing. You must get your own attorney for this hearing. Attorney's fees are available.
Private lawsuit: You can bring a lawsuit directly in state court only after the Commission has issued a letter of non-determination or held its hearing.

NEW YORK
Statute: N.Y. Executive Law §§290 to 301

State agency: New York State Division of Human Rights
55 West 125 Street, 13th Floor
New York, NY 10027
(212) 870-8566

Exclusions: Employers with fewer than four employees, domestic employment

Time limits: None is indicated in the state law. Call the agency to find out when you should file.

Exhaustion: No

Monetary damages: Compensatory damages can be awarded both by the Division and in a private lawsuit, but punitive damages can be awarded only in a private lawsuit.

Administrative procedure: There is an administrative hearing, and the state will provide you with an attorney.

Private lawsuit: You can bring a lawsuit directly in state court.

NORTH CAROLINA (has two state agencies)
Statute: Gen. Stats. of N.C. §143-422.1 to .3

For state and county employees and employees of the University of North Carolina:
State agency: North Carolina Office of Administrative Hearings
Post Office Drawer 27447
Raleigh, NC 27611
(919) 733-0431

Exclusions: Private employers

Time limits: 180 days

Exhaustion: Yes

Monetary damages: No compensatory or punitive damages can be awarded under state law.

Administrative procedure: There will be an administrative hearing, at which you must provide your own attorney. Attorney's fees are available.

Private lawsuit: You cannot bring a private lawsuit.

For private employees:
State agency: North Carolina Human Relations Commission*
21 West Jones Street
Raleigh, NC 27603
(919) 733-7996

Exclusions: Employers with fewer than 15 employees

Time limits: 180 days

Exhaustion: Yes

Monetary damages: No compensatory or punitive damages can be awarded under state law.

Administrative procedure: The Commission has no enforcement power. If your employer will not cooperate, the Commission will defer the claim to the EEOC.

Private lawsuit: You cannot bring a private lawsuit.

NORTH DAKOTA
Statute: N.D. Century Code Ann. §14-02, 4-01 to 21
State agency: North Dakota Department of Labor State Capitol
   Building
   600 East Boulevard
   Bismarck, ND 58505
   (701) 224-2660
Exclusions: Appointed staff of elected officials, domestic employ-
   ment, those employed by their parent, spouse or child
Time limits: 300 days
Exhaustion: No
Monetary damages: No compensatory or punitive damages can be
   awarded under state law.
Administrative procedure: There is no administrative hearing. After
   investigation and conciliation, if the Department finds that there
   is cause to believe harassment has occurred, you will be given
   the right to sue in state court.
Private lawsuit: You can bring a lawsuit directly in state court.

OHIO
Statute: Page's Ohio Rev. Code Ann. §4112.01 to 99
State agency: Ohio Civil Rights Commission
   220 Parsons Avenue
   Columbus, OH 43215
   (614) 466-5928
Exclusions: Employers with fewer than four employees, domestic
   employment
Time limits: Six months
Exhaustion: No
Monetary damages: Compensatory and punitive damages can be
   awarded in a private lawsuit. No compensatory or punitive
   damages can be awarded by the Commission.
Administrative procedure: The Commission will hold a hearing, at
   which the Attorney General will present the complaint. You may
   also have your own attorney, if you wish.
Private lawsuit: You may bring a lawsuit directly in state court.

OKLAHOMA
Statute: 25 Oklahoma Stats. §§1101 to 1802
State agency: Oklahoma Human Rights Commission
   2101 North Lincoln Boulevard, Room 480
   Oklahoma City, OK 73105
   (405) 521-2360
Exclusions: Employers with fewer than 15 employees, domestic
   employment, those employed by their parent, spouse or child,
   bona-fide nonprofit private membership clubs, Indian tribes

Time limits: 180 days

Exhaustion: Yes. If the Commission has not completed its administrative process in 180 days, you can request a right-to-sue letter.

Monetary damages: No compensatory or punitive damages can be awarded under state law.

Administrative procedure: The Commission will hold a hearing, at which the complaint will be presented by Commission staff. You may also have your own attorney, if you wish. Attorney's fees are available. The Commission's order has no legal effect without a corresponding order from the state court. The Commission must bring an action for review by the state court to get such an order.

Private lawsuit: You can bring a private lawsuit only with a right-to-sue letter.

OREGON

Statute: Or. Rev. Stats. §659.010 to .990

State agency: Oregon Bureau of Labor and Industry
  Civil Rights Division
  P.O. Box 800
  Portland, OR 97207
  (503) 229-6601

Exclusions: Domestic employment, those employed by their parent, spouse or child

Time limits: One year

Exhaustion: No

Monetary damages: Compensatory damages can be awarded by the Division. State Law is unclear as to whether compensatory damages can be awarded in a private lawsuit. No punitive damages are available under state law.

Administrative procedure: The Division will hold a hearing, and a Division attorney will present the complaint. You may also have your own attorney, if you wish. Attorney's fees are available.

Private lawsuit: You may file a lawsuit directly in state court. You must bring this suit within one year of the harassment, if you don't file a complaint with the Division.

PENNSYLVANIA

Statute: 43 Penn. Stats. Ann. §§951 to 962.2

State agency: Pennsylvania Human Rights Commission
  2971 East North 7th Street
  Harrisburg, PA 17110
  (717) 787-4412

Exclusions: Employers with fewer than four employees, agricultural workers, domestic employment, those employed by their parent, spouse or child

Time limits: 180 days

Exhaustion: No

Monetary damages: Compensatory damages can be awarded in a private lawsuit, but not by the Commission. No punitive damages can be awarded under state law.

Administrative procedure: The Commission will hold a hearing, at which you can have an attorney. However, only limited attorney's fees are available from the Commission.

Private lawsuit: You can bring a lawsuit directly in state court.

RHODE ISLAND

Statute: Gen. Laws of R.I. §28-5-1 to 40

State agency: Rhode Island Commission for Human Rights
10 Abbott Park Place
Providence, RI 02903
(401) 277-2661

Exclusions: Employers with fewer than four employees, domestic employment, those employed by their parent, spouse or child

Time limits: One year

Exhaustion: Yes. After 120 days, you can request a right-to-sue letter.

Monetary damages: Compensatory damages can be awarded both by the Commission and in a private lawsuit. Punitive damages can be awarded only in a private lawsuit.

Administrative procedure: The Commission will hold a hearing, at which you must be represented by your own attorney. Attorney's fees are available.

Private lawsuit: You can bring a private lawsuit only with a right-to-sue letter.

SOUTH CAROLINA

Statute: Code of S.C. title 1, §1-13-10 to 110

State agency: South Carolina Human Affairs Commission
P.O. Box 4490
Columbia, SC 29240
(803) 253-6336

Exclusions: Employers with fewer than 15 employees, bona-fide private membership clubs, Indian tribes, appointed staff of elected officials

Time limits: 180 days

Exhaustion: Yes. If the Commission doesn't bring a civil lawsuit within 180 days, you can get a right-to-sue letter.

Monetary damages: No compensatory or punitive damages can be awarded under state law.

Administrative procedure: There is no administrative hearing. If the Commission makes a finding of probable cause, it can bring a lawsuit against your employer. If the Commission doesn't bring suit within 180 days, you can bring a private lawsuit.

Private lawsuit: You may bring a private lawsuit only with a right-to-sue letter.

SOUTH DAKOTA

Statute: S.D. Codified Laws, Chapter 20-13
State agency: South Dakota Division of Human Rights
    500 East Capitol Street
    Pierre, SD 57501
    (605) 773-4493
Exclusions: None
Time limits: 180 days
Exhaustion: Yes. A right-to-sue letter is available after 60 days.
Monetary damages: Compensatory and punitive damages can be
    awarded in a private lawsuit, but not by the Division.
Administrative procedure: If the division finds probable cause to
    believe that discrimination has occurred, there will be an admin-
    istrative hearing. You must get an attorney for this hearing, but
    no attorney's fees are available.
Private lawsuit: You may bring a private lawsuit only with a right-
    to-sue letter. Attorney's fees are available.

TENNESSEE

Statute: Tenn. Code Ann. §4-21-101 to 408
State agency: Tennessee Human Rights Commission
    226 Capitol Boulevard, Suite 602
    Nashville, TN 37219
    (615) 741-5825
Exclusions: Employers with fewer than eight employees
Time limits: 180 days
Exhaustion: No
Monetary damages: Compensatory and punitive damages can be
    awarded, both by the Commission and in a private lawsuit.
Administrative procedure: You are entitled to an attorney at the
    administrative hearing. You can choose your own attorney, or
    have one appointed for you. Attorney's fees are available.
Private lawsuit: You can file a lawsuit directly in state court within
    one year. If you file a complaint with the Commission, you can
    withdraw it at any time to file your own lawsuit.

TEXAS

Statute: Tex. Stats. Ann., Article 5221(k) §§1.01 to 10-05
State agency: Texas Commission on Human Rights
    8100 Cameron Road, #525
    P.O. Box 13493
    Austin, TX 78753
    (512) 837-8534
Exclusions: Employers with fewer than 15 employees, appointed
    staff of elected officials
Time limits: 180 days
Exhaustion: Yes. After 180 days, you can bring a private lawsuit.

Monetary damages: No compensatory or punitive damages are available under state law.

Administrative procedure: If the evidence supports the complaint, the Commission will recommend a finding of harassment to an administrative panel. If two of the three members of this panel agree that harassment has taken place, conciliation will be attempted. If conciliation efforts fail, the Commission can decide to file suit in the state court to enforce its finding. You can join this lawsuit, with or without an attorney. The case for the complaint will be presented by Commission staff. Attorney's fees are available.

Private lawsuit: You must first file a complaint with the Commission. Once 180 days have passed, you then have a right to sue in state court. You can also sue in state court if the Commission determines that the complaint has no merit—that there is no reason to believe that harassment has occurred. Finally, if the Commission decides that harassment has taken place, but doesn't bring a suit in state court to enforce this finding, you may bring your own lawsuit to do so.

UTAH

Statute: Utah Code Ann. §34-35-1 to 7.1

State agency: Utah Industrial Commission, Anti-Discrimination Division
160 East 300 South
Salt Lake City, UT 84111
(801) 530-6801

Exclusions: Employers with fewer than 15 employees, religious organizations

Time limits: Must file within 180 days

Exhaustion: Yes

Monetary damages: No compensatory or punitive damages are available under state law.

Administrative procedure: You may have an attorney at the administrative hearing. Attorney's fees are available.

Private lawsuit: You cannot bring a private action.

VERMONT

Statute: 21 Vermont Stats. Ann. §495

State agency: Vermont Attorney General's Office
Civil Rights Division
109 State Street
Montpelier, VT 05609
(802) 828-3171

Exclusions: None

Time limits: Unclear. A federal district court recently held that there is a three-year statute of limitations. However, you may have as long as six years to file.

Exhaustion: No

Monetary damages: Compensatory and punitive damages can be awarded in a private lawsuit only.

Administrative procedure: There is no administrative hearing. If, after investigation and conciliation efforts, no solution has been reached, you must litigate in state court.

Private lawsuit: You may bring a lawsuit directly in state court.

VIRGINIA

Although there is a state law prohibiting harassment of state employees only, there is no state agency.

WASHINGTON

Statute: Rev. Code of Wash. Ann. §49.60.010 to .330

State agency: Washington State Human Rights Commission
Evergreen Plaza Building, Suite 402
711 South Capitol Way
Olympia, WA 98504
(206) 753-6770

Exclusions: Employers with fewer than eight employees, nonprofit religious organizations, domestic employment, those employed by their parent, spouse or child

Time limits: Six months

Exhaustion: No

Monetary damages: The Commission can award up to $1,000 in compensatory damages, but no punitive damages. Unlimited compensatory and punitive damages can be awarded in a private lawsuit.

Administrative procedure: There will be an administrative hearing, at which the Commission will represent the complaint. If you wish to have your own attorney, you may do so. Attorney's fees are available.

Private lawsuit: You may bring a lawsuit directly in state court.

WEST VIRGINIA

Statute: W Va. Code §5-11-1 to 19

State agency: West Virginia Human Rights Commission
1321 Plaza East, Room 106
Charleston, WV 25301
(304) 348-2616

Exclusions: Employers with fewer than 12 employees, domestic employment, those employed by their parent, spouse or child

Time limits: 180 days

Exhaustion: No

Monetary damages: Compensatory damages are limited to $2,500 from the Commission but are unlimited in state court. No punitive damages can be awarded under state law.

Administrative procedure: At the administrative hearing, the attorney general will present the complaint. You can have your own attorney, if you wish. If you do retain an attorney, attorney's fees are available from the Commission.

Private lawsuit: You can bring a lawsuit directly in state court.

WISCONSIN

Statute: Wis. Stats. Ann. §11.31 to 39

State agency: Wisconsin Equal Rights Division
Department of Industry, Labor and Human Relations
P.O. Box 8928
201 East Washington Avenue
Madison, WI 53708
(608) 267-9678

Exclusions: Those employed by their parent, spouse or child

Time limits: 300 days

Exhaustion: Yes

Monetary damages: No compensatory or punitive damages can be awarded under state law.

Administrative procedure: You may have an attorney at the administrative hearing. Attorney's fees are available.

Private lawsuit: You cannot bring a private lawsuit.

WYOMING

Statute: Wyoming Stats. Ann. §27-9-101 to 108

State agency: Wyoming Fair Employment Commission
Herschler Building
2nd East
Cheyenne, WY 82002
(307) 777-7261

Exclusions: Employers with fewer than two employees, religious organizations

Time limits: 90 days

Exhaustion: Yes. You can get a right-to-sue letter if the Commission decides that its investigation will take more than 200 days.

Monetary damages: Compensatory damages can be awarded in a private lawsuit, but not by the Commission. Punitive damages cannot be awarded under state law.

Administrative procedure: You may have an attorney at the administrative hearing if you wish; however, no attorney's fees are available.

Private lawsuit: You can bring a private lawsuit only with a right-to-sue letter.

Common Law Torts

Lawsuits based on common law torts may include intentional infliction of emotional distress and assault and battery. In some sexual harassment cases, these suits provide a remedy based on the common law of each state rather than on any statute or governmental agency regulation.

The same factual situation that is the basis for a sexual harassment claim under the Civil Rights Act or state FEP statutes may also serve as the ground for a tort action. Although not every case merits a claim of assault and battery or intentional infliction of emotional distress, these kinds of suits may compensate the victim of sexual harassment with substantial monetary damages—unlike Title VII of the Civil Rights Act, which limits the amount of money that can be collected.

One kind of tort action is called *assault and battery.* If the plaintiff brings an assault claim, she must prove that her harasser caused her to fear harmful or offensive physical contact. Both verbal and physical harassment can constitute assault. *Battery* is conduct that results in any harmful or offensive touching of another. Claims for assault and battery are frequently alleged in sexual harassment cases; usually, both claims are brought together. Examples of conduct that may rise to the level of a claim for assault and battery include grabbing, brushing against, and fondling the woman, as well as outright sexual assault and rape.

Another tort commonly alleged in sexual harassment cases is called *intentional infliction of emotional distress.* To prove such distress, a plaintiff must show that the conduct of her harasser was so shocking in character, or so extreme in degree, that a person of normal sensibilities would consider the action outrageous. This claim arises in most sexual harassment cases, because unwelcome physical conduct, as well as the creation of a hostile work environment, may be considered outrageous, and it is often left to the jury to decide.

Employers may be liable for other tort actions when they handle employee hiring or sexual harassment complaints carelessly. For example, an employer can be sued for defamation if it makes or condones false statements about an employee that tend to damage the employee's reputation. Defamation is either oral (*slander*) or written (*libel*). An employer could be sued, for example, for telling someone that an employee was fired for sexual harassment if the charge later turns out to be false.

Negligent hiring and retention claims also arise in the context of sexual harassment lawsuits. If an employer fails to take reasonable care before hiring an employee (for instance, by not performing appropriate reference and background checks) and that employee later causes damage to other employees, the employer may be liable for negligent hiring. Similarly, if an employer retains an employee with a demonstrated propensity for misconduct, it may be liable for negligent retention.

Finally, an employer may be liable for the tort of invasion of privacy if private and embarrassing details about the harasser or the victim are unnecessarily and publicly disclosed.

Summary of Significant Legal Cases

The following cases, summarized in chronological order, were selected to show the evolution of the legal and financial liabilities for sexual harassment. The list is not meant to be exhaustive but merely to show trends over the years.

Monge v. Beebe Rubber Co., 114 N.H. 130, 316 A.2d 549 (1974)

An employer's termination of an employment contract was found to be a breach of contract when the termination was motivated by malice because a female employee refused the sexual advances of her foreman. The case was decided under state contract law rather than Title VII and did not use the words *sexual harassment*.

Miller v. Bank of America, 600 F.2d 211 (9th Cir. 1979)

In one of the first appellate cases, Bank of America was found liable for a supervisor's sexual harassment, even though his behavior violated company policy and the bank was unaware of the sexual harassment. This liability was based on the concept of respondeat superior and was decided under Title VII of the Civil Rights Act.

Bundy v. Jackson, 641 F.2d 934 (D.D.C. 1981)

The court found that sexual insults and demeaning propositions constituted sexual harassment and were a form of sex discrimination, regardless of whether the plaintiff lost any tangible job benefits—such as wages or a promotion—as a result.

Wright v. Methodist Youth Services, Inc., 511 F. Supp. 307 (N.D. Ill. 1981)

This is the first case in which a court found that the termination of a man because he rejected sexual advances by his male supervisor was a violation of Title VII. The judge reasoned that a similarly sit-uated woman would not have had sexual demands made of her.

Rogers v. Loews L'Enfant Plaza Hotel, 526 F. Supp. 523 (D.D.C. 1981)

The plaintiff was sexually harassed by her immediate supervisor while working at a hotel restaurant. The court found that she was entitled to general and punitive damages under state tort law the-ories of intrusion, assault and battery, and intentional infliction of emotional distress.

NLRB v. Downslope Industries, Inc., 676 F.2d 1114 (6th Cir. 1982)

Under the National Labor Relations Act, the court found that free-dom from sexual harassment is a "working condition" for which employees may organize to protect themselves.

Davis v. United States Steel Corp., 779 F.2d 209 (4th Cir. 1986)

The inaction of a supervisor who observed an employee engaging in sexual harassment was found to be sufficient to make the company liable under the doctrine of respondeat superior. A super-visor has the responsibility to take the necessary corrective action.

Meritor Savings Bank v. Vinson, 477 U.S. 57 (1986)

This was the first U.S. Supreme Court case to find that sexual harass-ment is a form of sex discrimination under Title VII of the 1964 Civil Rights Act. The Court concluded that a claim of "hostile environment" sexual harassment is actionable under Title VII. Although the decision noted that employers cannot always be held liable for sexual harass-ment by management personnel, in this case the Court found that a grievance procedure and policy against discrimination, coupled with the employee's failure to use that procedure, did not immunize the employer from liability. The Court also allowed the introduction of evidence about the plaintiff's "provocative" clothing and behavior.

Delgado v. Lehman, 665 F. Supp. 460, 468 (E.D. Va. 1987)

This case is significant because of its holding that "sexual harassment need not take the form of overt sexual advances or suggestions, but may consist of such things as verbal abuse of women if it [is] sufficiently patterned to comprise a condition and is apparently caused by the sex of the harassed employee." In this case, a supervisor who was trying to protect his turf viewed women as threats. He went out of his way to demean the plaintiff and other women.

Hall v. Gus Construction Co., 842 F.2d 1010 (8th Cir. 1988)

The court held that the employer was liable for co-worker sexual harassment on the theory that the supervisor was the employer's agent. The foreman, as the agent of the company, had both actual and constructive knowledge of the harassment and failed to take appropriate action to stop the behavior.

Broderick v. Ruder, 685 F. Supp. 1269 (D.D.C. 1988)

In this precedent-setting case, an attorney who worked in an environment that was sexually offensive was found to be a victim of hostile work environment sexual harassment. She was forced to work in a department in which managers offered promotions and other preferential treatment to those who submitted to sexual advances. Broderick was deprived of promotions and job opportunities; when she and other women voiced their displeasure, management responded with hostility, and Broderick's job assignments were changed. The U.S. Securities and Exchange Commission was found liable in this situation because it failed to take action against supervisors when it had both actual and constructive knowledge of their conduct.

Shrout v. Black Clawson Co., 689 F. Supp. 774 (S.D. Ohio 1988)

The court held the employer liable for a supervisor's quid pro quo sexual harassment under the doctrine of respondeat superior. The supervisor made sexual remarks, touched the woman employee in offensive ways, refused to give her annual performance appraisals and salary reviews, and told her "things don't have to be this way" when she complained to him. She endured such behavior for four years before filing charges with the EEOC. She was awarded $75,000 in compensatory damages and $50,000 in punitive damages because of the employer's failure to take action when it knew or should have known of the harassment. An expert witness testified that an "open-door policy" was not sufficient to immunize the employer from liability and that it was reasonable to assume that lower-level women employees would hesitate to contact the company president with complaints of sexual harassment.

Paroline v. Unisys Corp., 867 F.2d 185 (4th Cir. 1989)

The Fourth Circuit ruled that "reasonable minds could differ as to whether Unisys'[s] response was reasonably calculated to end the harassment." The plaintiff offered evidence that previous reprimands of the harassing supervisor failed to deter him from continuing the behavior, and the court agreed.

Steele v. Offshore Shipbuilding, Inc., 867 F.2d 1311 (11th Cir. 1989)

In this case, the Eleventh Circuit held that an employer was not liable under the doctrine of respondeat superior because it took appropriate corrective action once it was informed of the sexual harassment. The court went on to find that the individual's actions constituted hostile environment sexual harassment and not quid pro quo sexual harassment, because he did not demand sexual favors in exchange for job benefits.

Waltman v. International Paper Co., 875 F.2d 468 (5th Cir. 1989)

This court found that a publicized sexual harassment policy and complaint procedure were insufficient to immunize the employer from liability because the employer told the plaintiff that she should expect such behavior when working with men. She was also told by human resources staff that they could not investigate her claims without revealing her identity and that any investigation would be detrimental to her. The court found that the employer's action was not reasonably calculated to end the harassment.

Ellison v. Brady, 924 F.2d 872 (9th Cir. 1991)

In *Ellison,* the Ninth Circuit became the first federal appeals court to rule that in determining whether the hostile work environment affected the employee's psychological well-being Title VII requires a "reasonable woman" standard. This standard may be more sensitive than the usual legal standard—that of a reasonable man—because a reasonable man might be less offended by sexually suggestive material than a reasonable woman would be. The court also decided that when an individual is harassed by a co-worker, the law is violated if the employer relocates the employee who was harassed rather than reassigning the harasser.

Robinson v. Jacksonville Shipyards, 760 F. Supp. 1486 (M.D. Fla. 1991)

In this Florida case, the judge also ruled on the effect of actions on a "reasonable woman." Here, the court found, the presence of calendars and posters featuring nude or scantily dressed women created an atmosphere of sexual harassment that unlawfully stereotyped women as sex objects. The court held that "a pre-existing atmosphere that deters women from entering or continuing in a profession or job is no less destructive to and offensive to workplace equality than a sign declaring 'men only.'" The court also ordered affirmative relief in the form of policy changes, training, and education. The case was appealed but was settled before the appeal was complete, and one of the issues raised was whether First Amendment free speech rights preclude the prohibition of visual sexual harassment.

Franklin v. Gwinnett County Public Schools, 112 S. Ct. 1028 (1992)

This was the first Supreme Court case to consider the issue of sexual harassment in schools. A high school student was harassed by her sports coach and teacher. The school conducted an investigation into her allegations. The teacher resigned on the condition that all matters pending against him be dropped, and the school complied with his request. Reversing the lower court decision, the Supreme Court ruled, for the first time, that monetary damages against schools are available in Title IX cases. (Title IX prohibits sex discrimination in educational institutions that receive federal funds.)

Jenson v. Eleleth Taconite Co., 842 F. Supp. 847 (D. Minn. 1993)

This was the first class-action (a suit brought by a group of individuals rather than a single plaintiff) sexual harassment case to reach a federal court. A group of female mine workers argued that the harassment was so pervasive, systemic, and severe that it discriminated against the entire group. At the mines, the workplace was filled with pornographic graffiti, photographs, cartoons, and other material that degradingly depicted women as sexual objects. The male workers also frequently spoke of their female co-workers in terms of body parts, commented on the women's sex lives, boasted of sexual exploits, and frequently propositioned the women. To succeed as a class action, the plaintiffs had to prove a "pattern or practice of sex discrimination." The court's decision integrated legal standards applicable to individual claims of sexual harassment with legal standards for class-action claims of sex discrimination, thereby producing a new legal standard applicable to class-action suits involving sexual harassment. *Jenson* represents a significant expansion of sexual harassment law, in that individual plaintiffs can now join forces to bring their claims.

Lehmann v. Toys "R" Us, Inc., 626 A.2d 445 (N.J. 1993)

Lehmann is significant because the case expands the boundaries of what constitutes a hostile environment. It is also useful reading because it contains an excellent survey and discussion of previous hostile environment cases. The plaintiff alleged that she had observed her supervisor inappropriately touching and groping other women and that he had asked her to lift her shirt and display her chest to another supervisor. In this case, the court found that the plaintiff's witnessing of sexual comments and touches was actionable. In addition, the court laid out in new detail the reasonable woman standard (first articulated in *Ellison,* discussed earlier in this section) and emphasized that the defendant had failed to properly investigate the plaintiff's claims.

Harris v. Forklift, 114 S. Ct. 367 (1993)

In an unusual, swift, short, and unanimous decision, the United States Supreme Court expanded the definition of hostile work environment by establishing that harassment may be actionable even if it does not cause severe psychological harm. In this case, Teresa Harris experienced constant verbal sexual harassment by the president of the company through sexual jokes, comments, and innuendos. He also humiliated her in front of clients and other employees. He suggested, for example, that they negotiate her raise in a motel room and asked Harris to reach into his front pocket for coins. Significantly, the court rejected the defendant's argument that in the male-dominated forklift industry, Harris should simply expect and tolerate such behavior. The lower federal courts had found that she needed to prove severe psychological harm to prove that her working environment was poisoned or hostile. At the Supreme Court level, as Justice Sandra O'Connor wrote for the majority, "it is not necessary for a plaintiff to have a nervous breakdown in order to be able to sue for sexual harassment." The court used the term "reasonable person" in describing the offensiveness of the behavior but left open the question of whether it meant for this to replace the use of the "reasonable woman standard."

Carr v. Allison Gas Turbine Div., 32 F.3d 1007 (7th Cir. 1994)

In this case, the plaintiff sued General Motors for the harassing behavior of her co-workers on the manufacturing line, which included sexual comments, innuendos, and physical threats with welding equipment. The defendants tried to argue that Carr had participated in some of the joking, including "talking like a man," and that, therefore, she could not sue. Judge Posner disagreed, holding that the plaintiff's "unladylike" behavior did not exonerate harassing male co-workers. In addition, he said General Motors should have foreseen that integrating women into the previously all-male factory environment would lead to sexual harassment and that the company should have taken steps through policies and training to prevent that from happening.

Johnson v. Los Angeles Fire Dept., 865 F. Supp. 1430 (C.D. 1994)

The court held that the department's policy of prohibiting *Playboy* in the workplace was unconstitutional on the grounds that it violated the First Amendment to the United States Constitution. The decision seemed to distinguish pure work environments such as *Jacksonville Shipyards* (see discussion earlier in this section) from the firehouse environment, which was, in addition to the place of employment for the firefighters, also the place where they ate, slept, and lived. In that unusual setting, the court seemed to imply, the First Amendment will take precedent over the sexual harassment policy.

Silva v. University of New Hampshire, 888 F. Supp. 293 (D.N.H. 1994)

Donald Silva, professor of English at the University of New Hampshire, was suspended from his position for one year without pay and was required to seek counseling for several classroom incidents in which he had used sexual analogies as a part of his lectures. He filed suit in federal court, claiming violation of his First Amendment rights. A New Hampshire district court judge issued a complex, 103-page order and a preliminary injunction, forcing the university to reinstate Silva until a complete trial and order had taken place. The case was settled out of court, making Silva's reinstatement permanent, removing the charge from his record, and granting him $60,000 in back pay and damages and $170,000 in legal fees. The case garnered considerable national media attention. *Silva* makes it clear that balancing free speech rights in the classroom with sexual harassment is a complex task with no clear lines. Basically, this case stands for the proposition that a university must be cautious in disciplining professors for such conduct, thereby balancing the rights of free speech with Title IX.

Future Trends in Sexual Harassment Law

Several trends point the way for the future of sexual harassment law. The first relates to sexual harassment in housing. The Rutgers Women's Law Clinic has taken the lead in investigating cases in which a landlord sexually harassed a tenant or required sexual favors in exchange for the provision of housing. Sexual harassment in housing constitutes sex discrimination in violation of both Title VII and Title VIII, the Fair Housing Act of the 1968 Civil Rights Act. Regina Cahan, author of *Home Is No Haven: An Analysis of Sexual Harassment in Housing*, stressed that "when sexual harassment occurs at work . . . the woman may remove herself from the offensive environment. When the harassment occurs in a woman's home, it is a complete invasion of her life" (Siegel 1992). The Women's Rights Litigation Clinic at Rutgers School of Law–Newark has prepared a pamphlet, "Stop Sexual Harassment in Housing," available in English and Spanish. (This organization is described in Chapter 5.)

Another trend is exemplified by a sexual harassment case filed in 1992 against Stroh's Brewery in Minnesota. In addition to complaints about a workplace rife with pinups and other sexually degrading material, one of the main allegations was that the company's media campaign contributed to the hostile work environment because the advertising used women's sexuality to sell beer. Stroh's dropped the advertising campaign and settled the lawsuit.

Also new are state laws that require companies of a certain size to post notices on the illegality of sexual harassment and on the procedure for filing a complaint with the state's human rights commission. A score of states, including Maine and California, either have or are considering such laws.

Inevitably, the Supreme Court will have to settle the confused issue of the First Amendment and verbal and pictorial sexual harassment. As noted in the earlier section on schools, as well as in the *Silva* case discussed previously, several lower courts have addressed this issue. The Supreme Court has not clearly decided the issue, other than to state as *dictum* (a legal aside in a written decision rather than a main part of the holding) in *R.A.V. v. City of St. Paul*, 505 U.S. 377, 389 (1992) that "words can in some circumstances violate laws directed not against speech but against conduct. . . . For example, sexually derogatory 'fighting words,' among other words, may produce a violation of Title VII's general prohibition against sexual discrimination in employment practices." Commentators have heavily criticized this dictum. See, for example, *Nadine Strossen, President, American Civil Liberties Union, Professor of Law, New York Law School, the Kenneth M. Piper Lecture: The Tensions between Regulating Workplace Harassment and the First Amendment: No Trump*, 71 Chicago-Kent L. Rev. 701 (1995).

Other issues over which great disagreement exists among the lower courts and that are currently awaiting clarification by the United States Supreme Court include the reasonable woman standard in hostile environment cases; the liability of schools and colleges for student-to-student harassment; and whether so-called third-party harassment, in which someone simply witnesses sexual harassment or romantic liaisons in the workplace, is legally actionable.

In recent years there has also been an explosion in the number of lawsuits by plaintiffs who were terminated or disciplined because of sexual harassment. This situation has forced companies to invest in time-consuming and painstaking investigations before they terminate an employee.

Finally, growing numbers of women are reporting harassment by e-mail in the form of explicit sexual graphics, obscene notes, and threats sent through their computers. An April 1995 article in the *New Republic* described the phenomenon, noting that "harassment of women is so common that women often pretend to be men to avoid sexually suggestive e-mail" (Chapman 1995, p. 14). In February 1995, a male student at the University of Michigan was arrested for sending on-line messages that contained graphic descriptions of the rape, torture, and murder of a female classmate.

Because of the rise in the number of sexual harassment lawsuits and million-dollar jury awards and the expansion of harassment cases to include harassment of employees by outsiders, harassment of superiors by subordinates, harassment of males by females, and harassment among members of the same sex, the inevitable backlash has set in. Several draft bills are circulating in Congress in an attempt to limit the damages in sexual harassment cases, either by restricting the amount of money available or by limiting the definition of sexual harassment.

Sexual Harassment Statistics

EEOC Statistics

Since 1980, 75 percent of the sex discrimination claims filed with the EEOC—more than 35,000 complaints—have been based on charges of sexual harassment. As a result of sexual harassment charges resolved by the EEOC in 1992, 1,340 people won $12.7 million; in 1993, 1,546 complainants won $25.2 million in monetary benefits from their employers, including back pay, remedial relief, damages, promotions, and reinstatements. This represents an increase of 98.3 percent in total monetary awards in a one-year period. Between 1989 and 1993, the number of sexual harassment charges filed in the United States increased by 112 percent ("Cost of Sexual Harassment" 1994). The number of cases rose from 6,000 in 1990 to over 15,000 in 1996 (Kaufman 1997).

Surveys on the Incidence of Sexual Harassment

Numerous studies have been conducted over the years on the incidence of sexual harassment. These studies have found widely varying results—from 15 to 80 percent of respondents have reported experiencing sexual harassment. Dr. Freada Klein, a sexual harassment expert and researcher, believes these disparate results happen for three reasons.

1. The studies used different definitions of the term *sexual harassment* or failed to define the term at all.
2. There were differences in how the respondents were selected. Respondents who "self-select" in response to a query in a magazine or newsletter, for example, may have different attitudes from those who are randomly selected.

3. The study results failed to show whether respondents were asked if they had experienced sexual harassment over a specific period of time. Asking whether a respondent has ever experienced sexual harassment may lead to a very different result than if respondents are asked whether they have experienced harassment within the past year.

The reader, therefore, should be cautious in drawing conclusions from any particular survey without determining the methodology employed. Following are the major findings from four of the more extensive studies that have been conducted on sexual harassment: the U.S. Merit Systems Protection Board study, the Gutek/L.A. study, the *Harvard Business Review/Redbook* study, and the Defense Department study. In addition, summary results are presented from a number of other studies on specific issues.

The U.S. Merit Systems Protection Board Study

A May 1980 (released in 1981) U.S. Merit Systems Protection Board (USMSPB) survey of over 23,000 federal executive-branch employees of both sexes (with a return rate of 85 percent) found that 42 percent of all female employees and 15 percent of all male employees reported having been sexually harassed. The most ambiguous forms of sexual harassment—"sexual comments" and "suggestive looks"—were reported the most often (USMSPB 1981).

A 1987 USMSPB follow-up study of approximately 13,000 federal employees found that 42 percent of all women and 14 percent of all men reported that they had experienced some form of uninvited and unwanted sexual attention. The most frequently experienced type of uninvited sexual attention was "unwanted sexual teasing, jokes, remarks, or questions" (USMSPB 1988). Figures 4.1 and 4.2 provide the details of some of the results of the earlier MSPB study. A 1994 MSPB follow-up study found similar numbers, with 44 percent of women and 19 percent of men reporting having received unwanted sexual attention during the preceding two years (see Figure 4.3). The survey reporters hypothesized that the numbers have not been reduced despite increased training on the issue, perhaps because some respondents are now more inclined to label certain kinds of behavior sexual harassment.

Figure 4.1 Overall Incidence Rate of Sexual Harassment (Percentage of Federal Employees Who Experienced Sexual Harassment between May 1978 and May 1980, by Severity of Harassment)

TOTAL FEDERAL WORKFORCE: 1,862,000
TOTAL VICTIMS 462,000 (25%)

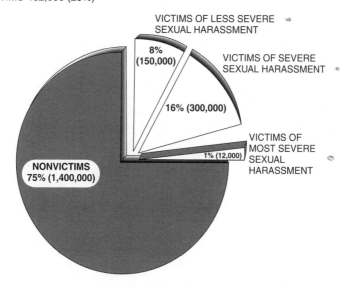

Note: These figures indicate the number of people harassed, classified by their most severe experience. Since many people reported that they had more than one experience, the number of harassment incidents is considerably larger.

Source: From a study conducted by the United States Merit Systems Protection Board, *Sexual Harassment of Federal Workers: Is It a Problem?* (Washington, DC: U.S. Government Printing Office, 1981).

The three MSPB studies also covered how employees define sexual harassment; employee responses to sexual harassment, including what actions employees think are the most effective in dealing with the issue and how they handled the problem; agency action to reduce incidences of sexual harassment; and how much sexual harassment costs the government. A discussion of the legal imperative to prevent sexual harassment, a review of the case law, and recommendations are also presented. The 1980 report also detailed victims according to age, marital status, racial and ethnic

Figure 4.2 Incidence Rate of Sexual Harassment among Women and Men (Percentage of Female and Male Federal Employees Who Experienced Sexual Harassment between May 1978 and May 1980, by Severity of Harassment)

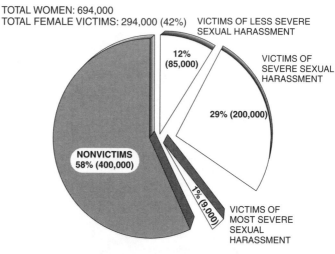

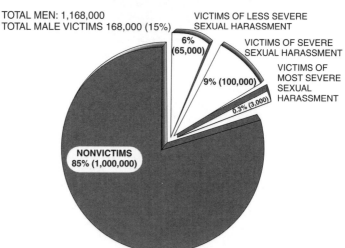

Note: These figures indicate the number of people harassed, classified by their most severe experience. Since many people reported that they had more than one experience, the number of harassment incidents is considerably larger.

Source: From a study conducted by the United States Merit Systems Protection Board, *Sexual Harassment of Federal Workers: Is It a Problem?* (Washington, DC: U.S. Government Printing Office, 1981).

Figure 4.3 Incidence Rate of Sexual Harassment among Men and Women (Percentage of Employees Who Experienced Sexually Harassing Behaviors in the Previous Two Years)

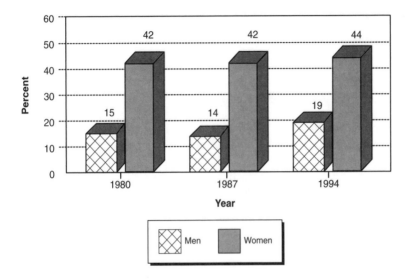

Source: Adapted from United States Merit Systems Protection Board, *Sexual Harassment in the Federal Workplace* (Washington, DC: U.S. Government Printing Office, 1981).

background, geographic location, annual salary, job classification, and other details. The sex, age, marital status, ethnic background, and other details about harassers were also studied.

The Gutek/L.A. Study

In 1978, a number of workers, selected by random sampling from the Los Angeles telephone directories, were interviewed by telephone. Although this survey may be somewhat out-of-date, it is included here because it is one of the few random, scientifically designed studies of sexual harassment. Forty-seven percent of the females and 46 percent of the males reported that they had experienced remarks of a sexual nature on their current jobs. Eleven percent of the women and 6 percent of the men reported that they had received requests for sexual activity on their present job (Gutek 1985).

Table 4.1 represents Barbara Gutek's findings, based on the results of the telephone survey, on the incidence of sexual harassment. Other factors Gutek studied include the nature and frequency of sexual harassment, the characteristics of harassers and the reactions of victims, workers' reports of sexual overtures, women's and men's attitudes about sexuality in the workplace, how different environments influence sexuality, explanations for sexuality in the workplace, and unequal sex ratios and sex role spillovers.

The *Harvard Business Review/Redbook* Study

Among the most pertinent data available on sexual harassment in private employment are those found in an article by Eliza Collins and Timothy Blodgett, "Sexual Harassment: Some See It . . . Some Won't," in the March–April 1981 issue of the *Harvard Business Review.* The article reported on a survey the *Review* conducted jointly with *Redbook* magazine. Questionnaires were mailed to 7,408 *Harvard Business Review* subscribers in the United States. Obviously, with such a mailing list, no claim can be made that the sample was random or unbiased. The sample was also skewed to ensure a large number of responses from females by including "virtually every female subscriber." Thirty-two percent of the questionnaires went to women, and 44 percent of the responses came from women. The overall response rate was 24.9 percent. Clearly, those who were most interested in the subject responded, and women tended to be more interested than men. A separate report on the survey was published by *Redbook* (Safran 1981).

The *Review* article reported that most people agreed on what sexual harassment was, but men and women seemed to disagree strongly on how frequently it occurred. Half of the women felt the amount of sexual harassment at work was greatly exaggerated, whereas two-thirds of the men felt that way. Two-thirds of high-level executives also felt the incidence of harassment at work was exaggerated. The *Review* reported that top management appeared isolated from harassment situations and that middle management was less aware of problems than were lower levels of management.

Considering the obvious bias in the survey method, it is interesting that only 10 percent of respondents reported that they had ever heard of a situation such as "Mr. X has asked me to have sex with him. I refused, but now I learn that he's given me a poor evaluation" (Collins and Blodgett 1981, p. 78).

Table 4.1 Experiences of Social-Sexual Behaviors

	Males (N = 405)	Females (N = 827)
Ever experienced on current job		
Complimentary comments	46.0%	50.1%
Insulting comments	12.6	12.2
Complimentary looks, gestures	47.3	51.6
Insulting looks, gestures	12.3	9.1
Nonsexual touching	73.5	68.9
Sexual touching	20.9	15.3
Expected socializing	2.7	2.8
Expected sexual activity	1.0	1.8
Ever experienced on any job		
Complimentary comments	60.7%	68.1%
Insulting comments	19.3	23.3
Complimentary looks, gestures	56.3	66.6
Insulting looks, gestures	19.3	20.3
Nonsexual touching	78.0	74.4
Sexual touching	33.3	33.1
Expected socializing	8.4	12.0
Expected sexual activity	3.5	7.7
Ever experienced and labeled it sexual harassment		
Complimentary comments	10.4%	18.9%
Insulting comments	12.1	19.8
Complimentary looks, gestures	8.1	16.2
Insulting looks, gestures	9.6	15.4
Nonsexual touching	3.5	3.6
Sexual touching	12.3	24.2
Expected socializing	7.4	10.9
Expected sexual activity	3.2	7.6
Have you ever experienced sexual harassment?	37.3%	53.1%

Source: Reprinted with permission from Barbara A. Gutek, *Sex and the Workplace: The Impact of Sexual Behavior and Harassment on Women, Men, and Organizations* (San Francisco: Jossey-Bass Inc., 1985).

Among the survey's major findings was the respondents' opinion that a supervisor's behavior was more serious and threatening than that of co-workers. Sexual harassment was seen as a power issue.

The study indicated that most respondents felt the EEOC guidelines were reasonable in theory, but some thought they would be difficult to implement because they were too vague.

Respondents felt it would be impractical to take action on what many women apparently believed were the most obnoxious and pervasive forms of harassment—innuendo and jokes—but 68 percent of male managers believed the EEOC guidelines would not be difficult to implement.

Some of the results of the *Harvard Business Review/Redbook* study detailing respondents' reports of the incidence of sexual harassment are presented in Tables 4.2 and 4.3.

The Defense Department Study

In this 1990 report, mandated by then Secretary of Defense Frank Carlucci in response to a recommendation of the Task Force on Women in the Military, about 20,250 responses were received from two confidential mail surveys of scientifically selected samples of active-duty members of the four military services and the U.S. Coast Guard in 1988 and 1989. The much larger 1988 survey targeted about 38,000 personnel in the active services. The survey was designed to focus on (1) the frequency of sexual harassment within the active-duty military; (2) the context, location, and circumstances under which sexual harassment occurs; and (3) the effectiveness of current programs designed to prevent, reduce, and eliminate sexual harassment.

In 1981, the Department of Defense (DOD) formally established its policy on sexual harassment, stating that "sexual harassment is unacceptable conduct and will not be condoned or tolerated in any way." Each of the services and the U.S. Coast Guard reissued that statement and established policies that emphasized the prevention of sexual harassment through extensive education and training. Survey questions covered the incidences and experiences of sexual harassment, actions taken to reduce sexual harassment, and the attitudes of leaders. Consistent with the department's policy, the language of the report calls reported experiences of uninvited and unwanted sexual talk and behavior, as perceived by respondents, *sexual harassment.*

The percentage of active-duty military personnel who had experienced at least one form of sexual harassment at work at least once in the year prior to the survey was estimated to be about 22 percent of the respondents. Female personnel (64 percent) were almost four times as likely as male personnel (17 percent) to have experienced some form of sexual harassment (see Figure 4.4).

The two most severe forms of sexual harassment reported were pressure for sexual favors and actual or attempted rape or

Table 4.2 Views on Extreme Behavior by Percentage of Total Respondents (1,846*)

	Not harassment	Possibly harassment	Sexual harassment	Don't know	Heard of or observed in company	Not heard of or observed in company
A. "I can't seem to go in and out of my boss's office without being patted or pinched."	1%	8%	90%	1%	14%	83%
B. "Mr. X has told me that it would be good for my career if we went out together. I guess that means it would be bad for my career if I said no."	2	17	79	2	12	85
C. "Mr. X has asked me to have sex with him, I refused, but now I learn that he's given me a poor evaluation."	1	20	78	1	10	87
D. "I have been having an affair with the head of my division. Now I've told him I want to break it off, but he says I will lose out on the promotion I've been expecting."	4	7	87	2	7	90

Source: From Eliza G. C. Collins and Timothy B. Blodgett, "Sexual Harassment: Some See It . . . Some Won't," *Harvard Business Review* (March–April 1981): 76–95. Reprinted with permission.

*In some cases throughout the exhibits not all people answered all questions.

Table 4.3 Views on Less Extreme Behavior According to Supervisor/Co-Worker* Split Sample

	Not harassment	Possibly harassment	Sexual harassment	Don't know	Heard of or observed in company	Not heard of or observed in company
A. "Whenever I go into the office, my supervisor (a man I work with) eyes me up and down, making me feel uncomfortable."	20%*	60%	16%	4%	61%	37%
	26	54	15	4	71	27
B. "My supervisor (a man I work with) starts each day with a sexual remark. He insists it's an innocent social comment."	5	46	44	4	35	63
	10	49	37	4	45	53
C. "Often in meetings my supervisor (a man I work with) continuously glances at me."	62	26	1	10	50	47
	65	26	2	6	61	36

Table 4.3 *continued*

D. "Every time we meet my supervisor (a man I work with) kisses me on the cheek."	4	43	46	7	11	86
	17	47	20	10	18	79
E. "My supervisor (a man I work with) asked me out on a date. Although I refused, he continues to ask me."	10	39	48	4	26	71
	33	41	20	5	42	56
F. "My supervisor (a man I work with) puts his hand on my arm when making a point."	43	44	3	10	59	36
	46	42	4	9	63	33

Source: From Eliza G. C. Collins and Timothy B. Blodgett, "Sexual Harassment: Some See It . . . Some Won't," *Harvard Business Review* (March–April 1981): 76–95. Reprinted with permission.

*Each column contains pairs of figures. The top percentage represents supervisor; the bottom percentage represents co-worker.

Figure 4.4 Percentage Experiencing Sexual Harassment from Someone at Work in the Last Year

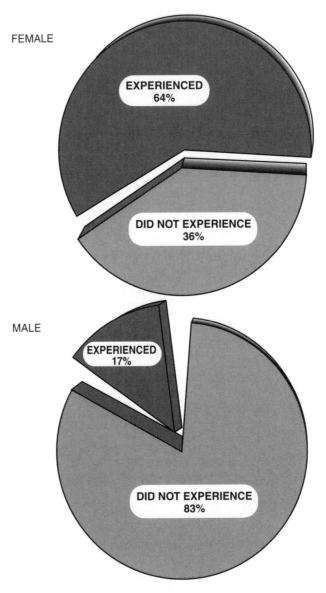

FEMALE

EXPERIENCED
64%

DID NOT EXPERIENCE
36%

MALE

EXPERIENCED
17%

DID NOT EXPERIENCE
83%

Source: From a study conducted by the Department of Defense, written by the Department of Defense Manpower Data Center, *Sexual Harassment in the Military: 1988* (Washington, DC: The Department of Defense, 1988). Available from the Assistant Secretary of Defense (Public Affairs) Room 2E777, the Pentagon, Washington, DC 20301-1400.

sexual assault. Fifteen percent of the female and 2 percent of the male respondents reported having experienced pressure for sexual favors. Five percent of the female and 1 percent of the male respondents reported having been the victims of actual or attempted rape or sexual assault.

Although verbal types of sexual harassment occur more frequently than other forms, just 4 percent of respondents (female, 9 percent; male, 3 percent) had experienced *only* verbal forms. The type of sexual harassment reported in the year prior to the survey by the majority of all victims (64 percent of female personnel and 17 percent of male personnel) was sexual teasing, jokes, remarks, or questions (female victims, 82 percent; male victims, 74 percent).

Female victims (88 percent) were more likely than male victims (73 percent) to report having experienced two or more of the ten forms of sexual harassment listed on the questionnaire. Female victims generally experienced sexual harassment more frequently than male victims, although frequency of occurrence varied by type of sexual harassment. See Table 4.4 for results of the types of behavior experienced as sexual harassment in the DOD study.

Miscellaneous Additional Studies of the Incidence of Sexual Harassment

- A 1975 survey of 155 women in Ithaca, New York, conducted by the Working Women's Institute found that 70 percent of the respondents had experienced some unwanted sexual advances (Siegel 1992).
- In 1976, *Redbook* magazine published a questionnaire on sexual harassment to which over 9,000 women responded. Eighty-eight percent of the respondents reported having experienced unwanted sexual attention on the job (Safran 1976).
- Of the more than 1,300 employers who responded to a 1992 sexual harassment survey conducted by Business and Legal Reports, 42 percent had received a complaint during the past year, and most of the complaints had resulted in disciplinary action against the wrongdoer (Business and Legal Reports 1992). Manufacturing employers were a bit more likely to have received a complaint than were nonmanufacturing or nonbusiness employers (44 percent in manufacturing compared with 42 percent in both nonmanufacturing and nonbusiness firms), and they also seemed more disposed to administer discipline (66 percent

Table 4.4 All Types of Sexual Harassment Received from Someone at Work during the Year Prior to the (DOD) Survey, by Gender

	All Services	
Responses	Female	Male
Type of Sexual Harassment:		
Actual or Attempted Rape or Sexual Assault	5%	1%
Pressure for Sexual Favors	15	2
Touching, Cornering	38	9
Looks, Gestures	44	10
Letters, Calls	14	3
Pressure for Dates	26	3
Teasing, Jokes	52	13
Whistles, Calls	38	5
Attempts To Get Participation*	7	2
Other Attention	5	1
None Experienced	36	83

The data in this table are weighted. Weighted data have been statistically adjusted to represent the active military population. Weighted statistics are estimates. The weighting scheme used slightly underestimates the total active force.

Percentages are rounded to the nearest whole number. Percentages of 0 may indicate less than 0.5 but not actually 0. Percentages will not sum to 100 because respondents could select more than one answer.

*"Attempts to get [respondent's] participation in any other kinds of sexually oriented activity."

Reference: Section II, Question 2: "Have you received any of the following kinds of *uninvited and unwanted* sexual attention *during the last 12 months* from someone where you work in the active-duty military?" (Abbreviated response options are given here under "Type of Sexual Harassment.")

Source: From a study conducted by the Department of Defense, written by the Department of Defense Manpower Data Center, *Sexual Harassment in the Military: 1988* (Washington, DC: The Department of Defense, 1988). Available from the Assistant Secretary of Defense (Public Affairs) Room 2E777, the Pentagon, Washington, DC 20301-1400.

of cases in manufacturing compared with 59 percent in nonmanufacturing and 54 percent in nonbusiness organizations).

Employers with more than 500 employees were the most likely to have received a complaint (56 percent), whereas organizations with fewer than 100 employees were the least likely to have received one (21 percent). Approximately three of every ten employers that had received a complaint found no basis for it, a finding that remained fairly consistent regardless of size or industrial category. Fewer than one in eight respondents had experienced the filing of a formal complaint with the government, but this still added up to over 100 formal charges for this population.

- A survey by *Working Woman* magazine in December 1988, conducted by sexual harassment expert Freada Klein and Klein Associates, Inc., surveyed Fortune 500 manufacturing and service companies. Directors of personnel, human resources managers, and equal opportunity officers who represented 3.3 million employees at 160 large corporations responded in depth to the 49-question survey. The survey reported a huge gap between the incidence of sexual harassment and the rate of complaints filed. Almost 90 percent of the companies surveyed had received at least one complaint in the past 12 months, and 25 percent had received six or more. Experts involved in the survey agreed that the numbers seemed unbelievably low, leading them to speculate that most workers do not report sexual harassment complaints. The survey found that companies received only 1.4 complaints per 1,000 women. This compares to 42 percent of women and 14 percent of men in the USMSPB study over a two-year period, as well as to Freada Klein's own studies, which showed that at least 15 percent of female employees had been sexually harassed in the past 12 months.

- A 1992 follow-up survey by *Working Woman* of 9,000 readers, as well as a simultaneous survey following up the 1988 survey of Fortune 500 companies, revealed that more than 60 percent of the readers said they had personally been harassed and more than a third knew a co-worker who had been harassed. Only one of four women reported the harassment, and most companies received fewer than five complaints a month; thus, the writers concluded that the vast majority of women who are harassed still do not feel they can safely report a problem. Only one of five women believed most complaints were given justice, whereas more than 70 percent of personnel managers thought they were.

- In a review of all of the available studies on the issue of sexual harassment, the National Council for Research on Women concluded that at least one of every two women will experience sexual harassment at some point during her academic or working life (Siegel 1992).
- A self-selected survey of the readers of *Glamour* magazine in 1981 found that 85 percent of respondents believed they had experienced some sort of sexual harassment on the job.
- Reviewing the results of several different measures of prevalence, Gutek (1985) suggested that up to 53 percent of women had been harassed at some point in their working lives.
- A random telephone survey of 400 people in the Chicago area found that nearly a third of the women and a fifth of the men reported having been sexually harassed at work. The study was conducted by the Medill School of Journalism and Northwestern University (Webb 1992).

The Incidence of Sexual Harassment among Particular Groups and Professions

The Military

Two-thirds of women in the military say they have been sexually harassed (Department of Defense 1990). In a 1987 report, investigators found that "the encouragement of a macho-male image contributes to behavior that is at best inappropriate and at worst mortally repugnant." The report indicated that both men and women in the navy and the marines sometimes demand sexual favors from lower-ranking servicewomen (Webb 1987). An analysis of sexual harassment complaints in the U.S. Air Force during 1987 revealed that offenders were "white, male, and also enlisted, but more often of a higher grade than the victims." The most frequent cases tended to be instances of a "hostile environment"; more severe cases, such as sexual propositions tied to job consequences and sexual assault and rape, were the least frequent (Popovich 1988). A similar analysis of a 1991 navy-wide survey revealed that 44 percent of female enlisted respondents and 33 percent of female officer respondents had been harassed during a one-year survey period (Culbertson, Rosenfeld, and Newell 1993).

A 1995 Pentagon survey of 90,000 active-duty service members indicated that violations had declined since the 1988 DOD study but still remained high (Gude 1996). The types of harassment ranged from rapes or assaults (reported by 4 percent) to teasing or jokes (reported by 44 percent). The percentage of women in each service who reported harassment was marines, 64 percent; army, 61 percent; navy, 53 percent; and air force, 49 percent.

In a reanalysis of the data gathered for the 1988 DOD survey, researchers concluded that sexual harassment is widespread throughout the armed services (in fact, DOD is repeating its survey). Moreover, they pinpointed a strong relationship between "hostile environment" harassment and individual incidents of sexual harassment. In those work situations in which respondents reported no environmental harassment, 99 percent reported no individual harassment (Firestone and Harris 1994).

Similarly, in a U.S. General Accounting Office (GAO) report on DOD service academies conducted in 1994 and 1995, women students at West Point and the U.S. Naval and Air Force academies reported sexual harassment at the same or higher rates than they had experienced four years earlier. The percentages of those who indicated that they had experienced one of ten forms of sexual harassment listed on the survey on a recurring basis were 78 percent at the U.S. Air Force Academy, an increase from 59 percent in the same survey in 1990–1991; 70 percent at the U.S. Naval Academy, up from 50 percent; and 80 percent at West Point, up from 76 percent. Between 36 percent and 42 percent of the female students at each academy said that at least once or twice in the past year they had been subjected to "physical, gender-related behavior that interfered with their performance or created a hostile environment, or unwelcome, deliberate physical conduct of a sexual nature"; 40–60 percent said they would hesitate to report sexual harassment for fear of reprisal (Schmitt 1995).

Blue-Collar Workers

A telephone interview study of 139 unskilled female auto workers revealed that 36 percent of the interviewees had experienced sexual harassment. In a small survey of coal miners, 53 percent of the women had been propositioned by their boss and 76 percent by co-workers; 17 percent had been physically attacked. Researcher Peggy Crull found that traditional women's work is more likely to be characterized by one extreme, the threat of losing a job for failing to comply with sexual demands; the other extreme—a sexually demeaning work environment—is the more typical mode of harassment for women working in formerly all-male settings (Crull 1984).

In "Blue-Collar Blues: The Sexual Harassment of Women Autoworkers," James Gruber and Lars Bjorn noted that in contrast to women in clerical work, for example, women autoworkers are likely to be highly visible and viewed as "outsiders" (Gruber and Bjorn 1982, p. 272). Gruber and Bjorn also pointed out that male autoworkers are apt to feel threatened by the "invasion" of women in the auto plant and by the fact that these women have similar jobs and earn similar wages to the men. "In situations where objective work conditions do not result in the subordination of women, it is quite likely that sexual harassment will occur as men attempt to regain an upper hand" (Gruber and Bjorn 1982, p. 272). In other words, when status differences between men and women are blurred, other means of creating differences between the sexes and of maintaining male dominance become salient (Gruber and Bjorn 1982, p. 290).

Professional Workers

The American Medical Women's Association (AMWA) issued a study in 1991 entitled "Gender Bias against and Sexual Harassment of AMWA Members in Massachusetts," which documented that within a one-year period 54 percent of respondents had encountered some form of sex discrimination. In addition, approximately one-fourth (27 percent) had experienced sexual harassment. Unwanted sexual attention not viewed as sexual harassment was experienced by more than twice as many respondents (55 percent) (Lenhart et al. 1991).

In "Women in Non-Traditional Occupations: Comparisons between Women Engineers and Dentists in Michigan," Kaisa Kauppinen-Toropainen of the Center for the Education of Women at the University of Michigan documented that 14 percent of the engineers surveyed reported having experienced unwanted pressure for sexual favors at work. Twenty-two percent mentioned the presence of sexually suggestive posters, pictures, or other materials of a sexual nature in the workplace (reported in Siegel 1992).

Several studies have documented sexual harassment of women in the legal profession. A *National Law Journal*/West Publishing survey in 1989 found that 60 percent of 900 female associates and partners in the country's top 250 law firms had experienced sexual harassment (*National Law Journal* 1989 [ABA 1992]). Thirteen women reported having been victims of rape or attempted rape. In "The State of the Legal Profession," a 1990 survey by the American Bar Association Young Lawyers' Division, the researchers found that 85 percent of 3,000 female lawyers reported having experienced or observed one type of harassment during the past two years, and 45 percent had experienced or observed five types during the same period (American Bar Association Commission on Women in the Profession 1992b).

In the field of journalism, a survey of women reporters and editors in Washington, D.C., conducted by Katherine McAdams in 1991, an assistant professor of journalism at the University of Maryland, found that 80 percent of the 102 journalists who responded to the questionnaire said sexual harassment on the job is a problem. Sixty percent of that group said they had personally been subjected to harassment (reported in Hoffman 1992).

At the United Nations, a survey of 875 women and men in both professional and general service (clerical) categories found that half of the women and 31 percent of the men reported that at some time they had either personally experienced sexual pressures or were aware that such pressures existed within the organization. The most specific situation in which such unprofessional conduct was reported was in the matter of promotion (reported by 62 percent), followed by recruitment (13 percent), obtaining a permanent contract (11 percent), and being transferred and going on missions (7 percent each) (Kelber 1977).

The 1992 *Working Woman* magazine survey discussed earlier concluded that "the higher a woman is in the corporate hierarchy, the more likely she is to be harassed" and "that's probably why *Working Woman* readers reported higher rates of harassment (60 percent) than respondents to other surveys, whose rates hover between 25 and 40 percent" (Sadroff 1992).

In 1993, a survey of females at the level of vice-president and higher in the largest U.S. service and industrial firms was conducted by the UCLA Graduate School of Management and the executive search firm of Korn-Ferry International. Of the more than 400 women who participated in the survey, nearly two-thirds reported having been sexually harassed (Walsh 1995).

According to a 1993 *New England Journal of Medicine* report, 77 percent of female family physicians in Ontario, Canada, reported having been sexually harassed by patients (Clancey 1994). Similarly, in a study of female attorneys conducted in 1993 by the journals *Inside Litigation* and *Of Counsel,* 39 percent of survey respondents reported having been harassed by clients, and 34 percent said opposing attorneys had harassed them (Clancey 1994).

Younger Women Workers

Young women are particularly vulnerable to sexual harassment by male superiors in the workplace. In the 1980 Merit Systems Protection Board random survey of women of all ages and educational backgrounds, women ages 16 to 19 reported the highest incidence of sexual harassment of any group. According to a 1992 *Working Woman* survey, almost 30 percent of the incidents reported occurred among women ages 18 to 24. Considering the small size of this age group in the workforce, this percentage is disproportionate.

Women of Color

According to the National Council for Research on Women (Siegel 1992), although historical and social science research documents white men's violence against women of color and same-race violence, there has been little reliable research on the dynamics between racism and sexual harassment. Several studies are currently underway to assess the incidence rates for women of color, including one being conducted by Dr. Michele Paludi. (See Chapter 3 for a brief biography of Paludi.)

In Schools and Colleges

In their 1984 survey of sexual harassment, Billie Wright Dzeich and Linda Weiner concluded that 20 to 30 percent of female college students experience sexual harassment. Yet they also found that the academic institutions in their study averaged only four complaints each during the 1982–1983 academic year (Dzeich and Weiner 1984).

Paludi and Barickman, in *Academic and Workplace Sexual Harassment* (1991), summarize the research on the incidence of sexual harassment in academic institutions (see Table 4.5).

A presentation at the 1985 American Psychological Association (APA) reported the results of a mail survey of graduate student

Table 4.5 Summary of Research on the Incidence of Sexual Harassment

Adams, Kottke, and Padgitt (1983): 13% of women students surveyed reported that they had avoided taking a class or working with certain professors because of the risk of being subjected to sexual advances; 17% received verbal sexual advances; 13.6% received sexual invitations; 6.4% had been subjected to physical advances; 2% received direct sexual assault

Chronicle of Higher Education Report of Harvard University (1983): 15% of the graduate students and 12% of the undergraduate students who had been sexually harassed by their professors changed their major or educational program because of the harassment

Wilson and Kraus (1983): 8.9% of the female undergraduates in their study had been pinched, touched, or patted to the point of personal discomfort

Bailey and Richards (1985): 12.7% of 246 graduate women surveyed reported that they had been sexually harassed; 21% had not enrolled in a course to avoid such behavior; 11.3% tried to report the behavior; 2.6% dropped a course because of it; 15.9% reported being directly assaulted

Bond (1988): 75% of 229 faculty experienced jokes with sexual themes during their graduate training; 68.9% were subjected to sexist comments demeaning to women; 57.8% of the women reported experiencing sexist remarks about their clothing, body, or sexual activities; 12.2 had unwanted intercourse, breast, or genital stimulation

Gutek (1985): 53.1% of private-sector workers surveyed reported being fired, not being promoted, not given raises, all because of refusal to comply with requests for sexual relationships

Source: Reprinted from *Academic and Workplace Sexual Harassment* by Michele A. Paludi and Richard B. Barickman by permission of the State University of New York Press. Copyright © 1991 by State University of New York.

members of APA's Division of Clinical Psychology and Division of Counseling. Of 246 women responding, 12.7 percent surveyed reported that they had been sexually harassed, 21 percent had not enrolled in a course to avoid such behavior, 11.3 percent had tried to report the behavior, 2.6 percent had dropped a course because of such behavior, and 15.9 percent reported having been directly assaulted (Siegel 1992).

According to Susan Strauss, in response to a 1991 sexual harassment questionnaire distributed to student leaders from 13 school districts at a Minnesota State Sex Equity Student Leadership conference:

- 80 percent of the students said they were aware of sexual harassment in their schools.
- 75 percent said they were aware of sexual harassment between students.
- 50 percent said they were aware of sexual harassment between students and staff.
- 26 percent said sexual harassment "goes on all the time."
- 50 percent said "it happens to a fair number of people."
- 6 percent said "it doesn't happen" (Strauss 1992, p. 3).

A study conducted by a Minnesota secondary vocational school in 1991 surveyed 250 students from four school districts. Approximately 50 percent of the teenage girls reported having been verbally and physically harassed at school; another 30 percent stated that they had been harassed at work (Strauss 1992).

In a 1993 *Seventeen* magazine/Wellesley College Center for Women poll, 89 percent of 4,200 girls ages 9 to 19 reported having experienced harassment such as pinching or grabbing, with 39 percent of the respondents experiencing at-school harassment on a daily basis. The poll indicated that the problem peaks between ages 13 and 16 (Stein, Marshall, and Tropp 1993).

Conversely, a survey conducted by the American Association of University Women in 1993, "Hostile Hallways," asked Louis Harris and associates to poll 8th to 11th graders. The survey showed that most at-school harassment occurred in the 6th through 9th grades, peaking in the 7th grade. The AAUW survey also found that 85 percent of girls and 76 percent of boys reported experiencing harassment at school (see Figure 4.5). Most harassment came from fellow students, but a small percentage of girls said they had been harassed by a teacher or another school employee (see Table 4.6). Sexual harassment of girls by boys included everything from obscene graffiti, jokes, and taunts to bra-snapping or skirt-flipping "days" and from groping and pinching to assembling lists of "sluts" or "dogs" (see Figure 4.6). In the poll, 33 percent of girls responding said they did not want to come to school after being harassed (see Figure 4.7) (AAUW 1993).

A cross-cultural study of grades K–12 in 1990 found that sexual harassment is pervasive in all school districts, urban and rural

Figure 4.5 Frequency of Sexual Harassment Experiences in School: Survey of 8th to 11th graders, 1993

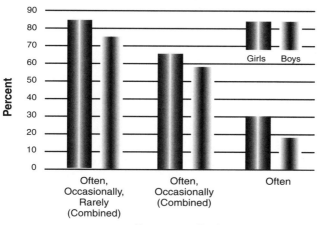

Source: Adapted from American Association of University Women, *Hostile Hallways: The AAUW Survey on Sexual Harassment in America's Schools* (Washington, DC: American Association of University Women, 1993). Reprinted with permission of American Association of University Women, 1111 16th Street N.W., Washington, DC.

(Linn et al. 1992). The same study found that sexual harassment also takes on racial tones and is less likely to occur when anyone is watching; it tends to happen in unsupervised areas.

Responding to popular-media skepticism about the high percentage of students who reported having experienced sexual harassment in the AAUW survey, researchers Eleanor Linn, Valerie Lee, Robert Croninger, and Xinglei Chen reanalyzed the original AAUW data, filtering out those incidents that do not fall within stricter definitions of sexual harassment. They found that 83 percent of girls and 60 percent of boys experienced and objected to sexually harassing behavior, results that remain close to the original AAUW numbers. The same researchers also created a severity scale for students' experience of sexual harassment and found that students defined severity by the frequency of harassing behavior, the age of the harasser (with harassment from adults experienced as more severe), and whether harassment was physical or verbal (with physical harassment more severe). Most important, they discovered that tolerance of sexual harassment within

Table 4.6   Who the Harassers Are: Results from AAUW
Survey, 1993

Harasser	Number	Percentage of All Harassers	Percentage Who are Male
Students	1,929	96.0	97.0
Administrators	8	0.4	100.0
Teachers or Counselors	58	3.0	98.0
Other School Staff	7	0.3	100

N = 2,002

Source: Adapted from Nan Stein, Nancy L. Marshall, and Linda R. Tropp, *Secrets in Public: Sexual Harassment in Our Schools* (Wellesley, MA: Wellesley College Center for Research on Women, 1993). Reprinted with permission of Center for Research on Women, Wellesley College.

N = number of harassers

schools is largely responsible for the fact that so many students are both harassers and harassees (Linn et al. 1996).

Psychological and Physical Effects of Harassment

Researchers have attempted to document the psychological and physical effects of harassment on victims. Gutek (1985) reported that 38 percent of the women in her Los Angeles study said the harassing incident affected their feelings about their jobs, and 28 percent said it affected how they related to other people at work. In general, Gutek found that harassment had a greater effect on a woman's work than it did on her private life, although about 15 percent of the women reported that the incident affected their health or their relationships with other men.

The women in the Gutek-L.A. survey were also asked how they felt right after the harassing incident. The two strongest reactions were disgust and anger: Over two-fifths of the women said they felt disgust, and about one-third said they were angry. Fewer women (under 15 percent) reported feeling anxious or hurt, and fewer than 10 percent said they felt very depressed, sad, or guilty. It may be significant, however, that they were reporting reactions

Figure 4.6 Types of Sexual Harassment Experienced in School: Survey of 8th to 11th graders, 1993

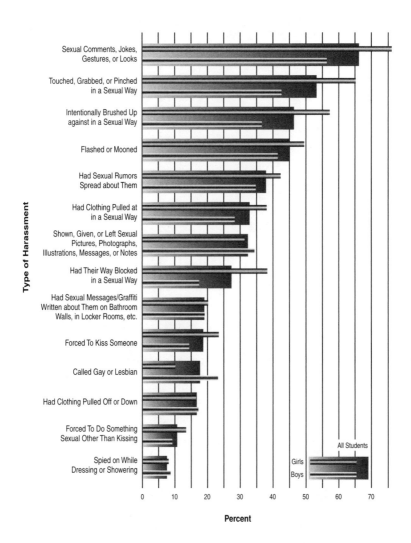

Source: Adapted from American Association of University Women; *Hostile Hallways: The AAUW Survey on Sexual Harassment in America's Schools* (Washington, DC: American Association of University Women, 1993). Reprinted with permission of American Association of University Women, 1111 16th Street N.W., Washington, DC.

Figure 4.7 Educational Impact of Victims of Harassment in
School: Survey of 8th to 11th Graders, 1993

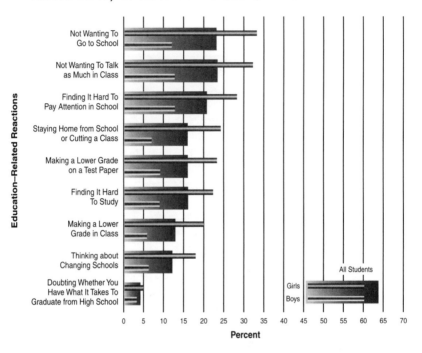

Source: Adapted from American Association of University Women, *Hostile Hallways: The AAUW Survey on Sexual Harassment in America's Schools* (Washington, DC: American Association of University Women, 1993). Reprinted with permission of American Association of University Women, 1111 16th Street N.W., Washington, DC.

Note: Base—the 81% of students who report some experience of sexual harassment in school.

to events that had occurred over a year earlier. Some initial feelings of hurt, Gutek speculated, may have turned to anger over time. In addition, many of the strong emotions the women felt at the time of the harassment may have been forgotten a year later.

Although many victims of sexual harassment publicly appear to brush off the harassment, the effects of stress as a result of harassment are significant. The American Psychiatric Association recognizes sexual harassment as a "severe stressor" (American Psychiatric Association 1987). As part of a growing list of identifiable effects, summarized by Deborah Siegel (1992), researchers have found anxiety attacks, headaches, sleep disturbance, disordered eating, gastrointestinal disorders, nausea, weight loss or gain, and crying spells. Fear, anger, anxiety, depression, self-questioning, and self-blaming are among the most common effects women describe.

Data from surveys of corporate employees indicate that employees who feel they have experienced sexual harassment, when compared to nonharassed employees, are substantially less positive about their employment (Klein 1991). Common responses include:

1. Less job satisfaction
2. Lower rating of their immediate supervisor
3. Less favorable view of company communication
4. Diminished confidence in the senior management team
5. Reduced organizational commitment
6. Increased likelihood of leaving the company

Federal working women in the USMSPB (1981) survey reported that unwanted sexual attention affected their lives. Thirty-six percent said it affected their feelings about work, 33 percent reported an impact on their emotional or physical condition, 15 percent said it affected their ability to work with others, 11 percent said it affected the quantity of their work, and 10 percent reported an effect on the quality of their work (USMSPB 1981, p. 81).

Conversely, the Department of Defense study (Department of Defense Manpower Data Center 1990, p. 30) found that the majority of respondents (85 percent of women, 94 percent of men) reported that they had not received or needed either counseling or medical assistance. Eleven percent of the women and 3 percent of the men, however, reported that counseling would have been helpful. The survey does not reveal why more of these victims did not seek or feel a need for medical assistance or counseling from a trained professional.

Paludi and Barickman (1991) reported on the "sexual harassment trauma syndrome" (formulated by Sandra Shullman in 1989), which has been applied to the effects of harassment on the physical, emotional, interpersonal, and career aspects of women's lives. Research has indicated that depending upon the severity of the harassment, between 21 percent and 82 percent of women report that their emotional condition, physical condition, or both deteriorated as a result of the experience. Furthermore, as with victims of rape who go to court, harassment victims may experience a second victimization when they attempt to deal with the situation through legal or institutional means. Stereotypes about sexual harassment and women's victimization blame women for the harassment (MacKinnon 1979). These stereotypes center around the myths that sexual harassment is a form of seduction, that women secretly want to be sexually harassed, and that women do not tell the truth (Paludi and Barickman 1991).

Finally, readers who responded to the *Working Woman* (1988) survey reported such ill effects as being fired or forced to quit their jobs (25 percent), experiencing seriously undermined self-confidence (27 percent), experiencing impaired health (12 percent), and suffering long-term career damage (13 percent) (Klein 1988).

More recently, some researchers have noted similarities between the symptoms seen in the aftermath of sexual harassment and those characteristic of posttraumatic stress disorder (PTSD) as defined by the American Psychiatric Association's (1987) *Diagnostic and Statistical Manual of Mental Disorders* (Gutek and Koss 1993). The first formal study of this subject was presented in a survey that found that women suffering from PTSD and depression were more likely to have been sexually harassed than those who had never experienced these problems (Koss et al. 1994). Similarly, in an analysis of data from a 1993 survey of employees of a public utility company in the northwest, in which 68 percent of the women reported having experienced at least one sexually harassing incident within a two-year period, those women who had experienced harassment were more likely to report symptoms associated with PTSD than were women who had not been harassed (Schneider and Swan 1994).

According to psychologist Sandra Shullman, traumatic experiences such as sexual harassment are frequently repressed. Victims may remember the experience in bits and pieces or may lose the chronological order of events, but their "descriptions of harassment may become clearer over time as the mind retrieves more memories" (Shullman 1991).

Both the 1987 and 1994 Merit Systems Protection Board surveys found that in addition to the substantial dollar amounts sexual harassment costs the federal government, very real and sometimes severe costs—both financial and emotional—are borne by employees who experience unwanted sexual attention. Table 4.7 reflects these findings.

Characteristics of the Harasser

Gutek (1985) studied the characteristics of both male and female harassers and found that the men who made advances toward

Table 4.7 Impact on Victims: Percentage of Respondents Who Experienced Sexual Harassment and Took or Experienced the Indicated Action, 1987 and 1994

	1987	1994
Used Sick Leave	13.0	8.0
Used Annual Leave	12.0	8.0
Took Leave without Pay	2.0	1.0
Received Medical or Emotional Help	2.0	3.0
Would Have Found Medical or Emotional Help Beneficial	12.0	7.0
Were Reassigned or Fired	2.0	2.0
Transferred to a New Job	5.0	2.0
Quit without a New Job	0.6	0.1
Suffered a Decline in Productivity	14.0	21.0

Source: Adapted from United States Merit Systems Protection Board, *Sexual Harassment in the Federal Workplace* (Washington, DC: U.S. Government Printing Office, 1995).

women were very different from the women who made advances toward men (see Table 4.8). The "average" man who made advances was very much like the "average" man in the survey, with the exception that the initiator tended to behave the same way toward other women workers. This was not the case with the average woman. The men described a female initiator as young, attractive, single, and not a supervisor. Gutek doubted that these women were in a position to harass anyone.

In a statement of the Ad Hoc Group for Public Information on Sexual Harassment, written by experts who gathered in Washington, D.C., to provide public information on sexual harassment during the October 1991 Senate Judiciary hearings, Louise F. Fitzgerald (reported in Siegel 1992, p. 27) reported that:

> Data from the major studies of victims . . . have suggested that most harassers are older than their victims (although some are younger); married (although some are single); and of the same race as their victims. Some harass many women (43 percent of U.S. Merit Systems Protection Board victims believed that their harassers had also harassed others), whereas others harass only once. Further, harassers are found in all types of occupations, at all organizational levels,

Table 4.8   Profile of Initiators

How Long Associated with Initiator?

	Less than 1 day	Less than 2 months	2–6 months	Over 6 months	Total (N)
Female Recipients	5.8	20.0	24.2	50.0	100% (310)
Male Recipients	5.6	23.8	25.2	45.5	100% (143)

Initiator Behaves This Way toward Others

	Yes	No	Total (N)
Female Recipients	71.0	29.0	100% (259)
Male Recipients	52.3	47.7	100% (109)

Initiator Is a Supervisor

	Yes	No	Total (N)
Female Recipients	44.8	56.3	100% (306)
Male Recipients	5.5	94.5	100% (139)

Initiator Age

	Under 30	30–39	40–49	Over 50	Total (N)
Female Recipients	19.0	31.8	26.0	23.1	100% (311)
Male Recipients	56.6	34.4	9.0	0.0	100% (145)

Initiator Married

	Yes	No	Total (N)
Female Recipients	65.4	34.6	100% (288)
Male Recipients	28.4	71.6	100% (131)

Attractiveness of Initiator

	Above average	Not above average	Total (N)
Female Recipients	41.8	58.2	100% (306)
Male Recipients	71.6	28.4	100% (141)

Source: Reprinted from Barbara A. Gutek, *Sex and the Workplace: The Impact of Sexual Behavior and Harassment on Women, Men, and Organizations* (San Francisco: Jossey-Bass Inc., 1985). Reprinted with permission.

among college professors as well as the business and professional world, and among individuals who live otherwise exemplary lives.

How Victims Respond

According to Klein (1988), most women who are sexually harassed do nothing: "Few incidents are reported to employers; the formal complaint rate across all companies is 1.4 per thousand women employees per year." This is a small percentage compared to the surveys that report the incidence of sexual harassment: "In most organizations, at least 90 percent of sexual harassment victims are unwilling to come forward for two reasons: fear of retaliation and fear of loss of privacy" (Klein 1991). Several surveys have supported Klein's opinions, including the survey of federal employees, which found that only 5 percent of those who had experienced sexual harassment had filed formal complaints or requested investigations (USMSPB 1988).

During the 1991 Senate Judiciary hearings, while considering the allegations that Clarence Thomas had harassed Anita Hill, many senators focused on the question of why Hill had not reported Thomas at the time the incidents allegedly occurred. According to sexual harassment experts quoted in Siegel (1992), Anita Hill's failure to complain ten years earlier is common behavior for victims.

Based on her surveys of victims, Barbara Gutek found three common reasons victims do not formally complain. Fifty percent of the women she surveyed reported that they did not believe anything would come of their complaints. Another 50 percent also reported that they were afraid they would be blamed for the harassment. Finally, victims reported that they were concerned about the harasser and did not want to hurt him. According to Gutek, women excused the harasser with statements such as "he's going through a bad time" (Gutek 1985). In the 1988 *Working Woman* survey, victims cited fear of retaliation as the chief reason for not reporting incidents of harassment (Klein 1988).

In all three U.S. Merit Systems Protection Board surveys, victims who responded with more assertive actions—such as telling or asking the harasser to stop or reporting the incident to a supervisor—invariably reported that the situation had improved. Table 4.9 shows the effectiveness of various actions actually taken by victims who responded to the 1994 USMSPB survey.

Table 4.9 How Well the Informal Actions Worked: Percentage of Victims Who Said the Indicated Action Made Things Better, Made Things Worse, or Made No Difference, 1994

	Better		Worse		No Difference	
	Men	Women	Men	Women	Men	Women
Asking or Telling the Person To Stop	61	60	15	8	25	32
Reporting the Behavior to a Supervisor or Other Official	33	58	16	13	52	29
Avoiding the Person	52	44	13	8	36	48
Threatening To Tell or Telling Others	55	37	0	14	46	49
Making a Joke of the Behavior	29	29	3	16	68	55
Ignoring the Behavioir or Doing Nothing	32	17	6	10	62	73
Going Along with the Behavior	18	7	17	37	65	57

Source: Adapted from United States Merit Systems Protection Board, *Sexual Harassment in the Federal Workplace* (Washington, DC: U.S. Government Printing Office, 1995).

Note: Respondents could choose more than one action.

Do Women Invite Harassment?

Only a few studies have openly addressed the issue of whether women invite harassment, with conflicting results. For example, 78 percent of the women and 86 percent of the men in the *Harvard Business Review/Redbook* study agreed or partly agreed with the statement "Women can and often do use their sexual attractiveness to their own advantage" (Collins and Blodgett 1981, p. 90). The article suggested that many believe women invite sexual harassment through their dress and their actions.

Reporting on the same study, however, *Redbook* found that male and female views differed. Only a third of the male respondents, compared to half of the women, defined the following statement as constituting sexual harassment: "Whenever I go to see Mr. X, I wear a tight skirt. It seems to help my career." Parenthetically, in the earlier *Redbook* survey, conducted in 1976, 30 percent of the

9,000 female respondents reported having used their sexual attractiveness to their own advantage (Safran 1981, p. 7). Of those who responded to the 1981 survey, two-thirds of the male respondents and three-fourths of the female executives did not believe a woman could avoid being the target of unwanted approaches if she dressed and behaved "properly."

Paradoxically, some evidence indicates that the more a woman is attuned to sex discrimination in the workplace, the less likely she is to encounter sexual harassment. In a 1991 study of 220 female lawyers from a midwestern city, researchers found that the respondents fell into two categories—careerist and feminist. They defined *careerists* as women who believed sexism no longer exists and that the law is an open, equally competitive arena. *Feminists* in this study viewed the legal profession as an uneven playing field, with women having lesser status than men. The authors found that 27 percent of the careerists were subjected to unwanted sexual advances, compared to only 12 percent of the feminists (American Bar Association Commission on Women in the Profession 1992b).

Gutek (1985) found that a common stereotype is to believe that some women are willing to use their sexuality to advance and thus to gain an unfair advantage over men competing for the same job. She found, however, "virtually no evidence that women benefit in this way." She also found comparable stereotypes about men—that they "sleep their way to the top or get jobs to find wives—[to be] exceedingly rare." She did find that a majority of both sexes agreed with the statement that if a man or a woman was propositioned at work, he or she could have done something to have prevented it. She found different results, however, from women who had experienced negative consequences as a result of sexual harassment; they were less likely than other women to believe that women cause overtures or propositions: "Whereas 71 percent of women who had not experienced any negative consequences of sexual harassment agreed that women cause or could prevent propositions, 60 percent of female victims agreed with the statement" (Gutek 1985, p. 103).

Paludi (1990) found that "there is ample evidence that women experience an enormous amount of guilt and self-blame surrounding harassment, just as they do over rape and incest." She suggested that one reason for this self-blame may be that women are—contrary to some popular theories—reluctant to view themselves as victims and would rather assume that they did something to cause the harassment. Ironically, such self-blame, Paludi concluded, gives victims a feeling that they have some degree of power over their experience.

Trainers who conduct sexual harassment workshops for students, businesses, and governments report that one of the questions most frequently asked is: "Don't women provoke men by wearing sexy clothes?" Dzeich and Weiner (1984, p. 66) pointed out that part of the problem for women is that "some people have trouble distinguishing seductive attire from that which simply emphasizes beauty and self-esteem":

> The sexual message of clothing is in the eye of the beholder, and women have suffered great misunderstanding from the opposite sex. A 1980 study at the University of California at Los Angeles found that of 432 blacks, whites, and Hispanics between the age[s] of 14 and 18, none viewed a male's open shirt, tight pants, tight swim trunks, or jewelry as indications that he was seeking sex. But males generally assumed that low-cut tops, shorts, tight jeans, or bralessness meant that a female was encouraging a sexual reaction. Females, however, contended that such dress simply indicated they were trying to be in style.

The authors concluded that sexual harassment is not caused by what women wear and is not excused by a man's misreading of the messages of attire:

> "Provocative dress" has nothing to do with sexual harassment. Whether women wear high collars, dresses that flatten their breasts, skirts that hide their ankles, or veils that cover their faces, they are forced to endure sexual harassment. It did not begin with tube tops and short shorts, and it will not cease as long as society insists on believing that men cannot restrain their sexual impulses and that women, by their dress, invite sexual advances.

Significantly, when the 1994 United States Merit Systems Protection Board looked at the question of which employees are at greater risk than others of being targets of unwanted sexual attention, it found that the likely targets were more likely to work exclusively or mostly with people of the opposite sex and to be supervised by members of the opposite sex. Employees of both sexes who reported having experienced unwanted sexual attention were more likely to be college educated than those who had not experienced such attention. Also, employees under age 35 had a greater chance of experiencing unwanted sexual attention than those who were older.

Differences in Men's and Women's Perceptions of Harassment

One of the most interesting results of the study of the difference in men's and women's perceptions of sexual harassment is the "gender gap" identified by Gutek (1985). She found that, in general, men are flattered by sexual advances at work, whereas women are insulted by them. Furthermore, she found that neither men nor women were aware of this difference.

Gutek reported different attitudes between the 178 men and 221 women as to whether social-sexual behavior at work was harassment. Reporting on the 1978 telephone survey discussed earlier, she found that higher percentages of women believed each of eight categories of behavior constituted harassment (see Table 4.10).

The *Harvard Business Review* (Collins and Blodgett 1981) reported that most people agreed on what sexual harassment was but that men and women seemed to disagree strongly on how frequently it occurred. Half of the women felt the amount of sexual harassment at work was greatly exaggerated, whereas two-thirds of the men felt that way.

Redbook, reporting on the same survey, found that male executives did not see sexual horseplay and subtle advances as clearcut harassment. Men in the Merit Systems Protection Board study had a tendency to think that victims were "somewhat responsible for bringing sexual harassment on themselves."

The 1994 Merit Systems Protection Board study asked whether "too much attention has been paid to the issue of sexual harassment in the past several years" (see Table 4.11). Thirty-two percent of the men surveyed said yes, whereas only 17 percent of the women agreed with the statement. Significantly, however, the survey showed that the emphasis on sexual harassment has not led to a chilling effect in the workplace. Only 18 percent of the men and 6 percent of the women indicated that fear of being accused of sexual harassment had made their organizations uncomfortable places in which to work (USMSPB 1995).

Table 4.10   What Is Sexual Harassment?

	Males	Females
Is Sexual Harassment		
Complimentary Comments	21.9%	33.5%
Insulting Comments	70.3	85.5
Complimentary Looks, Gestures	18.9	28.9
Insulting Looks, Gestures	61.6	80.3
Nonsexual Touching	6.6	7.3
Sexual Touching	58.6	84.3
Expected Socializing	91.1	95.8
Expected Sexual Activity	94.5	98.0

Source: Reprinted from Barbara A. Gutek, *Sex and the Workplace: The Impact of Sexual Behavior and Harassment on Women, Men, and Organizations* (San Francisco: Jossey-Bass Inc., 1985). Reprinted with permission.

Table 4.11   1994 Survey Item: "Too Much Attention Has Been Paid to the Issue of Sexual Harassment in the Past Several Years"

Response	Men	Women
Agree	32	17
Disagree	43	64
Neither Agree nor Disagree	23	16
Don't Know/Can't Judge	3	3

Source: Adapted from United States Merit Systems Protection Board, *Sexual Harassment in the Federal Workplace* (Washington, DC: U.S. Government Printing Office, 1995).

Note: Percentages have been rounded.

The Costs of Harassment to Employers

The 1981 Merit Systems Protection Board report concluded that sexual harassment had cost the federal government $189 million during the two-year period ending in May 1980. The losses included estimates of loss productivity and increased turnover. The 1988 update estimated costs of $267 million during the study period. The 1980 figures represented the costs of replacing employees who left their jobs ($36.7 million), paying sick leave to employees who missed work ($26.1 million), and reduced individual and work group productivity ($204.5 million) (USMSPB 1981).

The 1994 USMSPB update found harassment costs to the federal government to stand at an estimated $327 million during the two-year period from April 1992 to April 1994. The report noted that the increase reflected inflation and the rise in salaries more than an increase in the ill effects of harassment. Since the 1987 study, the report concluded that turnover and the amount of sick leave used had dropped significantly and that the severity and duration of productivity losses as a result of sexual harassment had also declined (USMSPB 1995).

The 1988 *Working Woman* survey (Klein 1988) found that the average total annual cost of sexual harassment of both men and women in Fortune 500 companies was $6,719,593 (excluding some costs, such as litigation). These costs included loss in productivity, turnover, and extra leave taken by victims. The study also found the average cost of sexual harassment to be $282.53 per employee per year for a typical Fortune 500 service or manufacturing firm with 23,784 employees and that a corporation of that size could begin to implement meaningful prevention efforts for $200,000 (a cost of $8.41 per employee).

Reporting on the *Harvard Business Review* survey, *Redbook* indicated that two of three executives believed unwanted sexual behavior was bad for business. They felt such behavior could hurt efficiency and lead to the turnover of trained and valuable employees (Safran 1981, p. 49).

Employers' Response to Harassment

According to the 1992 *Working Woman* survey, most Fortune 500 executives believe their companies are doing a good job in preventing and dealing with sexual harassment. Eighty-one percent reported having training programs on sexual harassment, compared with only 60 percent in the 1988 survey—although only half of *Working Woman* readers reported working for a company with such procedures.

The United States Merit Systems Protection Board's 1988 survey reported that no clear correlation exists between an agency's estimates of its training efforts on the issue of sexual harassment and the reported incidence of harassment in that agency. According to each agency's own estimate, on average a federal employee received a total of one to two hours of training on sexual harassment issues during the period 1980 to 1986. All agencies had (at that time) issued policy statements or other written guidance on sexual harassment.

According to the 1995 USMSPB update on harassment in the federal government, over 87 percent of federal supervisors and 77 percent of employees had received training in the area of sexual harassment. Around 78 percent of employees said they knew the channels to follow if they had been harassed and wanted to report it. All federal agencies have policies prohibiting sexual harassment, and 92 percent of federal employees are aware of those policies (USMSPB 1995).

The American Bar Association Commission on Women in the Profession (1992b) reported on a survey conducted by the American Management Association (AMA), which found that the top disciplinary actions taken against harassers were formal reprimand, probation or suspension, transfer of the harasser to a new position, counseling, and mediation between both parties. The same survey found that 52 percent of the AMA's 524 member companies had dealt with sexual harassment allegations during the past five years: 60 percent of the claims had resulted in disciplinary action against the harasser, and only 17 percent were dismissed without action.

Seventy-three percent of the respondents in the *Harvard Business Review/Redbook* study reported that they favored organizations establishing a policy against harassment, but only 29 percent worked in companies that had such a policy (Collins and Blodgett 1981). Some employers, however, were seriously concerned about the issue: One reported that three store managers had been fired in the past three years for sexual harassment.

Impact of Hill/Thomas on Harassment

Ronni Sadroff (1992) reported that in the nine months following Anita Hill's testimony, the number of inquiries to the EEOC increased 150 percent, and actual charges filed rose 23 percent. She also reported that *Working Woman* readers were far more likely than human resource executives to believe Hill rather than Thomas (59 percent to 38 percent). Women with more education and higher incomes and those in professional or managerial positions were the most likely to reject Thomas's story, as were women who had been harassed. The latter were also more sympathetic about the time lapse than were women who had never been harassed (63 percent versus 39 percent). In addition, more than half of the working women who had been sexually harassed said they could understand why Hill would continue to work for a man who treated her the way Thomas had. Two-thirds of the executives agreed that it was not unusual for a professional woman to continue to work with a man who had harassed her.

Almost half of the *Working Woman* readers believed publicity about the case had reduced the "comfort level" between women and men in the workplace. In addition, in 1992 more than half the readers intended to vote against their senator if he or she voted for Thomas's confirmation. In fact, the situation has been credited for the election of several women to the U.S. Senate in 1992, including Carol Moseley-Braun, an Illinois Democrat who won the primary election over Alan J. Dixon—a senator who voted to confirm Thomas. Braun was the first black woman to be elected to the Senate. As Eleanor Holmes Norton stated, "The greatest surprise of Anita Hill is that she managed to encourage other women even though she did not get justice for herself" (quoted in Sadroff 1992). Similarly, Alisa Solomon (1992) found that 81 percent of Fortune 500 companies now provide employees with sexual harassment training as a result of Anita Hill's testimony, compared to 60 percent in 1988.

Several surveys conducted since the hearings have shown an increase in the number of people who believe that Hill, not Thomas, was telling the truth. For example, a *Wall Street Journal*–NBC poll taken in September 1992 found that 44 percent of those surveyed believed Hill, up from 24 percent just after the hearings in 1991. Belief in Thomas's testimony dropped from 47 percent to 34 percent during that period (Cass 1992).

References

American Association of University Women (AAUW), *Hostile Hallways: The AAUW Survey on Sexual Harassment in America's Schools* (Washington, DC: American Association of University Women Educational Foundation, 1993).

American Bar Association Commission on Women in the Profession, "Sexual Harassment after Anita Hill," *Perspectives* 1, no. 2 (Spring 1992a): 1.

———, "Sexual Harassment Surveys Detail the Extent of the Problem," *Perspectives* 1, no. 2 (Spring 1992b): 2.

American Psychiatric Association, *Diagnostic and Statistical Manual of Mental Disorders*. 3d ed. 11 (Washington, DC: American Psychiatric Association, 1987).

Business and Legal Reports, Inc., "What To Do about Personnel Problems," *Business and Legal Reports, Michigan Edition* 2, no. 214 (July 1992): 1–3.

Cass, Connie (A.P. writer), "Hill: Sexism Taints Courts," *Rocky Mountain News* (October 13, 1992): 23A, col. 1.

Chapman, Gary, "The Flamers: The Internet and the Decline of Public Discourse," *The New Republic* 186, no. 4 (April 10, 1995): 13–15.

Clancey, Frank, "When Customer Service Crosses the Line," *Working Woman* (December 1994): 38.

Collins, Eliza G. C., and Timothy B. Blodgett, "Sexual Harassment: Some See It . . . Some Won't," *Harvard Business Review* 59, no. 2 (March–April 1981): 76–95.

Conte, Alba, *Sexual Harassment in the Workplace: Law and Practice* (New York: John Wiley and Sons, 1990).

"Cost of Sexual Harassment to Employees up Sharply," *Women in Public Services* 32, no. 4 (Spring 1994).

Crull, Peggy, "Stress Effects of Sexual Harassment on the Job: Implications for Counseling," *American Journal of Orthopsychiatry* 52 (1982): 539–544.

———, "Contrasting Sexual Harassment in Female- and Male-Dominated Occupations." In Karen Sacks and Dorothy Remy, eds., *My Troubles Are Going To Have Trouble with Me: Everyday Trials and Triumphs of Women Workers* (New Brunswick, NJ: Rutgers University Press, 1984): 218–228.

Culbertson, Amy L., Paul Rosenfeld, and Carol E. Newell, *Sexual Harassment in the Active-Duty Navy: Findings from the 1991 Navy-wide Survey* (San Diego: Navy Personnel Research and Development Center, 1993).

Department of Defense Manpower Data Center, *Sexual Harassment in the Military: 1988* (Washington, DC: Department of Defense, 1990). Available from the Assistant Secretary of Defense (Public Affairs), Room 2E777, the Pentagon, Washington, DC 20301-1400.

Dzeich, Billie Wright, and Linda Weiner, *The Lecherous Professor: Sexual Harassment on Campus* (Boston: Beacon Press, 1984).

Erickson, Kristen, "What Our Children Are Really Learning in School: Using Title IX To Combat Peer Sexual Harassment," 83 *Georgetown Law Journal* (April 1995): 1799.

Eskenazi, Martin, and David Gallen, *Sexual Harassment: Know Your Rights!* (New York: Carroll and Graf, 1992).

Firestone, Juanita M., and Richard J. Harris, "Sexual Harassment in the U.S. Military: Individual and Environmental Contexts," *Armed Forces and Society* 21, no. 1 (1994).

Gruber, James E., and Lars Bjorn, "Blue-Collar Blues: The Sexual Harassment of Women Autoworkers," *Work and Occupations* 9, no. 3 (1982): 271–298.

Gude, Karl, "Rape in the Ranks," *Newsweek* (November 15, 1996): 30.

Gutek, Barbara, *Sex and the Workplace: The Impact of Sexual Behavior and Harassment on Women, Men, and Organizations* (San Francisco: Jossey-Bass, 1985).

Gutek, Barbara, and Mary Koss, "Changed Women and Changed Organizations: Consequences of and Coping with Sexual Harassment," *Journal of Vocational Behavior* 42 (1993): 28.

Hoffman, Lisa, "Reporters Find Sexual Harassment an Impediment," *Denver Post* (June 23, 1992): 16, col. 2.

Kaufman, Lesli, "A Report from the Front," *Newsweek* (January 13, 1997): 31.

Kelber, Mim, "The UN's Dirty Little Secret," *Ms.* (November 1977): 51, 79.

Klein, Freada, *The 1988 Working Woman Sexual Harassment Survey Executive Report* (Cambridge, MA: Klein Associates, 1988).

———, *Testimony Before the Committee on Education and Labor,* House of Representatives, Hearings on H.R. 1, The Civil Rights Act of 1991 (Washington, DC: U.S. Government Printing Office, 1991).

Koss, Mary P., Lisa A. Goodman, Angela Browne, Louise F. Fitzgerald, Gwendolyn Puryear Keita, and Nancy Felipe Russo, *No Safe Haven: Male Violence against Women at Home, at Work, and in the Community* (Washington, DC: American Psychological Association, 1994).

Lenhart, Sharyn A., Freada Klein, Patricia Falcao, Elizabeth Phelan, and Kevin Smith, "Gender Bias against and Sexual Harassment of AMWA Members in Massachusetts," *JAMWA Journal* 46, no. 4 (July–August 1991): 121–125.

Linn, Eleanor, Valerie Lee, Robert Croninger, and Xinglei Chen, "The Culture of Sexual Harassment in Secondary Schools," *American Journal of Educational Research* (1996).

Linn, Eleanor, Nan D. Stein, Jackie Young, with Sandra Davis, "Bitter Lessons for All: Sexual Harassment in Schools." In James T. Sears, ed., *Sexuality and the Curriculum* (New York: Teachers College Press, 1992).

MacKinnon, Catharine A., *Sexual Harassment of Working Women* (New Haven, CT: Yale University Press, 1979).

National Law Journal, "Women in Large Firms: A High Price for Admission?" (December 11, 1989): 82. Reprinted in American Bar Association, *Lawyers and Balanced Lives: A Guide To Drafting and Implementing Sexual Harassment Policies for Lawyers* (Chicago: American Bar Association, 1992).

Omilian, Susan M., *Sexual Harassment in Employment* (Wilmette, IL: Callaghan, 1987).

Paludi, Michele A., ed., *Ivory Power: Sexual Harassment on Campus* (Albany: State University of New York Press, 1990).

Paludi, Michele A., and Richard B. Barickman, *Academic and Workplace Sexual Harassment: A Resource Manual* (Albany: State University of New York Press, 1991).

Petrocelli, William, and Barbara Kate Repa, *Sexual Harassment on the Job: What It Is and How To Stop It* (Berkeley, CA: Nolo Press, 1992).

Popovich, Paula M., "An Examination of Sexual Harassment Complaints in the Air Force for FY 1987" (Patrick Air Force Base, FL: Defense Equal Opportunity Management Institute, 1988).

Sadroff, Ronni, "Sexual Harassment: The Inside Story," *Working Woman* (June 1992): 47–51.

Safran, Claire, "What Men Do to Women on the Job: A Shocking Look at Sexual Harassment," *Redbook* (November 1976): 149, 217–223.

———, "Sexual Harassment: The View from the Top: The Joint *Redbook–Harvard Business Review* Report," *Redbook* (March 1981): 46–51.

Schmitt, Eric, "Study Says Sexual Harassment Persists at Military Academies," *New York Times* (April 5, 1995): B8.

Schneider, Kimberly T., and Suzanne Swan, "Job-Related, Psychological, and Health-Related Outcomes of Sexual Harassment," presentation at the Symposium on Sexual Harassment at the Ninth Annual Conference of the Society of Industrial and Organizational Psychology, April 1994, Nashville, TN.

Shullman, Sandra, *Sexual Harassment in the Workplace and the Impact of Sexual Harassment* (fact sheets) (Washington, DC: Women's Legal Defense Fund, 1991).

Siegel, Deborah L., *Sexual Harassment: Research and Resources* (New York: National Council for Research on Women, 1992).

Solomon, Alisa, "One Year after Anita Hill . . . Has America's Crash Course in Preventing Sexual Harassment Made a Difference?" *Glamour* (November 1992): 238, 239, 309–311.

Stacy, Neera Rellan, "Note, Seeking a Superior Institutional Liability Standard under Title IX for Teacher-Student Sexual Harassment," 71 *New York University Law Review* 1338 (November 1996).

Stein, Nan, Nancy L. Marshall, and Linda R. Tropp, *Secrets in Public: Sexual Harassment in Our Schools* (Wellesley, MA: Wellesley College Center for Research on Women, 1993).

Strauss, Susan, *Sexual Harassment and Teens: A Program for Positive Change* (Minneapolis, MN: Free Spirit, 1992).

United States Merit Systems Protection Board, *Sexual Harassment in the Federal Workplace: Is It a Problem?* (Washington, DC: U.S. Government Printing Office, 1981).

———, *Sexual Harassment in the Federal Government: An Update* (Washington, DC: U.S. Government Printing Office, 1988).

———, *Sexual Harassment in the Federal Workplace* (Washington, DC: U.S. Government Printing Office, 1995).

Wagner, Ellen J., *Sexual Harassment in the Workplace: How To Prevent, Investigate, and Resolve Problems in Your Organization* (New York: American Management Association, 1992).

Walsh, Sharon, "Decade of the Executive Woman: Hushing up Harassment," *Washington Post* (April 9, 1995): H1.

Webb, Susan, *Webb Report: A Newsletter on Sexual Harassment* (November–December 1987).

———, "Chicago Area Survey," *Webb Report* (August 1992).

Women's Legal Defense Fund, *Sex Discrimination in the Workplace.* 3d ed. (Washington, DC: Women's Legal Defense Fund, 1988).

Directory of Organizations

5

AFL-CIO: Union Privilege
1815 16th Street NW
Washington, DC 20006
(202) 637-5000
Fax: (202) 637-5058

Union Privilege is a nonprofit organization that provides various benefits to union members, including legal assistance and insurance. Membership is automatic for American Federation of Labor–Congress of Industrial Organization (AFL-CIO) local union members; the cost of membership in local unions varies. The organization offers a nationwide legal services plan free to most members of the AFL-CIO. Initial consultation and follow-up are also free, and other attorney's fees are discounted 30 percent. Many AFL-CIO locals also have their own legal services plans.

AFL-CIO Working Women's Department
815 16th Street NW
Washington, DC 20006
(202) 637-5390

The Working Women's Department was created in 1996 as a new department of the AFL-CIO. The department's charge is to be an activist voice for *all* working women and to inject the concerns of working women into the labor movement. Through political, program, policy, and outreach work at the local, state, and national levels, the department promotes the issues and concerns of working women. The department also runs a clearinghouse of resources for women; convenes coalition meetings of labor, civil rights, women's, and religious groups; and plans conferences related to its program activities.

Alexander Hamilton Institute
70 Hilltop Road
Ramsey, NJ 07446
(800) 879-2441

The Alexander Hamilton Institute is a private company specializing in human resource management issues. It serves primarily as a publishing company, producing a wide variety of personnel topics with a legal emphasis.

PUBLICATIONS: Two newsletters, *Personnel Legal Alert* and *Managers' Legal Bulletin,* which include articles on employment issues such as sexual harassment; two booklets for managers, *What Every Manager Must Know To Prevent Sexual Harassment* and *Conducting Sexual Harassment Investigations;* a video, *Sexual Harassment Is Bad Business;* and a wide variety of other material on personnel legal issues.

American Association of University Women (AAUW)
1111 16th Street NW
Washington, DC 20036
(202) 785-7700
Fax: (202) 872-1425

AAUW is a national organization of university graduates dedicated in part to furthering the education of women. Through its Legal Advocacy Fund, the association supports sexual harassment and other sex discrimination cases brought by women students, faculty, and staff against institutions of higher education. The Education Foundation sponsors research on women's education and discrimination against women in educational settings. At-large membership is $35 per year. Individual memberships through local organizations are $26 per year.

PUBLICATIONS: *How Schools Shortchange Girls,* a study of major findings on girls and education, including sexual discrimination issues; a variety of other publications relating to the education of girls and women.

American Bar Association (ABA)
750 North Lakeshore Drive
Chicago, IL 60611
(312) 988-5522
E-mail: http://www.abaanet.org

This national organization provides a number of educational, lobbying, and information services for and about attorneys. The association provides a booklet listing local lawyer referral services by state and county. (Many state bar associations also give legal referrals.) Dues for membership vary, ranging from $35 to $225, depending upon the number of years a lawyer has been in practice. The directory can be ordered by nonmembers from the ABA order department.

PUBLICATIONS: The ABA has recently published *Litigating the Sexual Harassment Case: A Guide for Plaintiff and Defense Attorneys.* The ABA publishes many other books and periodicals related to the practice of law, including a *Directory of Lawyers Referral Service.*

**American Bar Association Commission
on Women in the Profession**
750 North Lakeshore Drive
Chicago, IL 60611
(312) 988-5522
Fax: (312) 988-5688
E-mail: abacwp@abanet.org

The organization's mission is to secure the full and equal participation of women in the American Bar Association, the legal profession, and the justice system.

The ABA Commission on Women in the Profession was created in August 1987 to assess the status of women in the legal profession, identify barriers to advancement, and make recommendations to the ABA for action to address the problems identified. Recently, the commission has reevaluated its objectives and has identified new goals to accomplish its mission: to serve as a voice for the concerns of women lawyers, address impediments that prevent full and equal participation of women lawyers, serve as a catalyst for change, enhance the visibility and influence of the commission, develop opportunities for participation in the work of the commission, focus attention on the concerns of multicultural women, and forge coalitions with other groups to advance shared objectives. To meet these goals the commission engages in numerous ongoing projects, publishes regular reports, and presents programs at ABA meetings, some of which are described under Publications.

PUBLICATIONS: *Unfinished Business: Overcoming the Sisyphus Factor* documents the overt and subtle barriers that impede the full integration and equal participation of women in the law. *Elusive Equality: The Experiences of Women in Legal Education* distills findings from national hearings at which students, administrators, faculty members, and deans have provided their perspectives on gender influences in law schools. *Women in the Law: A Look at the Numbers* is a survey report of statistics currently available that document women's role in all sectors of the legal profession. Published in December 1995. *Directory of Associations of Women Lawyers* is a comprehensive directory that contains over 170 listings for national, state, and local, as well as multicultural, women's bar associations. *Lawyers and Balanced Lives: A Guide To Drafting and Implementing Workplace Policies for Lawyers* describes ways to make law firms "family friendly" for men and women; it includes fully drafted, comprehensive model policies, as well as suggestions for formulating and implementing those policies. The guide deals with parental leave, alternative work schedules, and sexual harassment policies. Published in 1990.

The commission regularly presents programs that address issues of concern to women lawyers. These have ranged from sexual harassment in the legal profession to the image of women in the media.

American Civil Liberties Union (ACLU)
Women's Rights Project
132 West 43rd Street
New York, NY 10036
(212) 944-9800

The ACLU is dedicated to the preservation and protection of individual civil liberties and civil rights. Most states have at least one office that provides legal assistance and referrals. The national Women's Rights Project litigates and provides litigation assistance in employment, education, and other gender discrimination issues. According to the national office, requests for assistance should be made first to a state or local ACLU office.

PUBLICATIONS: None specifically related to sexual harassment; a number of publications on general civil rights issues.

American Federation of State, County,
and Municipal Employees (AFSCME)
1625 L Street NW
Washington, DC 20036
(202) 429-5090
Fax: (202) 429-5088
E-mail: womensrights@afscme.org

The AFSCME is a national labor union with over 1 million members who work in state, county, and municipal government; the union provides a variety of support and educational services to members. The AFSCME is the second-largest union affiliated with the AFL-CIO and is the nation's fastest-growing union. It provides training workshops for members on the issue of sexual harassment, as well as on-site workshops for employees. The national union also assists with collective bargaining and helps to suggest language on sexual harassment issues to include in labor agreements. The union contends that full-time women workers still earn, on average, less than two-thirds as much as men and that at least half of this gap is caused by systematic underpayment in jobs that are filled primarily by women. The AFSCME works to obtain pay equity, which it defines as eliminating discrimination in pay for female-dominated jobs. The union also provides technical assistance to its members on domestic violence and work and family issues.

PUBLICATIONS: A booklet *Stopping Sexual Harassment, an AFSCME Guide,* which provides basic information for workers who believe they have been harassed, and *Domestic Violence: An AFSCME Guide for Union Action.*

American Federation of Teachers (AFT)
Human Rights and Community Relations Department
555 New Jersey Avenue NW
Washington, DC 20001
(202) 879-4434

The AFT represents the concerns of 908,000 teachers, school support staff, higher education faculty, nurses and other health professionals, and state and local government workers. The AFT is an affiliate of the AFL-CIO international union. Organized into local chapters, the union holds a national conference each year to consider educational, civil, human, and women's issues. As part of its resolution that states the organization's policies on the issue of sexual harassment, the group supports legislative and regulatory changes to ensure that no one will be denied unemployment compensation because of sexual harassment claims, as well as offering a separate resolution that supports training and education on student-to-student sexual harassment. Dues vary depending upon the local branch.

PUBLICATIONS: A variety of materials on various educational, civil, human, and women's issues, including a pamphlet, *Sexual Harassment: Unprofessional, Unacceptable, Unlawful,* and an *AFT Resource Guide on Sexual Harassment.*

American Psychological Association
750 1st Street NE
Washington, DC 20002
(202) 336-5500

This national organization of professional psychologists provides referrals to state and local associations that will furnish names of specialists who deal with the psychological problems associated with sexual harassment.

PUBLICATIONS: A brochure on sexual harassment that is available through the order department of the central office and on the World Wide Web; a report, *No Safe Haven,* which includes a chapter on sexual harassment.

American Society for Training and Development (ASTD)
1640 King Street
Alexandria, VA 22313
(703) 683-8100
Fax: (703) 683-8013

This national organization of professional workplace trainers supplies information and referral services on sexual harassment training. Dues for membership are $150 per year. Members include practitioners, managers, administrators, and researchers working in training and human resource development. The ASTD's Information Center is a member inquiry service that assists human resource practitioners in identifying resources for program development, professional development, or both. Information is available on sexual harassment awareness videos, books, and journal articles. Fees for services are different for nonmembers than for members.

PUBLICATIONS: None published by the ASTD; the organization provides information referrals to publications produced by other organizations.

Anderson-davis, Inc.
14901 East Hampden Avenue, Suite 220
Aurora, CO 80014
(303) 699-7074
Fax: (303) 699-7066

Anderson-davis is an educational services and consulting firm that specializes in the areas of sexual harassment, employment discrimination, effective speaking, and conflict resolution. Anderson-davis provides training programs and management briefings, policy and complaint procedure analysis, and training for in-house trainers and human resource professionals. It also produces videotaped trainers' manuals, a participant workbook, and a manual on how to investigate sexual harassment complaints. These resources are available in Spanish and French.

Asian-American Legal Defense and Education Fund (AALDEF)
99 Hudson Street, 12th Floor
New York, NY 10013
(212) 966-5932

Founded in 1974, AALDEF is a nonprofit group devoted to the protection of the legal rights of Asian Americans through impact litigation, legal advocacy, community education, and law student training. AALDEF provides legal advice and attorney referrals for Asians and Asian Americans on a wide variety of employment and other issues. It also conducts legal rights workshops and provides information on any new legal developments that concern the Asian American community. AALDEF has worked in the areas of immigration, labor, Japanese American redress, anti-Asian violence, and voting rights, as well as discrimination in employment. Annual dues range from basic ($50) to patron ($1,000).

PUBLICATIONS: A newsletter, *Outlook*, which may occasionally include articles on employment discrimination relating to the Asian American community.

Association for Union Democracy (AUD)
Women's Project
500 State Street, 2nd Floor

Brooklyn, NY 11217
(718) 855-6650

Open to members of any union for dues of $15 a year, the Association for Union Democracy provides nationwide attorney referrals, legal advice, counseling, and organizational assistance for women in unions. AUD is a pro-union civil liberties group that helps all union members to develop democracy within their unions. The Women's Project helps women with problems on the job and within their unions and offers training, workshops, and educational programs on sexual harassment for members and nonmembers.

PUBLICATIONS: None specifically on the subject of sexual harassment; *Union Democracy Review* and *$50+ Club News* are newsletters that contain occasional articles on sexual harassment and related discrimination issues.

Bureau of National Affairs (BNA) Communications
9439 Key West Avenue
Rockville, MD 20850
(800) 233-6067

The BNA is a private company that specializes in books, special reports, audio-video materials, and training programs on a wide variety of legal issues, including sexual harassment.

PUBLICATIONS: Videos include *A Costly Proposition, Intent vs. Impact, Myth vs. Facts,* and *Preventing Sexual Harassment,* all of which serve as training videos for the prevention of sexual harassment problems; also a wide variety of books and manuals on employment-related issues and sexual harassment. Call for current list; free previews available.

Business and Legal Reports, Inc. (BLR)
39 Academy Street
Madison, CT 06443
(203) 245-7448
E-mail: blrblr@aol.com

The BLR is a national publisher of regulatory compliance and employee training information. It has published approximately 200 books, which are updated each year, several of which are also available on CD ROM, as well as newsletters and videos that serve professionals in the areas of human resources, safety and health, the environment, and education. The goal of each publication is to interpret, in plain English, the many complex federal and state laws that pertain to the operation of U.S. businesses. The company's stated mission is "to help companies to problem solve in a proactive, rather than reactive, fashion."

PUBLICATIONS: Over 200 publications, including *HR Training Repros*, the book *How To Hire and Fire Legally and Fairly*, and the training guidebook *What Every Employer Should Be Doing about Sexual Harassment. What To Do about Personnel Problems in [Your State]* is a comprehensive offering of two-volume sets available for every state. Volumes are updated six times annually, and subscribers also receive a monthly newsletter that includes news on sexual harassment issues (also available on CD ROM). Three employee awareness training booklets—*Preventing Workplace Sexual Harassment, How To Recognize and Prevent Sexual Harassment in the Workplace,* and *What To Do about Sexual Harassment Complaints*—are also available. Videotapes include *Preventing Sexual Harassment in the Workplace.* Call, write, or e-mail for a current list.

Business and Professional Women/USA (BPW/USA)
2012 Massachusetts Avenue NW
Washington, DC 20036
(202) 293-1100

Founded in 1919 by the United States War Department as a vehicle to bring working women together to help with the war effort during World War I, the organization continued after the war with the goal of promoting women. BPW/USA members in 3,000 local organizations nationwide promote the advancement of working women through career development, networking, educational scholarships, and legislative advocacy. The national organization publishes a position paper on sexual harassment. Annual dues for members-at-large are $50; local dues vary.

Related organizations include the BPW Foundation, a nonprofit education and research organization that has awarded more than $5 million in scholarships, loans, and fellowships to approximately 7,000 women. The foundation also provides assistance to women entering nontraditional career fields and sponsors education and training for members on such topics as starting a business, leadership development, career strategies, work and family issues, and Workforce 2000.

Another related organization is the BPW Political Action Committee (BPW/PAC), which represents the collective power of individuals who support the BPW's national legislative agenda. One plank of the agenda is to eliminate all forms of violence and abuse against women; another is to secure pay equity, equal treatment, and economic equality in all areas of employment for all women. The political action committee provides contributions and endorsements to women and pro-women national candidates who support BPW's legislative priorities. The BPW/PAC is supported by voluntary contributions from BPW members. Membership benefits include networking opportunities, a reference library dedicated to working women's issues, a legislative hot line, and annual conventions and meetings that provide workshops and training, including a recent workshop on sexual harassment.

PUBLICATIONS: *A Crime of Power, Not Passion: Sexual Harassment in the Workplace*, a position paper on sexual harassment; a national magazine, *National Business Woman*, which may include articles on discrimination against women; a number of other publications and reports relating to women and work, including *You Can't Get There from Here: Working Women and the Glass Ceiling*.

CCH INCORPORATED
4025 West Peterson Avenue
Chicago, IL 60646
(312) 583-8500

CCH Incorporated is a private publishing company that offers material on many legal issues. It publishes a training manual on sexual harassment for managers and supervisors, as well as other publications on related personnel issues. Call or write for a current catalog.

PUBLICATIONS: *Sexual Harassment Manual for Managers and Supervisors*, a training manual; *Equal Employment Opportunity Manual for Managers and Supervisors*, a guide to EEO concepts and procedures; *Explanation of the Civil Rights Act of 1991*, a guide to the new law; and several other titles on legal issues in employment.

Center for Women in Government
State University of Albany, Draper Hall 302
135 Western Avenue
Albany, NY 12222
(518) 442-3900

Founded in 1978, the Center for Women in Government works to identify and remove barriers to employment equity for women in public service and to develop women's leadership in the public-policy arena. The center's program includes research, training, technical assistance, and policy education. The center provides sexual harassment training for New York state employees and serves workers nationwide through training, videos, digests of important sexual harassment cases and laws, and pamphlets on sexual harassment.

PUBLICATIONS: *Sexual Harassment—It's No Game,* a video-based training package designed for the public sector, along with a two- to three-hour written curriculum on the same subject; *Managing Sexual Harassment Problems: A Guidebook for Problem-Solvers,* a description of the types of sexual harassment and strategies for dealing with them; *Sexual Harassment: A Digest of Landmark and Other Significant Legal Cases,* a booklet describing legal avenues and summarizing key court decisions on the issue of sexual harassment.

Center for Women Policy Studies (CWPS)
1211 Connecticut Avenue NW, Suite 312
Washington, DC 20036
(202) 872-1770
Fax: (202) 296-8962

The CWPS is an independent, privately funded, national multi-ethnic feminist, policy research, and advocacy institution. Founded in 1972, the center has concentrated on complex, cutting-edge women's issues throughout its 25-year history. The center's central premises are that all issues affecting women are interre-lated, that sex and race bias throughout society must be addressed simultaneously, and that analyses of the status and needs of women must recognize their diversity—by race and ethnicity, eco-nomic status, disability, sexual orientation, and age. The center's programs combine advocacy, research, policy development, and public education to advance the agenda for women's equality and empowerment. CWPS programs address educational equity, eco-nomic opportunity for low-income women, work-family and workplace diversity policies, women and AIDS, reproductive rights and health, and violence against women.

PUBLICATIONS: An extensive list of publications; write or call for current catalog.

Coalition of Labor Union Women (CLUW)
1126 16th Street NW
Washington, DC 20036

(202) 466-4610
Fax: (202) 776-0537

CLUW is the only national organization for union women in the United States. CLUW is not a union but strives to make organized labor—and the public in general—more sensitive to the needs of working women and their families. CLUW has 75 chapters across the country and over 20,000 members representing more than 60 unions. The organization's goals include organizing the unorganized, promoting affirmative action in the workplace, stimulating political action and legislation on women's issues, and increasing women's participation in their unions. CLUW provides a referral service to other organizations, if necessary, and refers union members who have complaints about sexual harassment to the appropriate person within the local union.

A resource center with clippings, training materials, and a video library is available for members at CLUW offices. A hot line that provides counseling and referrals is provided for individuals who have sexual harassment complaints; CLUW receives one or two calls a week that relate to sexual harassment. The group also provides education on sexual harassment issues, organizes conferences and workshops, testifies and lobbies for legislation, supports strikes and boycotts, and publishes a newsletter and other written materials for union women. Finally, CLUW provides sample contract language, resolutions, and policies on sexual harassment, as well as legal referrals for individual members.

PUBLICATIONS: *The 9 to 5 Guide To Combating Sexual Harassment*, published with 9 to 5; a leaflet "Sexual Harassment: It's Not Funny, It's Not Flattery, and It's Not Your Fault" and a palm card with the same title; and a newsletter, *CLUW News*, which sometimes includes articles on sexual harassment and other discrimination issues.

College and University Personnel Association (CUPA)
1233 20th Street NW, Suite 301
Washington, DC 20036
(202) 429-0311

With an international membership of over 1,700 colleges and universities and other related organizations, CUPA serves more than 6,300 human resource administrators working in higher education. CUPA promotes the effective development and management of the personnel profession. It offers professional development programs and specialized workshops on personnel topics and provides publications, benefits, and legislative information services to help administrators be aware of current developments in the area of human resources. CUPA publishes a book and a video on sexual harassment.

PUBLICATIONS: *Subtle Sexual Harassment*, a training program that describes definitions, legal developments, and policy recommendations relating to sexual harassment and the university, and a companion videotape with the same title; and *Preventing Sexual Harassment on Campus: Policies and Practices for Higher Education*, a book with advice on tailoring policies for the institutional environment.

Communications Workers of America (CWA)
501 3rd Street NW
Washington, DC 20001-2797
(202) 434-1100

Calling itself "a union for the Information Age," the CWA, the largest telecommunications union in the world, represents 650,000 workers in private- and public-sector employment in the United States and Canada. More than 1,200 chartered local unions are affiliated with the CWA. Founded at meetings in Chicago and New Orleans in 1938, the CWA has gradually broadened its base from the telephone industry to other industries. CWA members are employed in telecommunications, printing and news media, public-service health care, cable television, general manufacturing, electronics, gas and electric utilities, and other fields. The CWA holds collective bargaining agreements for large employers such as AT&T and GTE.

The CWA considers sexual harassment offensive and dehumanizing and will not tolerate it in any form in any workplace—a position stated in the CWA Sexual Harassment Policy, adopted by the International Executive Board. Virtually all CWA contracts contain a nondiscrimination clause that prohibits discrimination on the basis of gender, and the contracts take the position that sexual harassment is discrimination on the basis of gender. The union provides internal training for union members and staff, as well as written materials on sexual harassment.

Equal Employment Opportunity Commission (EEOC)
303 East 17th Avenue, Suite 510
Denver, CO 80203

(800) 669-4000
(303) 866-1085

The EEOC is the federal agency charged with administering and enforcing the nation's equal employment opportunity laws. To contact the nearest EEOC office, call (800) 669-4000. For information regarding EEOC procedures and regulations, call (800) 669-EEOC. All information is printed in both English and Spanish.

PUBLICATIONS: Many different publications on equal opportunity issues, including a fact sheet on sexual harassment, *Facts about Sexual Harassment,* which includes information about how to file a charge; an annual report detailing the activities of the agency on many fronts, including sexual harassment claims.

Equal Rights Advocates (ERA)
1663 Mission Street, Suite 550
San Francisco, CA 94103
(415) 621-0672
(800) 839-4ERA (advice and counseling hot line)

One of the oldest and most active women's law centers in the United States, ERA is dedicated to the empowerment of women through the establishment of their economic, social, and political equality. ERA began in 1974 as a firm specializing in issues of sex-based discrimination and has evolved into a legal organization with a multifaceted approach to women's legal issues. Although court cases are a primary function, ERA also works to empower women to help themselves by providing practical advice and public education. ERA seeks to forge alliances with community groups and to build effective issue-oriented coalitions while emphasizing public education and media statements to inform public opinion.

The group sponsors legal action and offers legal advice and counseling in both English and Spanish to women who are the objects of discrimination. Some of the organization's major cases have included, for example, a precedent-setting peer-on-peer sexual harassment case in a school and a case that helped workers to obtain pregnancy-related disability benefits. ERA provides counseling and referrals to attorneys and other women's groups nationwide for victims of sexual harassment and gender discrimination. Memberships vary from a student/low-income membership at $15 per year to an advocate membership of $1,000.

PUBLICATIONS: Various pamphlets on women's issues, as well as *The Equal Rights Advocate,* a newsletter that sometimes addresses issues of sexual harassment; *The Affirmative Action Handbook: How To Start and Defend Affirmative Action Programs,* a joint publication of Equal Rights Advocates and the San Francisco Lawyers' Committee for Urban Affairs; and a booklet and video, *Keeping the Door Open: Why Women Should Support Affirmative Action.*

Federally Employed Women (FEW)
1400 Eye Street NW, Suite 425
Washington, DC 20005-2252
(202) 898-0994
Fax: (202) 898-0998
E-mail: fewinc@few.org

Formed in 1968, FEW is a national nonprofit membership organization of federally employed women, with chapters throughout the United States. According to its bylaws, FEW shall be "operated exclusively for the charitable and educational purposes of taking action to end sex discrimination and toward the advancement of women in employment in the federal government." FEW provides education and training for career development; it also lobbies on legislation of interest to the group, such as the Equal Rights Amendment and bills that relate to health care and violence against women. The group provides written materials on how federal workers can stop sexual harassment, find and select an EEO attorney, and go to court. Dues vary, depending upon the type of membership.

PUBLICATIONS: A booklet, *Combating Sexual Harassment: A Federal Worker's Guide;* and *News and Views,* a newsletter that sometime contains articles relating to sexual harassment.

Fund for the Feminist Majority
1600 Wilson Boulevard
Arlington, VA 22209
(703) 522-2214 (general information)
(703) 522-2501 (sexual harassment hot line)

The Feminist Majority was founded by former National Organization for Women president Eleanor Smeal with the goal of involving more women in "areas of power," including politics, business, and government. The organization's ongoing "Feminization of Power" campaign, a nationwide effort, seeks "to inspire unprecedented numbers of feminists to seek leadership positions, to promote a National Feminist Agenda, and to heighten awareness and visibility of the feminist majority." The organization consists of two separate groups, the Fund for the Feminist Majority and the Feminist Majority Foundation.

The Fund for the Feminist Majority (FFM) is a lobbying and political advocacy group. The FFM is a nonprofit organization dedicated to increasing the percentage of feminist women in elected office, as well as to advancing the National Feminist Agenda. The fund also supports education, lobbying, and public relations efforts on these issues. The group's hot line recommends resources and organizations that deal with the subject of sexual harassment. The Feminist Majority Foundation is the organization's research and education arm, which, in addition to developing educational materials and activities, pursues projects on the use of initiatives and referenda for women's rights and contraceptive research and development.

PUBLICATIONS: *Training Resources on Sexual Harassment,* a list of resources on the subject of sexual harassment; *Organizational Resources,* a list of organizations that deal with the subject; *The Feminist Majority Report,* a quarterly newsletter; and *The Feminization of Power,* photographs and biographies of women in political office and public life in the United States and abroad who have "made a feminist difference."

Haimes Associates, Inc.
437 West Chestnut Hill Avenue
Philadelphia, PA 19118
(215) 248-4920
Fax: (215) 248-4331

Haimes Associates is a private firm that provides training aids on equal employment and discrimination issues, including a handbook for managers and supervisors on the issue of sexual harassment. Its handbooks are brief, to the point, and easy to understand for the layperson. They are intended for lower levels of management and supervision and are priced economically to permit broadscale distribution within an organization.

PUBLICATIONS: Handbooks for managers and supervisors on the following topics: *Sexual Harassment, The Americans with Disabilities*

Act, Drug Abuse in the Workplace, EEO, and *Effective Interviewing and EEO.*

Institute for Women at Work
School of Industrial and Labor Relations, Cornell University
16 East 34th Street, 4th Floor
New York, NY 10016
(212) 340-2800

The institute is a division of the New York State School of Industrial-Labor Relations at Cornell University. It serves as an intellectual, research, and education center with the stated purpose of providing a "forum to examine and evaluate the economic, political, social, and educational issues that connect women and their work." The institute focuses on women's status in the workplace and on the economic status of women. It offers seminars and training on the wage gap, the family, discrimination, and work and publishes a bibliography of sexual harassment resource materials. Occasional training seminars on sexual harassment are also offered, primarily for union members. For a fee, the institute will conduct and collect research on the issue of sexual harassment in specific industries.

PUBLICATIONS: *Sexual Harassment Bibliography,* a collection of written resources on the subject; and *Research Surveys on Sexual Harassment in the Workplace,* a list of surveys on the issue.

McGrath Systems, Inc.
211 East Victoria Street, Suite B
Santa Barbara, CA 93101
(805) 822-1212

McGrath Systems is a sexual harassment and employment law training company specifically designed to focus on public education. Founded by attorney and school law expert Mary Jo McGrath, the company provides training on preventing sexual harassment, sexual harassment investigations, employee supervision, evaluation and documentation, and the McGrath Template Communication System. The Communication System seeks to foster honest and direct feedback for employees while protecting the legal rights and responsibilities of managers and employees. The company's products and services seek to unite the legal rights and responsibilities of the workplace with the human dynamics of the workplace.

PUBLICATIONS: A variety of videotapes and manuals related to sexual harassment, employment law, and communications issues, including the video training series, *Sexual Harassment: Minimize the Risk.*

NAACP Legal Defense and Education Fund, Inc.
99 Hudson Street
New York, NY 10013
(212) 219-1900

The NAACP works to advance the rights of African Americans. Legal counseling is offered, as are referrals for workers or students seeking to bring sexual harassment claims.

PUBLICATIONS: Various publications relating to fund-raising and capital punishment; none specifically on the issue of sexual harassment.

National Education Association (NEA)
Human and Civil Rights Department
1201 16th Street NW
Washington, DC 20036
(202) 833-4000

The NEA is a national membership organization for teachers that seeks to advance the career development of teachers and works on a variety of education issues. The group provides training, videos, and brochures on sexual harassment, available to union members only.

PUBLICATIONS: *Sexual Harassment,* a brochure and training packet on the subject.

National Employment Lawyers Association (NELA)
600 Harrison Street, Suite 535
San Francisco, CA 94107
E-mail: http//www.nela.org.

The National Employment Lawyers Association is a nonprofit, professional membership organization of more than 3,000 lawyers from around the United States who represent employees in employment matters. The association's primary mission is to serve the needs of its members, including providing education and training. NELA also promotes federal and state legislation on employment issues. Membership ($125–$175 annually) is restricted to legal professionals who practice in the area of employment law on behalf of plaintiff employees.

To request a state listing of employment lawyers, send a written request along with a self-addressed letter-size envelope with 55 cents in postage to the National Employment Lawyers Association at the address shown here. The organization cannot respond to telephone, e-mail, or fax requests.

PUBLICATIONS: *Employee Rights Litigation: Pleading and Practice* (Matthew Bender) and *The Employee Advocate Newsletter* and *Employee Advocate Supplement* (quarterly, distributed to members); two educational seminars (in spring and fall) and one annual convention (in June) held each year.

National Resource Center for Consumers of Legal Services
P.O. Box 340
Gloucester, VA 23061
(804) 693-9330
Fax: (804) 693-7363

A nonprofit organization, this resource center is organized to assist all types of groups in establishing plans for providing high-quality, low-cost legal services. The center provides education, research, and information on this issue. Membership is open to any person or organization interested in delivery of legal services and includes information on legal service plans, sponsoring organizations, bar associations, and interested individuals. Dues are scaled according to ability to pay and degree of involvement. The center provides nationwide legal referrals to attorneys. It also publishes materials on how to choose a lawyer.

PUBLICATIONS: A variety of resources on legal services plans, as well as a pamphlet, "Choosing and Using a Lawyer."

National Women's Law Center
11 Dupont Circle NW, Suite 800
Washington, DC 20036
(202) 588-5180
Fax: (202) 588-5185

The National Women's Law Center is a nonprofit organization that has been working since 1972 to advance and protect women's legal rights. The center focuses on major policy areas of importance to women and their families, including child support, employment, education, sexual harassment in the workplace and in the military, reproductive rights and health, child and adult dependent care, public assistance, tax reform, and social security—with special attention given to the concerns of low-income women.

PUBLICATIONS: The center publishes several special publications, fact sheets, and policy papers on a variety of subjects, including *Breaking Down Barriers: A Legal Guide to Title IX* and *Sexual Harassment of Women in the Military.* Copies are available for free, or for a nominal fee, upon request.

National Women's Political Caucus
c/o The Capitol Hill Women's Political Caucus
P.O. Box 599, Longworth Building
Washington, DC 20515
(202) 986-0994

Founded in 1971 to encourage women's participation in the political process, the caucus is dedicated to increasing the number of women in politics. The District of Columbia chapter has produced a model sexual harassment policy for congressional members and an honor roll of members of Congress who have adopted sexual harassment policies. The group also conducts a seminar for staff members who work on Capitol Hill and participates in the orientation of new Congress members. Originally, to receive the support of the caucus, women congressional candidates must have supported choice in abortion rights, the Equal Rights Amendment, and federal funding for child care. The criteria for caucus support are now expanding and changing from these original goals.

PUBLICATIONS: A model sexual harassment policy for Congress members; an honor roll of members of Congress who have adopted sexual harassment policies.

NAWE: Advancing Women in Higher Education
1325 18th Street NW, Suite 210
Washington, DC 20036
(202) 659-9330

One of the oldest organizations for women in education, NAWE provides support and career development for women who work in higher education. The association's stated mission is to provide "educational opportunities and professional support for all women—not just younger women, minorities, the disadvantaged, and the disabled but those in the mainstream as well—throughout their careers." This nonprofit group conducts two conferences a year for members and also sponsors a conference for women student leaders. Other programs provide assistance in professional development, scholarly research, and legislative advocacy.

PUBLICATIONS: *Initiatives,* a trade journal, which sometimes includes articles about sexual harassment on college campuses.

9 to 5, National Association of Working Women
231 West Wisconsin Avenue, Suite 903
Milwaukee, WI 53203-2308
(414) 274-0925 (general information)
(800) 522-0925 (job problem hot line)

In the early 1970s, when Karen Nussbaum was a clerk-typist at Harvard University, a young man walked into her office, looked directly at her, and asked, "Isn't anyone here?" At that moment, Nussbaum realized what her working life lacked: respect. She helped to form 9 to 5, a national nonprofit membership organization dedicated to attaining respect for U.S. office workers, with local chapters throughout the country. (This group served as a source of material for the popular movie with the same name.) A toll-free confidential telephone hot line, staffed by trained job counselors, provides information and referrals on how to deal with sexual harassment and other problems on the job. During the confirmation hearings for Clarence Thomas, 9 to 5 received more than 14,000 calls in five business days from working women seeking help in combating sexual harassment on the job. Discrimination and harassment top the list of job problems reported on the hot line.

The group publishes books and reports on sexual harassment, available at a discount to members. Members also receive legal referrals to attorneys who specialize in sexual harassment. A newsletter published five times a year sometimes provides articles on the subject of sexual harassment. The group assists employers across the country with training and workshops on the issue. Some local chapters offer sexual harassment support groups and referrals to training resources. National dues are $25 annually.

PUBLICATIONS: A book, *The 9 to 5 Guide To Combating Sexual Harassment;* two pamphlets, "Sexual Harassment: What Every Working Woman Needs To Know from 9 to 5" and "Is Your Organization Able To Deal with Sexual Harassment? Skills for Managers from 9 to 5"; and *9 to 5 Newsline,* a newsletter published five times a year that sometimes includes articles on sexual harassment.

NOW Legal Defense and Education Fund (NOW LDEF)
99 Hudson Street, 12th Floor
New York, NY 10013
(212) 925-6635
World Wide Website: www.nowldef.org

For the past 27 years, attorneys at NOW LDEF—a national non-profit public-interest advocacy organization funded by grants and private donations—have pursued equality for women and girls in the workplace, schools, the family, and the courts through litigation, education, and public information programs. NOW LDEF's docket of 70 cases covers a wide range of gender equity issues.

Some of the workplace sexual harassment cases the NOW LDEF has worked on include *Harris v. Forklift Systems, Inc.* (1994), the second U.S. Supreme Court case to address sexual harassment in employment, which found that plaintiffs in sexual harassment cases need not prove psychological injury to prevail; *Robinson v. Jacksonville Shipyards* (1991), a case involving a woman welder in which a federal court ruled that pervasive pornography in the workplace constitutes hostile environment sexual harassment; *Townsend v. Indiana University,* a case involving lost wages and unpaid medical leave caused by trauma resulting from sexual assaults and harassment; and *Bowman v. Heller,* in which the U.S. Supreme Court let stand a lower court decision awarding damages to a woman who had been sexually harassed by a co-worker who pasted her picture on photographs of naked women in graphic sexual poses and circulated them throughout the office.

Since 1993, the NOW LDEF has worked extensively on sexual harassment in schools. In April 1993, the NOW LDEF and the Wellesley College Center for Research on Women released the results of a survey on sexual harassment in schools conducted through *Seventeen* magazine. The NOW LDEF was cocounsel in *Doe v. Petaluma City School District* (1993; modified 1996), the first federal case in the United States to recognize a claim for student-to-student sexual harassment. The NOW LDEF has appeared as amicus in numerous cases concerning girl's rights to be free from sexual harassment and sex discrimination in the schools, including *Franklin v. Gwinnett County Public Schools* (1992), the first U.S. Supreme Court case that addressed sexual harassment in schools; *Patricia H. v. Berkeley Unified School District* (1993), a case involving teacher-to-student sexual harassment; and *Davis v. Monroe County Board of Education* (1994), *Seamons v. Snow* (1996), and *Rowinsky v. Bryan Independent School District* (1996), appellate court cases involving student-to-student sexual harassment.

PUBLICATIONS: The NOW LDEF has over 15 legal resource kits that contain bibliographies, fact sheets, resource lists, statistical information, and articles or pieces relevant to the particular topic. The following resource kits are available for $5.00 each by writing to the NOW LDEF: *Employment Sexual Harassment and Discrimination, Policies and Procedures on Sexual Harassment in the Schools, Sexual Harassment in Housing, Sexual Harassment in the Schools,* and the *Sexual Harassment Policies Manual.*

Pacific Resource Development Group
145 N.W. 85th Street, Suite 104
Seattle, WA 98117
(800) 767-3062
(206) 782-7015
Fax: (206) 782-4501
E-mail: pacres@nwlink.com
Website: http//seattlelive.com/pacres.htm

Pacific Resource is a private company devoted to education and training on the subject of sexual harassment. The organization is headed by trainer and consultant Susan Webb. The group produces employee handbooks and videotape training packages on sexual harassment, a monthly newsletter, and training manuals for managers. Workshops presented by the group have been offered to more than 60,000 employees in more than 1,500 companies and organizations nationwide. The group also provides a train-the-trainer program for companies that want their own personnel to conduct sessions and training for investigators to facilitate in-house complaint resolution.

PUBLICATIONS: *Sexual Harassment . . . Shades of Gray: Guidelines for Managers, Supervisors, and Employees,* a handbook that explains the basic principles of sexual harassment, definitions, prevention, and training; a videotape training package, *Sexual Harassment: Shades of Gray,* a monthly newsletter on sexual harassment, *The Webb Report;* a series of booklets on sexual harassment; a *Resource Manual;* a *Training Manual;* and an *Investigator's Manual.* Two new books are available: *Step Forward, Sexual Harassment in the Workplace* and *Shockwaves: The Global Impact of Sexual Harassment.*

Society for Human Resource Management (SHRM)
606 North Washington Street
Alexandria, VA 22314
(703) 548-3440

The SHRM is a membership organization for human resource managers, with over 80,000 members worldwide. The organization provides its members with government and media representation, education and information services, conferences and seminars, and publications that assist human resource practitioners. The organization publishes a variety of written information for members, including advice on developing sexual harassment policies, as well as a library and computer database on personnel issues. There are more than 400 local chapters. Dues are $160 annually, with additional chapter dues.

PUBLICATIONS: *HR Magazine* and *HR News,* a newsletter, both of which sometimes contain articles on sexual harassment and related discrimination issues; and *HR Legal Report,* a quarterly newsletter that provides in-depth analysis of current legal issues for human resource professionals and contains occasional discussions of sexual harassment and discrimination.

Tele-Lawyer
18377 Beach Boulevard, Suite 325
Huntington Beach, CA 92648
(800) 835-3529

This private company provides legal advice over the telephone at a reasonable per-minute charge. Staff lawyers will also review documents, such as employment contracts, and do legal research on issues, including sexual harassment. Tele-Lawyer was founded by Huntington Beach lawyer Michael Cane in 1989. He and 35 other attorneys work the telephones ten hours a day, five days a week. For a cost of three dollars a minute, charged to the caller's telephone bill or credit card, the lawyers answer questions about a variety of subjects, including, for example, how to file an EEOC claim or a small-claims court lawsuit, how to handle a speeding ticket, and what to do about a threatening letter from the Internal Revenue Service.

United Auto Workers Union (UAW)
Women's Department
8000 East Jefferson
Detroit, MI 48214
(313) 926-5212

Different groups have come together under the UAW umbrella, from auto workers to state workers to nursing home workers. The goals of the Women's Department are to help bring women into active participation in their local unions, to encourage women to run in union elections, to teach women skills for bargaining, and to develop leadership and education. Although the Women's Department still conducts some workshops on sexual harassment, it is currently developing revised written and video training materials and new workshops for UAW and other union members.

PUBLICATIONS: Currently revising materials to be used for training and in workshops.

Wider Opportunities for Women
815 15th Street NW, Suite 916
Washington, DC 20005
(202) 638-3143
Fax: (202) 638-4885

This national nonprofit organization works to achieve economic independence and equal opportunities for women and girls through education, training, and employment. The group offers publications related to sexual harassment and provides consulting services for employers and unions on the issue of sexual harassment.

PUBLICATIONS: *Sexual Harassment Solutions,* a booklet that profiles successful policy on sexual harassment and includes a fact sheet on sexual harassment; and *The Employer* and the *Union Manual,* two publications that contain proven strategies for integrating and retaining women into trades and technical jobs, including chapters on sexual harassment prevention.

Women Employed Institute
22 West Monroe, Suite 1400
Chicago, IL 60603
(312) 782-3902

This membership organization provides career development, networking opportunities, and support for Chicago working women, as well as conducting research into and advocacy around various issues that affect women's economic advancement. The group offers weekly telephone counseling on employment issues, including sexual harassment, and can provide referrals to local attorneys. Women Employed also provides sexual harassment prevention training for area employers.

PUBLICATIONS: *Sexual Harassment: The Problem That Isn't Going Away*, a study of women who were harassed on the job in the Chicago area that explores their courses of action and the outcomes of their situations; *Sexual Harassment and Your Rights on the Job*, a fact sheet on the issue; and *Women Employed News*, a newsletter for members that occasionally addresses the issue of sexual harassment.

Women's Bureau
U.S. Department of Labor
200 Constitution Avenue NW
Washington, DC 20210
(800) 827-5335
Fax: (202) 219-5529

The Women's Bureau of the U.S. Department of Labor focuses on a variety of issues relating to women and work, including sexual harassment. It has a publication on sexual harassment, published in English and Spanish, as part of a series of *Don't Work in the Dark—Know Your Rights* publications. The bureau can also provide resources on sexual harassment.

PUBLICATIONS: *Sexual Harassment Resources*, a list of materials relating to sexual harassment.

Women's Law Project
125 South 9th Street, Suite 401
Philadelphia, PA 19107
(215) 928-9801

The Women's Law Project is a nonprofit, feminist, legal advocacy organization that was founded in 1974. The project works to abolish discrimination and injustice and to advance the legal and economic status of women and their families. Since 1974, the project has worked in the fields of health, reproductive freedom, employment, domestic relations, housing, insurance, credit, and education. Through lawsuits, education, and working with the government, the project hopes to break new ground on these legal issues. It provides a telephone counseling service, as well as information on sexual harassment and how to find a lawyer.

PUBLICATIONS: None specifically on sexual harassment; a variety on other issues relating to women and the law.

Women's Legal Defense Fund
1875 Connecticut Avenue NW, Suite 710
Washington, DC 20009
(202) 986-2600

The Women's Legal Defense Fund works for "policies that reflect the realities women face in their everyday lives"—policies that provide equal opportunity, reproductive freedom, quality health care, and economic security. Founded in 1971 to increase opportunities for women, the Women's Legal Defense Fund works in Congress, the courts, the administrative branch of government, and the states; at the grassroots level; and with the media to advance public policy for women. Dues vary from single membership, $50–$90, to the Capital Club, $5,000. The fund sponsors public education, written information, advocacy, and target litigation on sexual harassment.

PUBLICATIONS: A poster entitled *Sexual Harassment in Your Workplace: Your Legal Rights;* a newsletter, *WLDF News,* which frequently includes articles on sexual harassment and related discrimination issues; and *Sexual Harassment in the Workplace,* a fact sheet on the issue.

Women's Rights Litigation Clinic
Rutgers School of Law–Newark
15 Washington Street
Newark, NJ 07102-3192
(201) 648-5637

Founded as a temporary student-initiated undertaking in 1972 and institutionalized as a permanent enterprise in 1973, with Nadine Taub as director, the clinic has focused on litigation and legal counseling relating to women's rights. Open to both second- and third-year students, the Women's Rights Litigation Clinic offers a legal-practice experience to students who, working with attorney-instructors, have achieved a number of important victories, particularly in the areas of gender equality and reproductive rights. The clinic has received requests for assistance from individuals and organizations throughout the United States, as well as inquiries regarding its activities from Europe and Australia.

The clinic litigated the landmark case of *Tomkins v. Public Service Electric and Gas Co.* (1977), in which the court found sexual harassment to be an impermissible form of sex discrimination in employment. It filed an amicus curiae (friend of the court) brief in *T. L. v. Toys "R" Us* (1988), a case that extended the definition of hostile environment in which the Appellate Division of New Jersey adopted the standard of a "reasonable victim" rather than a "reasonable operator." The clinic filed another amicus brief in *Thoreson v. Penthouse Ltd.* (1989), upholding a lower court award to an employee of *Penthouse* magazine of $60,000 in compensatory damages for demands by her boss that she sleep with two of the men he did business with. Students also field a high volume of calls from women, counseling them on claims of sexual harassment and other work-related issues. Early in its existence, the clinic was involved in establishing the right to sue for sexual harassment experienced by students in colleges and universities. It may be the first organization in the United States to have focused on sexual harassment in housing and to have provided community education and outreach on the issue, including publishing a brochure on the subject in English and Spanish, holding meetings with tenant organizations, and giving a presentation to the New Jersey Commission on Sex Discrimination. The clinic is funded by grants, private donations, and recovery of fees from lawsuits; it also receives some funding from Rutgers Law School.

PUBLICATIONS: "Stop Sexual Harassment in Housing," a flyer on the issue and what to do about it, published in English and Spanish.

Selected Print Resources

6

An attempt has been made in this section, as in other chapters of this book, to present all points of view on the issue of sexual harassment. Few articles, however, and no entire books take the position that sexual harassment should be viewed as a personal, rather than a legal, problem; question the extent of government regulation in this area; warn about the risk of false charges; or represent the point of view of the alleged harasser. An attempt, therefore, has been made to present representative samples of books that question the feminist position on sex roles or sex discrimination in the section entitled "Related Gender Issues." In addition, because the entire issue of sexual harassment has come to the forefront only since the early 1970s, the number of books and monographs available on this issue is necessarily limited. Since the issue has changed and evolved so rapidly, many works are already outdated. Some are still listed in this chapter because they present a particular point of view or have historical significance. Before relying on facts or legal precedent in any particular work, however, check the date it was published.

Anthologies

Mahoney, M. R., et al. **"Gender, Race, and the Politics of Supreme Court Appointments: The Import of the Anita Hill/Clarence Thomas Hearings."** *Southern California Law Review* 65 (March 1992): 1279–1582.

In this 300-page symposium, scholars from a number of different disciplines leap into the Hill/Thomas debate with a score of articles. English and classics professors, for example, discuss the backdrop of the drama in terms of myth and storytelling, historians address the historical context, and political scientists consider the political maneuvering behind the hearings. Also reprinted is an address by Anita Hill delivered before the National Forum for Women in State Legislatures. A sample of the titles reveals some of the anthology's content: "Cringing at Myths of Black Sexuality," "October Tragedy," and "Roman Oratory, Pornography, and the Silencing of Anita Hill." None of the contributors to this collection pulls any punches; all appear to be squarely in Anita Hill's camp or, at the least, critical of the way the Senate handled the proceedings. The writing is colorful and passionate, providing ample evidence of how deeply affected many people were by this uniquely American drama.

Morrison, Toni, ed. *Racing Justice, Engendering Power: Essays on Anita Hill, Clarence Thomas, and the Construction of Social Reality*. New York: Pantheon Books, 1992. 475p. ISBN 0-679-74145-3.

This volume attempts to frame the entire Clarence Thomas/Anita Hill controversy within the broader context of race and gender. Toni Morrison contributes an introduction and brings together 18 provocative and original essays, all but one written specifically for this book, by prominent academicians—black and white, male and female. These writings address not only the racial and sexual aspects but also the historical, political, cultural, legal, psychological, and linguistic aspects of a single revelatory moment in U.S. history. The diverse contributors include, for example, A. Leon Higginbotham Jr., a judicial colleague of Clarence Thomas's, and Carol M. Swain, an assistant professor of politics and public affairs at Princeton University's Woodrow Wilson School. As Toni Morrison emphasizes in the introduction:

> For insight into the complicated and complicating events that the confirmation of Clarence Thomas

became, one needs perspective, not attitude; context, not anecdotes; analysis, not postures. For any kind of lasting illumination the focus must be on the history routinely ignored or played down or unknown.

This complex, thoughtful, and challenging book provides such insight and illumination. Although she notes that what happened was upsetting and serious, Morrison concludes that

Regardless of political alliances, something positive and liberating has already surfaced. In matters of race and gender, it is now possible and necessary, as it seemed never to have been before, to speak about these matters without the barriers, the silences, the embarrassing gaps in discourse. It is clear to the most reductionist intellect that black people think differently from one another, it is also clear that the time for undiscriminating racial unity has passed. A conversation, a serious exchange between black men and women, has begun in a new arena, and the contestants defy the mold. Nor is it as easy as it used to be to split along racial lines, as the alliances and coalitions between white and black women, and the conflicts among black women and among black men, during the intense debates regarding Anita Hill's testimony against Clarence Thomas's appointment prove.

National Association of College and University Attorneys. *Sexual Harassment on Campus: A Legal Compendium.* Washington, DC: National Association of College and University Attorneys, 1988. 201p. Bibliography. ISBN 9998954150.

This compendium pulls together in one source some of the leading law review and journal articles on sexual harassment in higher education. It also includes the sexual harassment policies and procedures of several universities and organizations and provides guidance for administrators on drafting sexual harassment policies. The work includes a selected bibliography and outlines major court cases. It also contains an analysis of leading Supreme Court cases and a selection of articles from the *Journal of the National Association for Women Deans, Administrators, and Counselors* on such subjects as implementing a sexual harassment program at a large university. The anthology is a useful source for identifying avenues for further research on sexual harassment in colleges.

Paludi, Michele A., ed. *Ivory Power: Sexual Harassment on Campus.* Albany: State University of New York Press, 1990. 298p. Index, bibliography. ISBN 0-7914-0457-9 (cloth); 0-7914-0458-7 (paper).

Paludi, a research psychologist and director of the research collective on sexual harassment at Hunter College, edited this collection of scholarly papers, which starts from the premise that the most reliable data indicate that 30 percent of women students are sexually harassed by at least one instructor during their college years. (When definitions of *sexual harassment* include gender harassment—sexist comments and behavior—the incidence is 70 percent.) This collection covers the myths and realities of sexual harassment on campus; definitions and measurement; methods of studying the problem; the impact of harassment on victims' cognitive, physical, and emotional well-being; studies of the men who become harassers; and how administrators should handle complaints. Extensive appendixes detail sample references on the subject, including audiovisual materials, workshop ideas, and training materials.

One unique feature of the book is its emphasis on the experiences of graduate women and women faculty and administrators. The collection takes a sociological perspective on understanding and eliminating sexual harassment while also addressing the interface of racism and sexism on college campuses and the legal issues involved in academic sexual harassment cases. *Ivory Power* is an important work on the study of sexism and of women's professional advancement—or lack thereof.

Paul, Ellen Frankel, Lloyd R. Cohen, Linda C. Majka, Alan Kors, Jean Bethke Elshtain, and Nicholas Davidson, **"Sexual Harassment or Harassment of Sexuality?"** *Society* 28, no. 4 (May–June 1991): 4–45.

In this journal symposium, several authors present articles that question the basic idea of allowing sexual harassment claims to rise to the level of legal complaints. In an article entitled "Bared Buttocks and Federal Cases," for example, Ellen Frankel Paul, a professor of political science, argues that "for women to expect reverential treatment in the workplace is utopian"; Frankel also complains that "sexual harassment is a notoriously ill-defined and almost infinitely expandable concept" and insists that "women must develop a thick skin to survive and prosper in the workplace."

Similarly, contributor Lloyd Cohen, a law professor at Chicago-Kent School of Law, agrees that the definition of *sexual harassment* has become "more, rather than less, elusive with use" and expresses his concern that the threat of legal sanctions will drive men away from necessary and proper courtship rituals. "Even if it were possible theoretically to define a category of sexual harassment as evil, it may still not be sensible to impose legal sanctions on such behavior," he concludes, because for a number of people in our mobile society the workplace represents "by far the best avenue for finding and pursuing romantic interests."

Alan Kors, a history professor at the University of Pennsylvania, laments the rise and strictures of sexual and racial harassment policies in the university and worries that they will impinge upon the rights of free speech and academic freedom. Philosophy and political science professor Jean Bethke Elshtain comments on the collision of attempts to restrict pornography with the rights of free speech. Finally, Nicholas Davidson, author of *The Failure of Feminism*, provides a critique of *Feminism and Sexual Harassment*, arguing that the feminist position on the issue represents an unreconcilable conflict between the desire for equal treatment of the sexes and the supposed need for protection from sexual advances.

> On the one hand, feminists have endlessly assured us, women are "strong," . . . just as tough as men. . . . On the other hand, if women are just as tough as men . . . why do they need the protection of special "sexual harassment" laws? After all, could a woman not just say no?

Such contradictions, he argues, mean that "women's liberation has, in a sense, produced women's oppression." In all, this lively series of articles provides a much-needed counterpoint to the scores of books and periodicals that simply assume—without much analysis—that seeking legal redress for sexual harassment claims is a worthy ideal.

Sumrall, Amber Coverdale, and Dena Taylor, eds. *Sexual Harassment: Women Speak Out.* Freedom, CA: Crossing Press, 1992. 321p. ISBN 0-89594-544-4 and 0-89595-2.

This book, dedicated to Anita Hill, arose out of the anger of Elaine Goldman Gill, a co-owner of Crossing Press, after she had watched the Clarence Thomas confirmation hearings. The editors called—in newspapers, on radio stations, and on college campuses—for submissions from women detailing their own experiences with sexual harassment. Hundreds of manuscripts arrived in response. The editors described the accounts as "painful, angry, humiliating, humorous, and empowering."

> Women all over the country—in their homes, at work, in the laundromat, at the hairdressers, in classrooms—watched Anita Hill's testimony, and the repeated questions, insinuations, disbelief, and laughter from the senators. For countless numbers of women, the Hill-Thomas hearings opened the gates of denial, and long-repressed memories came tumbling out.

In this book, women write of their experiences and how they responded to them. Some women were depressed or had physical symptoms, some fought back, some denied the harassment, some found humorous or other ways to deal with the harasser. The stories, which are presented alphabetically, are interspersed with quotations from and cartoons by women. The book includes a resource section for women who have experienced harassment.

The responders are a varied and interesting lot. They range from a 68-year-old woman who was forced to leave several jobs because of harassment to a 45-year-old woman who recalls having been fondled at age 12 by an electrician who was working in her school. Women from a wide variety of careers, from writers to police officers, relate the harassment they have suffered and its consequences for their lives. Although it is not a scientific survey of women harassment victims, the book provides valuable samples of women's experiences in this area and may comfort other women who have suffered the same fate. This book is unique in the literature on sexual harassment because it allows women to express their pain, outrage, and eventual power in their own words. Yet some readers may be troubled by the book's ironclad feminist stance. As Andrea Dworkin, an authority on rape, wrote in the introduction:

> Outside, the woman is public in male territory, a hands-on zone; her presence there is taken to be a declaration of availability—for sex and sexual insult. . . . The verbal assaults and some physical assaults are endemic in the environment. . . . None of us can stand up to all of it; we are incredulous as each new

aggression occurs. We hurry to forget. It can't have happened, we say; or it happens all the time, we say—it is too rare to be credible or too common to matter. We won't be believed or no one will care: or both.

Swisher, Karin L., ed. *What Is Sexual Harassment?* San Diego: Greenhaven Press, 1995. 91p. Index, bibliography. ISBN 1-56510-299-1 (cloth); 1-56510-266-5 (paper).

This book is part of an anthology series that focuses a wide range of viewpoints on a single controversial issue and attempts to provide in-depth discussions by leading voices on each perspective. Brief bibliographies and a few organizations to contact are included. The editor describes the spectrum of points of view as follows:

> At one end of the spectrum stand those who believe that the response to harassment is an absurd overreaction and that an adult should simply cope with or leave a situation where harassment is a problem. At another extreme stand those who would cite a construction worker for a wolf whistle or a suggestive remark, believing that everyone should be free from unwanted sexualized behavior.

The authors range from syndicated newspaper columnist Ellen Goodman, who argues that the "reasonable woman" definition of sexual harassment makes good sense, to J. H. Foegen, a business professor, who argues that "broad definitions of sexual harassment are harmful to business." The writers discuss what they believe is the most useful definition of sexual harassment in schools, colleges, and academia. The collection provides a brief but useful overview of the subject from various viewpoints.

Bibliographies

Crocker, Phyllis L. **"Annotated Bibliography on Sexual Harassment in Education."** *Women's Rights Law Reporter* 7, no. 2 (Winter 1982): 91–106.

Prepared as part of the Sexual Harassment in Education Project of the NOW Legal Defense and Education Fund, this bibliography includes 131 items: reports; articles; books, legal cases, and papers; organizational publications; works in progress; and resources. The major focus is on higher education, although a few entries deal with secondary and vocational education and with sexual harassment in therapy. Articles that reflect a hostile or frivolous viewpoint are listed "because they illuminate some of the unstated but deeply held beliefs with which organizers and litigators have to contend." The annotations list contact persons, which makes the work useful for locating obscure material. Unfortunately, with a 1982 publication date, the list obviously does not include more recent material.

Gartland, Patricia, and Winfred Bevilacqua. **"Sexual Harassment: Recent Research and Useful Resources."** *Journal of the National Association for Women Deans, Administrators, and Counselors* 46, no. 2 (Winter 1983): 47–50.

This select, partially annotated list of 37 items includes books and handbooks, resource agencies, audiovisual materials, and a dozen journal articles that reflect the range of literature available on sexual harassment in 1983. The list focuses on handbooks published by professional associations and resource agencies, and about half covers harassment in higher education.

Jacobs, Daniel J. **"Sexual Harassment and Related Issues: A Selective Bibliography."** *Record of the Association of the Bar of the City of New York* 46, no. 8 (December 1991): 930–939.

This extensive list of 167 entries focuses on the most recent articles available at the time about legal issues that arise in sexual harassment cases. It mainly covers legal periodicals, although it also includes a few general publications, some books, and some government publications. The listings are not annotated.

McCaghy, M. Dawn. *Sexual Harassment: A Guide to Resources.* Boston: G. K. Hall, 1985. 181p. Index. ISBN 0-8161-8669-3.

McCaghy, a former reference librarian at Bowling Green State University who also holds a bachelor's degree in sociology, compiled this comprehensive bibliography, which includes sources to mid-1983 and a few 1984 references. The extensive subject categories include the feminist perspective, a general overview, the legal perspective, and management response, among others. Each source listing provides a balanced discussion of the contents. Training and audiovisual materials are also listed and summarized. The work includes a comprehensive author-title index and a separate subject index. An excellent reference work, the book's only drawback is that it is out-of-date in this fast-changing field, but it is included here because it is the only hardback, readily available bibliography on the subject of sexual harassment.

NOW Legal Defense and Education Fund. **"Sexual Harassment in the Schools Resource Kit."** New York: NOW Legal Defense and Education Fund, 1992. 5p.

This short list of annotated entries on sexual harassment in schools focuses on secondary education, although some listings cover colleges and universities. The booklet was prepared by the Project of Equal Education Rights of the NOW Legal Defense and Education Fund. The entries include news articles, magazine articles, scholarly publications, books, pamphlets, surveys, and resource organizations. An annotation of the major Supreme Court cases on sexual harassment in schools is also included. Because the issue of sexual harassment and young people is relatively new, this bibliography is especially valuable because it compiles the few sources that are available.

Books, Monographs, and Selected Articles

Sexual Harassment

American Association of University Women (AAUW) Educational Foundation and Harris/Scholastic Research. **"Hostile Hallways: The AAUW Survey on Sexual Harassment in America's Schools."** Washington, DC: The AAUW Educational Foundation, 1994. 25p.

Commissioned by the American Association of University Women and conducted by Louis Harris and Associates to ensure that the survey's methodology, implementation, and questionnaire would meet the highest standards of the survey research community, this report has been well publicized and has attracted much commentary—both positive and negative. The extensive study of 1,632 field surveys completed by public school students in grades 8 through 11 from 79 schools across the continental United States included representative samples for Hispanic, white, and African American students. Critics have questioned the study's conclusion that 4 of 5 students have experienced some form of sexual harassment as based on too broad a definition of harassment. Later researchers (see Linn et al. [1996] in the Introduction of the present book), however, have reexamined and reaffirmed this study's basic conclusions.

Other important findings include that of those who have experienced harassment, 1 in 4 report having been targeted "often." The most common forms of harassment reported were sexual comments, jokes, gestures, or looks—76 percent of girls and 56 percent of boys reported having experienced such harassment. At the other extreme, 11 percent reported having been forced to do something sexual other than kissing. Particularly compelling are the findings that the harassment significantly influenced students' abilities to study, made them feel less confident about themselves, and even made some doubt that they had what it takes to graduate from high school. The format of the report is useful, with many graphs, quotes, and a conclusion that suggests the need for future action. This report is a significant contribution to the field. Before this study, although many studies of sexual harassment in workplaces and colleges had been conducted, little was known about harassment in junior and senior high schools.

Berns, Walter. **"Terms of Endearment: Legislating Love."** *Harper's* (October 1980): 14–20.

Berns, a resident scholar at the American Enterprise Institute, wrote this short piece just before the first EEOC guidelines on sexual harassment became final. Berns criticizes the guidelines for not defining sexual harassment and predicts that the requirement that the employer must provide an environment free from "sexual contamination" will eventually lead to dress codes for women, lest they provoke men. Although he admits that the regulations relate to behavior in the workplace, Berns argues that

> Many lovers who end up in the bedroom meet in the workplace. [The EEOC's] purpose is the prevention of sexual harassment, not the inhibiting of romance; but in its efforts to identify the one, the commission will intrude upon the other. This will interfere with the easy and sometimes playful familiarity that characterizes the relationships of men and women.

Berns believes the government should respect "the privacy of erotic relationships" and notes that "traditionally, love has been seen to be none of the government's business." The article is a playful, witty critique of the early EEOC guidelines.

Black, Beryl. *Coping with Sexual Harassment.* New York: Rosen Publishing Group, 1987. 149p. Index, bibliography. ISBN 0-8239-0732-5.

This book is one of the few that discusses incidents of sexual harassment experienced by young people at work and ways of coping with this problem. Written in an engaging style, the book presents the story of a fictional teenager who is sexually harassed at her first job. Excerpts from her diary and her letters to an advice column, "Ted and Monica," tell her story. The fictional columnists reply to her and solicit letters from their readers. The readers' letters reveal their own views on the subject of harassment, as well as their experiences with both male and female homosexual and heterosexual harassment at work and in school. "Ted and Monica" respond with advice from psychological experts and an exposition of the law and EEOC guidelines. Without writing down to the reader, the book manages to impart a great deal of information in an innovative format. A list of organizational resources and a short book list are included. The book emphasizes the serious consequences of sexual harassment; in fact, some readers may find a few of the scenarios exaggerated, as when several teens kill themselves or their harassers. Young people, however, will probably be drawn into the many stories presented, as well as the diverse points of view.

Bouchard, Elizabeth. *Everything You Need To Know about Sexual Harassment.* Revised ed. New York: Rosen Publishing Group, 1992. 64p. Index, bibliography, glossary. ISBN 0-8239-1490-9.

One of a series of books for young people on social issues, this work presents clear and concise definitions of sexual harassment in education and employment and explains how victims can handle the problem and where to go for help. Bouchard, a Chicago writer and teacher, explains the topic in a format that uses fictionalized examples of sexual harassment, followed by questions and answers about the scenarios. In addition to these real-life situations, subjects covered include how to spot sexual harassment, why it happens, who it happens to, how to avoid sexual harassment, choices for action, and how to cope with harassment. Large type and numerous topic headings make this book easy, yet accurate and helpful, to read. Particularly helpful are the glossary, which explains words that may be new to younger readers; the list of sources for help, such as the Equal Employment Opportunity Commission and various women's organizations; and a short list of suggestions for further reading. A balanced discussion of the Anita Hill/Clarence Thomas case is included. Photographs of the dramatized situations help hold the reader's interest. The advice on avoiding harassment is practical; it includes suggestions on how to keep the relationship on a business level and to say "no" assertively right from the start, how to ask a harasser to stop, how to write him or her a letter, how to file an EEOC complaint, and when to seek legal advice.

Brock, David. *The Real Anita Hill.* New York: Free Press, 1993. 438p. Index. ISBN 0-02-904655-6.

In this best-selling book, Brock expands his 1992 article with the same title that was published in the *American Spectator.* He continues to provide fuel for the view that Anita Hill manufactured or exaggerated her charges against Clarence Thomas. After extensively investigating Hill's background and conducting interviews with her former colleagues, students, and professors, Brock seems to present two, somewhat conflicting theories about why Hill lied: one, that Hill used the situation to further her own political ambitions and legal career, as well as to retaliate against Thomas because he had once passed her over for a promotion; and two, that one of Hill's friends had confused Thomas with another supervisor Hill had also accused of sexual harassment and had passed this information to the media, at which point Hill was too embarrassed to straighten out the misunderstanding and continued the charade all the way to the United States Congress. Brock also contends that opponents of Thomas (including pro-choice groups) pursued Hill to come forward to thwart the nomination.

Some of Brock's allegations are too bizarre to be believable, such as those from two of Hill's former law school students, who claimed they had found pubic hair (how would they know it was?) in papers she had returned to them. These and other stories about Hill are offered to show that she, rather than Clarence Thomas, had strange ideas about sexual relationships and may be "a bit nutty and a bit slutty." Brock also claims Hill once lied about a minor traffic accident. Feminist defenders of Hill will undoubtedly dismiss this piece as unproven gossip or worse, but it is included here because it presents an opposing view to that expressed by the many women's magazines and women's groups that have declared Anita Hill to be a wronged feminist heroine.

Chaiet, Donna. *Staying Safe at School.* New York: Rosen Publishing Group, 1995. 64p. Index, bibliography, glossary. ISBN 0-8239-1864-5.

It is a sign of the times that this brief work begins with the statement "School is meant to be a safe environment in which you can learn from your teachers and fellow students." Two of the five chapters deal with sexual harassment, including "Dealing with

Unwanted Touching" and "Coping with Verbal Abuse." The book is written in a clear style with large print and should serve as a good guide to prevention of harassment for young people. The book includes a glossary of terms, useful discussions of body language, directive language, and step-by-step prevention techniques. Realistic photos contribute to the user-friendly format. Chaiet is a practicing attorney who also teaches self-defense and safety classes for young people.

Collins, Eliza G. C., and Timothy B. Blodgett. **"Sexual Harassment: Some See It . . . Some Won't."** *Harvard Business Review* 59, no. 2 (March–April 1981): 76–95.

This report summarizes the results of a joint survey, with *Redbook* magazine, of more than 1,800 business executives drawn from *Harvard Business Review* subscribers. The researchers designed questions to probe perceptions of what harassment is, how frequently it occurs, and how management responds. The text is well written, and memorable quotations are interspersed with the survey results, which gives the study an interesting style. The survey pinpointed differences in men's and women's perceptions, most notably with regard to how much harassment actually occurs, how top managers respond to various situations, and how they ought to respond. Opinions about EEOC guidelines and company policies were also solicited. At the time of the survey (1981), most respondents of both sexes favored company policies governing harassment, but few worked for companies that had such policies. The study is a classic that is often cited as one of the few to address the thoughts and views of top executives rather than those of workers.

Conte, Alba. *Sexual Harassment in the Workplace: Law and Practice.* New York: John Wiley and Sons, 1990. 556p. Index. ISBN 0-471-50743-1.

This comprehensive legal treatise covers all facets of the law in the area of sexual harassment. Conte surveys the options available to victims under various laws and guides attorneys through administrative and judicial proceedings. The book provides a state-by-state breakdown of relevant common and statutory law and discusses the issues unique to the area of sexual harassment. Extensive discussions of most sexual harassment cases are included, along with sample legal forms for various phases of litigation. Although it is written in a style general readers can follow, the book probably offers too much legal detail and analysis for the lay researcher. Nevertheless, if specific legal citations, analysis, or practice pointers are required, this is the resource to use. Note, however, that the main book includes only pre-1990 cases; yearly supplements are published as updates.

Danforth, John C. *Resurrection: The Confirmation of Clarence Thomas.* New York: Viking, 1994. 225p. Index. ISBN 0-670-86022-0.

In 1991 Senator Danforth pledged to be Clarence Thomas's guide and sponsor through the latter's confirmation process to the U.S. Supreme Court. Danforth, Thomas's longtime friend and mentor, was unprepared for the maelstrom that would erupt over Anita Hill's allegations of sexual harassment. This highly personal account of Danforth's role as Thomas's advocate and friend presents a unique view of the historic proceedings. Danforth admits that he pulled no punches in finding and encouraging all efforts to destroy Hill's credibility. The book is centered on his own, as well as Thomas's religious faith, and Danforth questions whether such tactics were consistent with that faith. Although the discussion is somewhat confused, the answer appears to be "yes." Danforth defends his fight as not only a "good" fight, which he admits may sometimes have been undertaken for the wrong reasons, but also a "just" fight. Danforth believes an injustice was done to Thomas and that remedying that injustice made any means used to do so appropriate.

According to the senator, Thomas was near collapse at one point in the hearings, beaten down by the publicity, the questioning, and some vague, unnamed past sins. Danforth took him into his Senate office to play a tape of "Onward Christian Soldiers," after which he, Thomas, and their wives joined hands in prayer. Danforth asked that Thomas receive God's help because he could no longer help himself and that God's will be done in the hearings. What occurred after that prayer, Danforth believes, was nothing short of a resurrection. Thomas—buoyed by the support of his friends and by the prayer—marched into the Senate hearings and gave his famous speech in which he compared the confirmation process to a "high-tech lynching." Danforth concludes that both he and Thomas felt the ultimate confirmation was clearly God's will.

Although Danforth asserts that "if there is any lesson to be learned from the Thomas-Hill matter, it must be that service of a good cause does not justify the wanton destruction of a person, whether that person is Clarence Thomas or Anita Hill," he continues to insist that he was fighting not only a "good" cause but a "just" one and that he "fought dirty in a fight without rules." Yet he admits that he "fought ineffectively," for he believes that nothing he did to destroy Hill's credibility had "any bearing on the outcome" but that the outcome was a result of the prayer uplifting Thomas so that "when Clarence left [Senator Danforth's] office for the Caucus Room, it was not as a martyr with his eyes fixed on heaven. It was [as] a warrior doing battle for the Lord." This book is included here because of its highly personal perspective on this historic event, even though those who believe Anita Hill may be enraged by Danforth's account, as well as by his religious views.

Dzeich, Billie Wright, and Linda Weiner. *The Lecherous Professor: Sexual Harassment on Campus.* Boston: Beacon Press, 1984. 219p. Index, bibliography. ISBN 0-8070-3100-3.

Of the 6 million women who enter college each year, these authors estimate that 1 million will experience some form of sexual harassment by male professors. With experience as both professors and administrators, Dzeich and Weiner provide the first book-length account of this issue and suggestions for solving the problem. The writers dismiss many myths, such as the idea that college women ask for sexual harassment by dressing provocatively or by using sex to advance their academic careers. Their research reveals otherwise; they quote, for example, an ombudsman at a southern college:

> We very seldom get the campus-queen type in our office. My guess is that they are less likely to be harassed than those who are average in appearance. I think professors avoid them for the same reason a lot of college men hesitate about asking them out. They don't know how to act with them, and they're afraid of being rejected.

Similarly, the authors assert that

> The assumption that a student's clothes are an invitation to teachers rather than male peers is wishful and muddled thinking by college professors. . . . Whether women wear high collars, dresses that flatten their breasts, skirts that hide their ankles, or veils that cover their faces, they are forced to endure sexual harassment. It did not begin with tube tops and short shorts, and it will not cease as long as society insists on believing that men cannot restrain their sexual

impulses and that women, by their dress, invite sexual advances.

Drawing on in-depth interviews with students, faculty members, deans, and department heads at colleges and universities across the United States, the authors researched all aspects of this issue, including the characteristics of academia that contribute to harassment, what a typical harasser is like, the effects of harassment on both male and female students, and the professional dilemmas faced by women faculty members. The authors also define sexual harassment by analyzing the power differences between students and teachers. Finally, they detail positive steps students, parents, administrators, and faculty members can take to diminish the incidence of sexual harassment. Although the book provides the kind of in-depth material suitable for an academic researcher, the general reader will also find it useful because it is written in a readable style and contains a lively mix of quotations from students, faculty, and administrators.

Eskenazi, Martin, and David Gallen. *Sexual Harassment: Know Your Rights!* New York: Carroll and Graf, 1992. 224p. Index, bibliography. ISBN 0-88184-816-6.

One of a crop of books that sprouted after the Clarence Thomas confirmation hearings, this work consists mainly of a collection of writings from other sources, including a reprint of a speech given by Anita Hill as part of a panel on sexual harassment and policymaking at the National Forum for Women in State Legislatures convened by the Center for the American Woman and Politics in late 1991. Another contributor is attorney and sexual harassment pioneer Catharine MacKinnon, with a reprint from her 1979 book *Sexual Harassment of Working Women* that details the incidence of sexual harassment and the experience of women who have been sexually harassed. *Sexual Harassment* includes special sections on federal employees and educational institutions; the National Organization for Women Legal Resource Kit on the issue is also reprinted. The EEOC guidelines, a question-and-answer section written by the authors, a list of resources, a bibliography, and an index complete the book. Although it clearly answers the most basic questions about what sexual harassment is and what to do about it and is laudable for its reasonable price ($9.95 in 1992), the book suffers from a somewhat jumbled composition of material from a wide variety of sources.

Estrich, Susan. **"Sex at Work."** *Stanford Law Review* 43 (April 1991): 813–862.

This major law review article by Susan Estrich, the Robert Kingsley professor of law and political science at the University of Southern California, traces the history of sexual harassment cases starting from the law on rape. As she states:

> While the crime of rape is centuries old, the federal cause of action for sexual harassment is an invention of our times. . . . The very existence of such a cause of action is a triumph for feminist scholars and practitioners, as well as for victims of sexual harassment.

Estrich is one of a handful of legal theorists who argue that the law is dominated by age-old male biases and who attempt to shape the direction of the law in terms relevant to women. In this article she addresses "the most persuasive and painful evidence of the durability of sexism in the law's judgment of the sexual relations of men and women." Rather than provide a legal treatise on sexual harassment, Estrich intends to "reveal the attitudes and understandings underlying legal doctrine in this area." In so doing, she seeks to change the future direction of the law. In her review of hundred of cases, Estrich finds a pervasive and sexist attitude; this bias assumes that sexual behavior at work is normal and even desirable. She argues that this attitude leads to unacceptable problems of proof for women in sexual harassment cases. She recommends, for example, that the requirement that the woman prove advances are "unwelcome" be eliminated as "gratuitous and personally humiliating." She does not believe courts should protect the right of a few to have "consensual" sex in the workplace (a right, she argues, few women, according to the studies, even want) at the cost of exposing the "overwhelming majority to oppression and indignity at work." She recommends that companies implement policies against sexual relationships among employees in the workplace, at least those between an employee and his or her direct supervisor. Although some may find Estrich's proposals for legal reform to be radical, the depth of her scholarship and analysis is impressive.

Farley, Lin. *Sexual Shakedown: The Sexual Harassment of Women on the Job.* New York: McGraw Hill, 1978. 228p. Index. ISBN 0-07-019957-4.

Now out of print, this classic book was the first published on the issue of sexual harassment and is still widely available in libraries and private collections. The work grew out of journalist Farley's experience teaching a class on women and work at Cornell in 1974. No research was readily available as class material, so

Farley turned to small "consciousness-raising groups." Although the groups consisted of women from different backgrounds, from affluent to poor, Farley found that

> When we had finished, there was an unmistakable pattern to our employment. Something absent in all the literature, something I had never seen although I had observed it many times, was newly exposed. Each one of us had already quit or had been fired from a job at least once because we had been made too uncomfortable by the behavior of men.

After naming the problems women faced on the job *sexual harassment,* Farley set about to learn how widespread the problem was and what the issue meant. Writing from a feminist perspective, Farley emphasizes that "job segregation" by sex is sustained largely by male sexual harassment, which, Farley believes, rolled back the momentum of affirmative action and created a female ghetto. Sexual harassment comes about because "assertions of male dominance are socially sanctioned." She concludes that job segregation is the primary mechanism in a capitalist society that maintains the superiority of men over women, because it enforces lower wages for women in the labor market, and lower wages encourage women to marry.

The book presents many individual women's stories and takes the position that much female turnover in jobs is caused by sexual harassment rather than the traditional stereotypes that women lack seriousness toward work, become pregnant, or leave because of sheer flightiness. Farley finds that the only hope is for women to become equal partners in the workforce. To do so, she suggests, women must organize, help each other to file claims of sexual harassment, if necessary, and take assertiveness courses. Farley provides historical and economic analyses, discusses legal remedies, and examines union and employer reactions to the issue of sexual harassment. The author's stance is unabashedly feminist; she views U.S. society as "first, last, and foremost a patriarchy" in which the historical function of sexual harassment has been to keep women "in line." Nevertheless, her arguments are supported by case studies, interviews, and extensive research documented by nine pages of endnotes.

Gay, Kathryn. *Rights and Respect: What You Need To Know About Gender Bias and Sexual Harassment.* Brookfield: Millbrook Press, 1995. 128p. Index. ISBN 1-56294-493-2.

Gay, the author of more than 50 books for young people, presents a well-researched guide to sexual harassment with a particular emphasis on sexual harassment in schools and colleges. The book includes extensive citations from cases, surveys, and statistics, as well as articles and public statements by writers on both sides of the issue. She includes personal stories of young people who have been harassed, most of whom requested anonymity. A clean writing style and a balanced perspective make this slender work a good overview of the subject. The discussion of some of the more controversial studies of harassment and gender bias in schools is especially useful and balanced. Bibliographical notes direct the reader to more detailed sources; a short but handy list of organizational resources is also included. Gay presents an overview of how the entire subject of sexual harassment is evolving yet emphasizes that training and education are resulting in changed attitudes. As one of her high school sources concluded after taking part in a sexual harassment prevention program, "Harassment is basic disrespect—so who needs it?"

Gutek, Barbara A. *Sex and the Workplace.* San Francisco: Jossey-Bass, 1985. 216p. Index, bibliography. ISBN 0-87589-656-1.

Gutek, a professor of psychology, business administration, and executive management and a key figure in sexual harassment research, publishes extensively on the dynamics of sexual harassment in the workplace. This book presents a review of a comprehensive program of research on sex at work and the interactions between women and men in the workplace. The book is based on findings from several studies, primarily from a large random-sample survey of 1,257 working men and women in Los Angeles County conducted over a six-year period beginning in 1978. This study revealed generalized information on sexual behavior— including sexual harassment—which workers have problems with harassment, how they react to harassment, and, most uniquely, the kinds of organizational conditions that foster such problems.

The book includes a historical overview of the issues of sex at work, how sex segregation of work and pay differentials between men and women affect the psychological experiences of working women and men, the characteristics of harassers, and the reactions of victims of harassment. Also presented are the verbatim comments of men and women who reported having experienced sexual overtures from the opposite sex. One of Gutek's most frequently quoted and important findings has been the giant gender gap in attitudes: Men consistently say they are flattered by sexual overtures from women at work, whereas women consistently say they are insulted by sexual propositions from men. Gutek, who is an academician, never offers an opinion without citing research that supports her view. One of her conclusions is that when men and women work together in equal numbers in the same jobs, virtually no social-sexual problems exist. By contrast, she finds, sexual harassment is much more prevalent when women and men are segregated in certain jobs. In general, Gutek concludes, women are hurt by sex in the workplace, but men are not: "Contrary to popular belief, women do not use sex at work nearly as frequently as men do." This is an essential, well-researched work.

Hodgson, Harriet. *Powerplays: How Teens Can Pull the Plug on Sexual Harassment.* Minneapolis: Deaconess Press, 1993. 164p. Index, bibliography. ISBN 0-925190-67-5.

Hodgson, a former teacher and the author of 12 books for parents and children, notes that at the time she wrote this book, little had been written about sexual harassment and teens, so she turned to teens and experts for firsthand information. She recounts her own experience of harassment by an eighth-grade teacher in her introduction to the book. The book covers the difference between flirting and harassment, why some students may be vulnerable, how harassers "prime" or prepare their victims for harassment and abuse, facts about harassers and victims, how to use anger as power, how to report harassment, and how to gather legal evidence, as well as ways parents can help and tips on prevention. Women's advocates may object to the section on what makes some teens more vulnerable to harassment or abuse. Although the writer does not "blame the victims," her emphasis on prevention through one's attitude and demeanor walks a thin line. This book is a thorough review of problems for teens, but its strength is its extensive citation of expert opinions and the many stories from actual teens.

Jones, Constance. *Sexual Harassment.* New York: Facts on File, 1996. 280p. Index, bibliography, appendix. ISBN 0-8160-3273-4.

This reference book, part of the Facts on File "Library in a Book" series, seeks to provide students, librarians, teachers, and other researchers with a concise and objective introduction to this controversial subject. The author strives to present all sides of the controversy and includes a historical survey, a chronology of events and court cases, a bibliography, and short biographies of notable individuals. The volume also includes an appendix that contains the full text of several important cases, EEOC guidelines, and laws. A list of organizations includes contact information and short descriptions of the groups' focus.

The extensive bibliography lists books, articles, and videos by subject in a somewhat confusing manner. Although the work purports to present an objective view of the complex problem of sexual harassment, the author takes a stance consistent with most feminist writers on the subject, making comments such as "sexual harassment, a form of discrimination meant to keep women 'in their place,' mirrors society's timeless violence against women." Many conservative commentators would disagree with that statement, as well as with others such as "sexual harassment is first about power and second about sex."

Klein, Freada. **"The 1988 Working Woman Sexual Harassment Survey Executive Report."** Cambridge, MA: Klein Associates, 1988. 36p.

This report summarizes the results of a survey conducted at the behest of *Working Woman* magazine; a shorter report was published in that periodical. In March 1988, a 49-item questionnaire was sent to the heads of human resources at the Fortune 500 service and manufacturing companies. This writing summarizes the methodology and results of the survey. One of the most important findings is that sexual harassment costs a typical Fortune 500 company $6.7 million per year ($282.53 per employee per year); these costs include turnover, absenteeism, reduced productivity, and the use of internal complaint mechanisms. In contrast, the report emphasizes that preventive steps can be taken for around $200,000. Another significant finding is that most incidents of sexual harassment are not reported to employers. The study also details the percentage of respondents that have written policies on harassment and the effect of top management's commitment to end sexual harassment. The report includes recommendations for human resource professionals. This survey is among those most often cited as providing reliable data on sexual harassment.

Langelan, Martha J. *Back Off! How To Confront and Stop Sexual Harassment and Harassers.* New York: Fireside, 1994. 380p. Bibliography, appendixes. ISBN 0-671-78856-6.

This book aims to be a "direct-action" guide to tactics for victims of sexual harassment. Langelan, past president of the D.C. Rape Crisis Center and an economist at the U.S. Department of Transportation, is also a self-defense instructor and conducts harassment-confrontation classes for women. She takes the position that traditional responses such as appeasement and aggression do not work in sexual harassment situations because of the dynamics of sex and power in those situations. Among the options she recommends are nonviolent personal confrontation techniques, group confrontations, administrative remedies, and formal lawsuits. Clearly, however, she favors self-help and informed confrontations over lawsuits and administrative complaints, with their attendant emotional and financial costs to the complainant.

The book is filled with emotional and empowering success stories about women—from an eight-year-old schoolgirl who successfully stopped a schoolyard bully from harassing her to an organized group of 50 women who confronted a dockworker about an attempted rape. Many of the stories will make women laugh or cheer, because many of the experiences are so common at work or on the street. A chapter on men as allies is especially interesting and unique in the literature on sexual harassment; it contains stories of men who have confronted other men who were harassing women.

One of the most memorable stories comes from Catharine MacKinnon, who wrote the book's introduction. When MacKinnon was in law school at Yale University, she lived in a "bombed-out" area of New Haven, where a "daily gauntlet" of men hung out around the corner bar. Tired of hearing sexual invitations in both English and Spanish, as well as lewd noises every time she walked by, she made up yellow cards that stated in both languages, "You have just offended a woman. This card has been chemically treated. Your prick will fall off in three days." For years afterward, when the men saw her coming all talking ceased, and they became "engrossed in their shoelaces or [in] the pigeons on the roof."

Extensive appendixes include descriptions of the law, resources for reading, and organizations. This is a useful, original work.

MacKinnon, Catharine A. *Sexual Harassment of Working Women.* New Haven: Yale University Press, 1979. 312p. Index. ISBN 0-300-02298-0 (cloth); 0-300-02299-9 (paper).

Written by a well-known feminist scholar, this book is widely credited as the first to articulate a legal basis for the thesis that sexual harassment is a form of sex discrimination and is, therefore, illegal. Published before most of the legal precedent on the issue, the book addresses whether sexual harassment could be considered a violation of the Equal Protection Clause of the Constitution or discrimination in employment because of sex under Title VII of the Civil Rights Act of 1964 or other laws. The work also considers whether a woman who quits her job because of sexual harassment should be entitled to unemployment compensation and whether an employer is responsible for the actions of its employees who engage in sexual harassment. This book was one of the first to frame the problem of sexual harassment within the context of the inferior position of women in the labor market, as well as to provide a factual account of the nature and extent of sexual harassment and to show how harassment grows out of and reinforces the traditional social roles of men and women in U.S. society. Because no systematic studies of sexual harassment had been conducted at the time the book was written, MacKinnon was forced to rely on evidence from women's observations of their own lives.

MacKinnon never waivers from her feminist stance. She states, for example, that "one thing wrong with sexual harassment (and with rape) is that it eroticizes women's submission. It acts out and deepens the powerlessness of women as a gender, *as women.*" Arguing that "an analysis of sexuality must not be severed and abstracted from analysis of gender," MacKinnon concludes that "women want to be equal and different, too," that is, we must accept that women in the workplace face different issues before we can correctly understand sexual harassment.

Although the book is out-of-date in this rapidly changing legal field and its complex style may be difficult reading for the layperson, the book is impressive because it was the first to attempt a legal analysis of the issue of sexual harassment. The book fulfills the author's expressed goal: "to bring to the law something of the reality of women's lives."

Martindale, Melanie. **"Sexual Harassment in the Military: 1988."** Arlington, VA: Defense Manpower Data Center, 1990. 56p.

This report summarizes the results of the first large-scale study of sexual harassment in the military, conducted in 1988. A wealth of data is presented, including the incidence of sexual harassment in the military; the context, location, and circumstances under which sexual harassment occurs; and the effectiveness of current military programs to prevent and deal with harassment. The major finding is that 64 percent of the women and 17 percent of the men in military service had experienced sexual harassment in the year preceding the study. The respondents were not asked directly and explicitly about "sexual harassment" but about specific, behaviorally described "uninvited and unwanted sexual attention" received at work. The presentation of the data and survey results is straightforward, complete with graphs and tables. The author does not take a position on the meaning of the results or make recommendations for future action.

Massachusetts Department of Education, Division of Curriculum and Instruction. **"Who's Hurt and Who's Liable: Sexual Harassment in Massachusetts Schools: A Curriculum and Guide for School Personnel."** Quincy: Massachusetts Department of Education, Bureau of Operational Support, 1986. 87p.

Developed by Nan Stein, a sex equity/civil rights specialist for the Massachusetts Department of Education, this curriculum was the first to be offered to secondary schools on the subject of sexual harassment and has been used as a model by schools across the United States. The curriculum provides information for all members of the school community: students, teachers, counselors, and administrators. The guide defines sexual harassment, explains the legal issues involved, describes administrative strategies, suggests student activities and classroom lessons, and includes other materials that relate to the issue. The curriculum takes the position that sexual harassment in schools is a pervasive problem and an obstacle to equal educational opportunities.

Mayer, Jane, and Jill Abramson. *Strange Justice: The Selling of Clarence Thomas.* Boston: Houghton Mifflin, 1994. 406p. Index. ISBN 0-395-63318-4.

Written by two respected writers for the *Wall Street Journal,* this book is based on hundreds of interviews with participants, friends, relatives, politicians, and attorneys who were a part of the Hill-Thomas controversy. The writers started with the same question that plagued most of the rest of the country: Who was telling the truth in this "he said–she said" controversy? After years of investigation, the writers, who are trained investigative reporters for the *Wall Street Journal*—which is known for its conservative editorial policy—concluded that the facts back Anita Hill's account.

Mayer and Abramson reached this conclusion because they identified many other potential witnesses who would have backed Hill's descriptions of Thomas's behavior, women who had experienced similar incidents and Thomas's friends who knew of his long-standing interest in pornography and his penchant for discussing that predilection in public. The authors also uncovered several other contemporaneous witnesses whom Hill had spoken with while the harassment was occurring who were never interviewed or called to testify.

This extensively documented book tells the story of a carefully orchestrated campaign by Thomas backers to make sure these witnesses would never be called and that Thomas would be confirmed, no matter what the cost. *Strange Justice* includes an almost hourly chronicle of the days leading up to the confirmation hearings, as well as of the hearings themselves.

The authors were granted a rare, extensive private interview with Anita Hill, although Thomas refused their repeated requests for an interview. In often shocking detail, the book reveals Thomas's ten-year campaign for a seat on the High Court and the doubts the White House expressed but then concealed as the Bush administration cleverly manipulated the Senate, collaborated with the religious right, and manufactured "grassroots" support from the black community. The authors also document Thomas's performance on the Court so far—a performance that has disappointed some of his supporters—including his public speeches to conservative groups and his officiation at Rush Limbaugh's wedding. Thomas told friends when he was confirmed at age 43 that he has no intention of stepping down early but plans to serve for 43 years. It will take him that long, he stated, to get even.

Whether readers agree or disagree with the authors' conclusions, there is much to admire in this exhaustively researched and brilliantly written book.

McIntyre, Douglas I. *Sexual Harassment in Government.* Ann Arbor, MI: University Microfilms, 1984. 342p. Bibliography.

This Ph.D. thesis, originally submitted to the Department of Government at Florida State University, is a statistical survey on the issue of sexual harassment, based on a random sample of female employees of the state of Florida. Unlike many studies that have been conducted on sexual harassment, this one followed scientific, objective survey techniques. In addition, the thesis reviewed national information on sexual harassment—including case law, other surveys, and the EEOC guidelines—and considered recommendations for national policy and the obligations of, and suggested action by, employers. The book is particularly useful as a model of how a sexual harassment survey should be conducted, because it includes extensive discussions of the methodology and the original survey material.

Meyer, Mary Coeli, Inge M. Berchtold, Jeannenne L. Oestreich, and Frederick J. Collins. *Sexual Harassment at Work.* New York: Petrocelli Books, 1981. 200p. Bibliography. ISBN 0-89433-156-6.

This book, written from a management perspective, presents a good introduction to the scope of the problem of sexual harassment and is one of the first comprehensive source books on the subject. Sparked by the 1980 EEOC regulations that first suggested that organizations could be held legally responsible for sexual harassment, the book defines the problem and provides case studies, sample policy statements for organizations, suggested awareness training, tips on how employees can handle harassment, and lists of organizations, legal precedent, and other resources. Although somewhat dated and apparently out of print, the book is widely available in most libraries.

Women activists, however, may be put off by the management-oriented tone of the book, which presents as many examples of sexually harassed men as of harassed women (other experts have concluded that sexual harassment by women is rare) and continually emphasizes that the harassee has a responsibility to communicate clearly with the harasser. The book also rejects the feminist argument that sexual harassment is another example of a purposeful attempt to oppress women, arguing instead that it is a sometimes innocent and baffled response by men to confusing social evolution and technological change; that is, harassment is perpetrated by those who cannot adapt or respond to changing roles. The book remains one of the few works to acknowledge and emphasize the complexity of the issue of harassment, stressing that men and women may view the same situation differently without pointing the finger at easy victims or villains.

Morris, Celia. *Bearing Witness: Sexual Harassment and Beyond— Everywoman's Story.* Boston: Little, Brown, 1994. 326p. Index. ISBN 0-316-58422-3.

Bearing Witness constitutes a series of Morris's personal essays—powerfully told—about the stories of many women who have been sexually harassed. Morris's interviews are both moving and terrifying. From Anita Hill to heretofore anonymous factory workers, Morris gives a voice to the headlines and legal cases. Arguing that women have moved from "what did she do to deserve it" and "why did she stay" to "why did he do it" and "what can we do to change all that," Morris submits that women and men must work together to solve this collective social issue. To press the pace of change on important women's issues, Morris argues, women must "learn to use the collective 'we.'"

Morris states that she started writing this book after she and millions of women around the country had experienced a "shock of recognition" in the wake of the Hill-Thomas hearings and had "admitted openly that men could be very dangerous to our health." She also realized that men and women had experienced the hearings differently. What was needed, she decided, was "corroborating testimony: stories that might demonstrate how common—how even tame—Hill's initial experiences with Clarence Thomas had been." She looked at neither polls nor surveys but searched instead for "authentic voices." This book is the result of her nationwide search. Clearly writing from the perspective that the women's accounts are as true as they are common, Morris gives a literary voice to this side of the debate on sexual harassment.

Neville, Kathleen. *Corporate Attractions: An Inside Account of Sexual Harassment.* Washington, DC: Acropolis Books Ltd., 1990. 301p. Index. ISBN 0-87491-952-5 (cloth); 0-87491-953-3 (paper).

Kathleen Neville was an advertising sales executive and reporter with a Buffalo, New York, television station in 1981 when she was sexually harassed by her boss, who demanded sexual favors in return for continued employment. This book is an unflinching and engrossing account of the six-year legal battle that ensued when she was fired after she refused his advances. Neville was twice victimized—once by her harasser and then by the legal system—as a federal district court judge and an appellate court found that she had been sexually harassed but was fired for unrelated reasons, even though she had years of outstanding performance evaluations.

Neville offers tips for other victims on reporting the initial harassment, communicating with the harasser and co-workers, and selecting a competent attorney—with the hope that others will be able to avoid her painful experience. She also details "new rules for the workplace" to help both men and women workers to avoid harassment claims. The book exposes the physical, emotional, and financial costs of both the harassment and the lengthy legal process. Neville learned the hard way that she, not her harasser, ended up on trial. This account will make any victim think twice before pursuing a harassment claim.

Omilian, Susan M. *Sexual Harassment in Employment.* Wilmette, IL: Callaghan, 1987. 177p. Index. ISBN 0-8366-0013-4.

Although this book is aimed at attorneys representing a plaintiff or a defendant in a lawsuit based on sexual harassment, the clear language—mostly free of legalese—makes it accessible to the layperson. This comprehensive report analyzes most of the court decisions up to the time of its publication that had considered the issue of sexual harassment and includes a consideration of questions yet to be answered (in 1987) by the courts. Omilian also discusses a long list of cases in which the victim could not prove a sexual harassment claim and includes tips for both sides in litigating a sexual harassment case. The book lacks a glossary of legal terms, which would have made it even more useful to a layperson, and the text may provide more detail than is needed by the average researcher. Still, the work offers a wealth of information about individual cases and legal analysis. Unfortunately, because of its publication date, this work does not include more recent sexual harassment cases that have significantly changed the face of the law in this area.

Paludi, Michele A., and Richard B. Barickman. *Academic and Workplace Sexual Harassment: A Resource Manual.* Albany: State University of New York Press, 1991. 215p. Index. ISBN 0-7914-0829-9 (cloth); 0-7914-8030-2 (paper).

Paludi is a research psychologist who has published a number of works on sexual harassment, developmental psychology, and women's issues. She directed the Research Collective on Sexual Harassment at Hunter College. Barickman helped to establish the Hunter panel on sexual harassment; he has also written on the issue of sexual harassment and gender. Despite the title, this work focuses mainly on sexual harassment on campus rather than in the workplace. Written from a feminist perspective, the book takes the position, for example, that there is no such thing as a consensual sexual relationship between a student and a faculty member because of the disparity in power between the two. The authors provide extensive results from various studies, such as the incidence of sexual harassment claims and the psychological impact of harassment. The work is important and useful because of the depth of research offered. The book is written in an academic style but suffers from a lack of clear organization; the writers constantly interrupt the text in a confusing manner with tables and study results. In addition, much of the book consists of articles previously published in other journals, which results in some repetition.

Petrocelli, William, and Barbara Kate Repa. *Sexual Harassment on the Job: What It Is and How To Stop It.* Berkeley, CA: Nolo Press, 1992. 198p. Index. ISBN 0-87337-1771-1.

This book is part of a series published by Nolo Press on "how-to" legal issues. The authors provide a clear guide to understanding the laws on sexual harassment, deciding whether an employee has a claim, following the complaint process, and even such rarely covered matters as reading legal citations and managing an attorney. Although the book does include sample sexual harassment policies and tips for employers on finding the right training consultant or materials, the focus is on employees who believe they may have been harassed. The language is easy for the layperson to understand. The book includes a useful list of resources, as well as a state-by-state compendium of laws relating to harassment. An excellent guide through the legal thicket of laws and policies in this area, the book is well designed and includes lively quotations from a variety of experts and commentators on the subject of sexual harassment. The authors take the position that sexual harassment is not about sex but about power: "Sexual harassment is a male tactic to make a woman vulnerable in the workplace. It often works."

Phelps, Timothy M., and Helen Winternitz. *Capitol Games.* New York: Hyperion, 1992. 458p. Index, bibliographical note. ISBN 1-56282-916-5.

Timothy Phelps, the *Newsday* Supreme Court reporter who broke the story on Anita Hill's allegations of sexual harassment against Clarence Thomas, and coauthor Helen Winternitz, an award-winning journalist and author, present a blow-by-blow description of events leading up to the hearing on Thomas's nomination and the behind-the-scenes maneuvering during and after the hearings. A classic piece of investigative reporting, *Capitol Games* answers questions not covered by the televised proceedings, including why Angela Wright, who had also accused Thomas of sexual harassment, did not testify and why the Democratic senators failed to control the hearing process. The book also provides the backgrounds of and disagreements among the legal and public relations teams that advised both Hill and Thomas. Insider accounts of how Thomas positioned himself as a black conservative, how he was selected as a candidate for the Supreme Court, and how the radical right backed his cause provide fascinating background information on this justice. Hill's legal career and family background are also scrutinized. The authors take no position on the issue of who was telling the truth during the hearings but focus instead on providing readers with enough facts and information to allow them to make their own decisions. The book serves as a chronicle of the nomination spectacle that captivated the American public in fall 1991, as well as providing an engrossing account of the mix of race, sex, and politics that fueled the proceedings.

Rutter, M. D. *Sex, Power, and Boundaries: Understanding and Preventing Sexual Harassment.* New York: Bantam Books, 1996. 255p. Index, bibliography. ISBN 0-553-09954-X.

Rutter, a physician and psychiatrist with professional expertise in sexual and boundary incidents (he authored *Sex in the Forbidden Zone: When Men in Power—Therapists, Doctors, Clergy, Teachers, and Others—Betray Women's Trust* [1989]), draws on actual incidents, in-depth research, and legal decisions to answer questions about what constitutes appropriate behavior in the face of rapidly changing sexual politics, boundaries, and laws. He reviews the basics on sexual harassment from a legal perspective and discusses training options and policy. Because of his training in psychology, Rutter takes more of a mediation perspective in resolving disputes and suggests a training model whereby the men and women in a work group agree on what constitutes appropriate behavior for that organization. Many attorneys and human resource professionals avoid such an approach because it can lead to inconsistent results in a large organization and to the possibility of a failure to proscribe legally actionable behavior.

Rutter's main contribution to the sexual harassment literature is to provide an explanation of the problem from a psychological perspective, including the damage harassment can cause, as well as an examination of the issue of boundaries and an explanation of how different people and cultures can have such different perceptions of what constitutes appropriate personal boundaries. The notes include a wealth of citations to the psychological and medical literature on this subject.

Segrave, Kerry. *The Sexual Harassment of Women in the Workplace, 1600 to 1993.* Jefferson. NC: MacFarland and Company. 272p. Index, bibliography. ISBN 0-7864-0007-2.

This unique book seeks to document the history of sexual harassment. Starting from the premise that most working women will experience sexual harassment at some point during their working lives, the author finds that this premise "was true as far back as one can see." This extensive work includes fascinating bits of historical perspective that are not documented in any other source. For example, Segrave quotes industrial psychologist Ordway Tead, who wrote in 1918 that the presence of women in the workplace was a sexual fringe benefit for male co-workers and supervisors. Tead placed sex along with security and recognition as major incentives for male workers.

Segrave documents the harassment of working women as domestics and as mine and factory workers during wars and before and after the Industrial Revolution. She also considers the various psychological and historical perspectives of each era on why sexual attention in the workplace was or was not considered a problem. Finally, she documents a pervasive thread that indicates that this kind of attention is about an uncontrollable male libido rather than male power.

Siegel, Deborah, and Marina Budhos. *Sexual Harassment: Research and Resources.* Revised ed. New York: National Council for Research on Women, 1995. 90p. Bibliography, appendixes. ISBN 1-880547-20-1.

Originally published in 1992 and revised twice since then, most recently in 1995, this useful research guide contains an overview of the definitions, laws, surveys, and other research available on the topic of sexual harassment. This report contains some of the most up-to-date references available on the issue of sexual harassment. Much of the text consists of quotations from experts who were interviewed especially for this publication; it therefore offers material not found in any other book on the subject. Extensive appendixes provide information on researchers and expert witnesses, organizations, conferences, and even guidelines for organizational forums on the issue. A selected bibliography and list of available videos is also included. This book is a useful compilation of information on sexual harassment.

Stein, Nan, Nancy Marshall, and Linda R. Troop. **"Secrets in Public: Sexual Harassment in Our Schools."** Wellesley, MA: Wellesley College Center for Research on Women, 1993. 26p.

This volume contains the results of a study conducted by *Seventeen* magazine for the Wellesley College Center for Research on Women and the NOW Legal Defense and Education Fund. Over 4,200 girls completed and returned the surveys published in *Seventeen* in September 1992. Although critics of the survey methodology may argue that its accuracy is questionable because the girls were self-selected, the numbers mirror the more scientific AAUW study discussed earlier in this chapter. For example, the earlier study, like the latter, also found that 89 percent of respondents had experienced some kind of harassment. Almost 99 percent of the respondents to the *Seventeen* survey were girls, and they were overwhelmingly (89 percent) Caucasian.

One of the most interesting results this book reports is that the students, when asked what they thought schools should do about harassment, suggested taking the matter much more seriously and providing security. The report has many useful quotes from respondents. Nan Stein was one of the first researchers in the country to identify, study, and research student-to-student harassment. She has been published extensively in educational journals, has written and published her own classwork outline, and is frequently quoted by the popular media.

Strauss, Susan. *Sexual Harassment and Teens: A Program for Positive Change.* Minneapolis: Free Spirit, 1992. 149p. Index, bibliography. ISBN 0-915793-44-X.

This book, designed to sensitize students, faculty, and staff to the issue of the sexual harassment of teens, includes a complete course for sexual harassment training designed for grades 7 through 12. Strauss is a trainer and organizational development specialist with a hospital in Minneapolis who has also designed and directed educational programs on sexual harassment and assisted in developing school policies on the issue. The book includes 40 reproducible forms and handouts, as well as a sexual harassment survey. The curriculum is designed to help adults identify and solve sexual harassment problems in any school, community organization, youth group, or other gathering of young people. Case studies, activities, and a review of the laws and guidelines on sexual harassment, as well as suggested policies, procedures, and a list of resources, are provided. Designed for educators, this book covers the basic information needed to teach sexual harassment awareness to young people and provides an actual curriculum presented in a clear, concise format. The program was developed as a result of studies conducted in Minnesota schools, which revealed that 50 percent of teenage girls reported having been verbally and physically harassed at school.

United States Department of Defense, Office of the Inspector General. *The Tailhook Report: The Official Inquiry into the Events of Tailhook '91.* New York: St. Martin's Press, 1993. Appendixes. ISBN 0-312-10392-8.

Subtitled "The Shocking Details behind the Scandal That Has Rocked the Nation," a title bestowed presumably by the publisher rather than the government, this report provides the details of the September 1991 convention at which over 4,000 U.S. Navy and Marine Corps aviation officers met at a hotel in Las Vegas for the 35th Annual Tailhook Symposium. According to the report, during that weekend parties and drunken behavior raged out of control and caused widespread damage to the hotel. In addition, at least 90 victims of indecent assault were identified, 140 officers were referred for possible court-martial or disciplinary action, and several top navy officials were demoted, transferred, or resigned. The report describes in fresh detail the scope and investigative methodology, the background of the Tailhook association, the witnesses, navy cooperation with the investigation, the assaults— including the so-called gauntlet—and the Tailhook ritual behavior, such as the infamous "ballwalking." The report concludes with a frank discussion of officer attitudes and leadership issues, including a section on the "failure of leadership." Extensive appendixes range from the convention agenda to the actual witness statements and assault reports. *The Tailhook Report* is an important historical record of this event.

United States Merit Systems Protection Board. *Sexual Harassment in the Federal Workplace: Is It a Problem?* Washington, DC: U.S. Government Printing Office, 1981. 202p. Bibliography, appendixes.

This study, which was mandated by Congress, was the first on this topic to be scientifically designed and to draw on a nationwide sample. Around 23,000 federal workers were sent questionnaires in 1980; over 20,000 responded. Replete with statistical data, tables, and graphs, this pivotal report examines the extent and impact of sexual harassment in the federal workplace, its victims and perpetrators, awareness of the problem, and the perceived effectiveness of various remedies. The study found that harassment was widespread in the federal workplace: 42 percent of female employees and 15 percent of males reported experiencing harassment during the two-year period studied. Extensive details are presented on the characteristics of both victims and harassers, as well as the costs of harassment to the government and its effect on victims. Appendixes include the research methodology, the survey questionnaire, official policy documents, and a survey of the literature. A 14-page annotated bibliography is included.

———. **"Sexual Harassment in the Federal Government: An Update."** Washington, DC: U.S. Government Printing Office, 1988. 49p.

This report updates the more detailed 1981 offering described in the previous entry. For this study, a questionnaire was sent to a representative cross-section of approximately 13,000 federal employees, of whom 8,523 responded. The report found an increase in employees' inclination to define certain types of behavior as sexual harassment but no decrease in the amount of harassment experienced. By the time of this study, all federal agencies reported having sexual harassment policies in place. The report includes an update of the material presented in the 1981 volume, as well as new material on agency actions taken to reduce sexual harassment and a review of the case law. Recommendations for further government action are offered.

————. **"Sexual Harassment in the Federal Workplace: Trends, Progress, Continuing Challenges."** Washington, DC: U.S. Government Printing Office, 1995. 73p.

In this updated version of previous studies, the Merit Systems Protection Board surveyed federal workers in 1994 about their views and experiences of sexual harassment, their attitudes toward and beliefs about relationships in the workplace, the effects sexual harassment has had on them, the efforts they used to combat harassment, and the programs agencies used to combat harassment. Where applicable, the report compares the findings to those in the surveys published in 1981 and 1988. The present report concludes that although the workplace is more sensitive to the issue of sexual harassment, the problem has "by no means disappeared." The survey found that 44 percent of women and 19 percent of men responding had experienced unwanted attention during the previous two years—a finding similar to that in the study published in 1988. The present report states that this increase may be attributed to increased awareness of what constitutes sexual harassment, which has led to a higher level of reporting. Only 6 percent of those who receive such attention report it. The report concludes that sexual harassment cost the government an estimated $327 million during the two-year period studied. Among the more interesting findings was the fact that most employees do not think the emphasis on sexual harassment has made their workplaces uncomfortable, contrary to the predictions of many critics of sexual harassment policies and training.

Wagner, Ellen J. *Sexual Harassment in the Workplace: How To Prevent, Investigate, and Resolve Problems in Your Organization.* New York: American Management Association, 1992. 148p. Index, glossary. ISBN 0-8144-7787-9.

Wagner, an attorney and human resource consultant, presents a useful guide for management that is refreshingly free from legal jargon. The book includes a step-by-step approach to investigating a claim of sexual harassment within an organization. It also covers avoiding pitfalls, such as defamation or wrongful discharge claims; deciding on appropriate discipline or counseling; instituting termination procedures; handling personnel files and reference requests; and preventing future claims. Included are sample policy statements and interview questions, training guides, a complete glossary of legal terms, and a straightforward explanation of legal precedent free from legalese. The book includes one of the few discussions of the relatively new legal claim of "paramour preference" and explains how sexual favoritism can open the door to third-party claims of sexual discrimination.

Webb, Susan L. *Step Forward: Sexual Harassment in the Workplace.* New York: Mastermedia, 1991. 116p. ISBN 0-942381-51-2.

Susan Webb is a consultant and trainer who specializes in the area of human relations. She frequently provides expert witness testimony and training on the subject of sexual harassment and conducts investigations into allegations of harassment and other interpersonal conflicts. This slim volume is an easy-to follow manual that discusses what employees and management need to know about harassment. Filled with interactive quizzes, this book offers answers to the standard questions on the issue, including "What is sexual harassment," "How can I be sure it's sexual harassment," "Whose fault is it," and "Don't women harass men, too?" Included are suggestions for limiting liability, training guidelines, and an analysis of future trends. The book provides a number of quick lists, such as "a six-step program for managers to help them stop sexual harassment," "the ten factors for assessing an incident," and "how to conduct an investigation." The history of sexual harassment and the important cases on the issue are also discussed briefly. This is one of the few books that includes a survey of sexual harassment studies from around the world. The book was published just after the Clarence Thomas confirmation hearings, and it mentions the controversy and comments on the rise in the level of interest in sexual harassment those hearings engendered. In a section about the future, Webb mentions that many who work in the human rights field believe that in poor economic times, all forms of harassment and discrimination occur more frequently. A section on the costs of harassment summarizes some of the more dramatic awards to those who have won cases involving harassment claims.

Zimmerman, Jean. *Tailspin: Women at War in the Wake of Tailhook.* New York: Doubleday, 1995. 336p. Index, bibliography. ISBN 0-385-47789-9.

This well-written, lively, and engrossing book documents the U.S. Navy's history that led to the Tailhook scandal. This full-length chronicle of the scandal and its aftermath explores the link between the convention in Las Vegas and the legal ban on women in combat. Zimmerman traces the role of female warriors throughout history as she introduces today's women jet pilots, for whom the term *armor-plated ceiling* has been more than a metaphor. She also profiles these women's male counterparts and describes and brings alive for the reader mixed-gender ships and the flight lines on which navy men and women fight a unique kind of gender war. This book is sure to be read for years to come as an important work of both military history and feminist scholarship.

Related Gender Issues

American Association of University Women Educational Foundation. *How Schools Shortchange Girls.* Washington, DC: American Association of University Women Educational Foundation, 1992. 116p. ISBN 0-8106-2501-6.

In this significant report, which was researched by the Wellesley College Center for Research on Women, the AAUW presents a persuasive and startling examination of how girls are disadvantaged in U.S. schools, grades K–12. The book includes recommendations for educators and policymakers, as well as concrete strategies for change. Ironically, AAUW's first national study—undertaken in 1885—was initiated to dispel the commonly accepted myth that higher education was harmful to women's health. This more recent report explodes the truth behind another myth—namely, that girls and boys receive equal educations. The findings support the premise that Title IX of the 1972 Education Amendments, which prohibits discrimination in educational institutions that receive federal funds, has not solved the problem of equal education. The report is a synthesis of the available research at the time on the subject of girls in school and presents compelling evidence that girls are not receiving the same quality of education as boys. The research documents a wide range of findings—for example, that teachers are more likely to call on boys than on girls and that the curriculum lacks positive women role models. One of the recommendations of the report is that schools need to implement policies against sex discrimination and sexual harassment to ensure equal educational opportunities for girls.

Davidson, Nicholas. *The Failure of Feminism.* Buffalo, NY: Prometheus Books, 1988. 392p. Index, bibliography. ISBN 0-87975-408-4.

Nicholas Davidson, a writer with degrees in history from the University of Massachusetts at Amherst and the University of Chicago, presents this extensively annotated assault on feminism.

He answers the question "Has feminism failed?" with a resounding "yes." Davidson argues that some of our most basic assumptions about gender originated in the scientific confusion of the nineteenth century and submits that we need a new recognition of the centrality of both masculinity and femininity in the human experience. If we fail "to achieve a workable gender balance," he argues, our civilization may not survive. "It is not enough to tolerate gender," writes Davidson, "we must celebrate it." After he explores the history of feminism, Davidson insists that the feminist perspective has led to such ills as a lack of spontaneity in sex and frigidity in women. Although he does not directly address the issue of sexual harassment, he argues that male aggression in sex and other areas is a force of nature that will never change.

Davidson's book is offered here for its thorough and widely read critique of the feminist perspective, which holds that "the human condition is a product of men's oppression of women. Women must resist this oppression by refusing to submit to sex on men's terms," and his conclusion that "the belief that gender is a purely cultural construct is fast becoming a peculiar archaism." He draws on examples such as the Israeli kibbutzim to argue that even there the attempt to eliminate sex roles has failed. One puzzling note appears in one of his final conclusions: that women (although apparently not men!) should have the choice of whether to work full-time or part-time or to be full-time housekeepers. Many feminists would argue that this is what they have been working toward all along. *The Failure of Feminism* is a contentious book that is sure to provoke discussion and thought.

Faludi, Susan. *Backlash: The Undeclared War against American Women.* New York: Crown, 1991. 552p. Index. ISBN 0-517-57698-8.

Faludi, a Pulitzer Prize–winning journalist, presents a witty and exhaustively researched indictment of the media and the political and legal establishments, which she alleges have manufactured a backlash of public opinion in response to the gains women have made since the early 1970s. She submits a persuasive account of how such supposed phenomena as unmarried and unhappy women in their thirties, the rise in female infertility, and a return to the fashions of the 1950s are all attempts to keep women in their place and to, in effect, punish females for the few advances that have been achieved. Although the book contains few specifics on sexual harassment, Faludi does discuss several major cases and details the retaliation all of the women in her examples have suffered for daring to come forward with sexual harassment claims. More important, however, the book serves as one view of the context in which sexual harassment claims are brought and validates the feminist position that holds that perpetrators of sexual harassment are intentionally seeking to thwart the economic and professional progress of women. This controversial book quickly became a classic in the field of women's studies.

Farrell, Warren. *The Myth of Male Power.* New York: Simon and Schuster, 1993. 512p. Index, bibliography. ISBN 0-671-79349.

Farrell is the only man to have been elected three times to the board of the National Organization for Women, although he no longer serves on the board. Described as "the Gloria Steinem of men's liberation" by the *Chicago Tribune*, he is also the author of *The Liberated Man* and the best-seller *Why Men Are the Way They Are*, a professor, and a popular workshop leader. In this work, which is sure to enrage some feminists, Dr. Farrell argues that male power is largely a myth because of the special obligations imposed on men, such as the expectation that men will support a family and be drafted. Farrell defines *power* as "control over one's own life" and concludes that the male's obligation to earn more money than a woman if he wants her to love him does not lead to power or control over the man's life. He asserts that because of historical sex roles, neither men nor women have had control over their lives. The work is included in this listing because of Farrell's widely publicized thesis that a woman's fantasy of meeting and being taken care of by a successful man fuels much of men's drive to succeed and their resulting insensitivity.

On the issue of harassment, Farrell contends that women expect to date, and even marry, men whom they meet at work; he believes this expectation leads to confused signals in the workplace. As an example, he points to the many popular romance novels in which the heroine initially resists the advances of her supervisor or boss but eventually submits to him and lives happily ever after. Men, he contends, are confused about how to interpret the mixed messages they receive at work, which may lead to claims of sexual harassment. When the issue of sexual harassment initially surfaced, he argues, we were told "men don't 'get it'" when, in fact, *neither* sex "gets it." Men do not understand women's fears of harassment, which stem from their passive role; women do not understand men's fears of sexual rejection, which stem from the initiating role. Both sexes are so preoccupied with their own vulnerability that neither sex "'gets' the other sex's vulnerability." Farrell devotes an entire chapter to sexual harassment, asserting that

When . . . women complained they were being sexually
harassed, the government radically expanded its protection of women by expanding its prosecution of men.
Simultaneously, construction sites with shaky scaffold-
ing and coal mines with shaky ceilings were left unin-
spected—and the men left unprotected. In brief, men
were left unprotected from premature death while
women were protected from premature flirtation.

Allowing claims for sexual harassment, Farrell argues, is a double-
edged sword for women, because

Paying an equal wage to a woman who is a few hundred times more likely than a man to sue for harass-
ments and hazards is not to an employer's advantage.
*The overprotection of women and the underprotection of
men, then, soon leads to discrimination against hiring
women* [emphasis in original].

The book is loaded with statistics and footnotes with which
Farrell attempts to prove his points. Although some of Farrell's
positions and examples may be exaggerated or calculated to provoke, the book is one of the few that questions the wisdom and
effectiveness of government legislation against sexual harassment
and is thus an important contribution to the debate and guaran-
teed to inspire lively discussion.

Paglia, Camille. *Sexual Personae.* London and New Haven, CT:
Yale University Press, 1990. 718p. Index. ISBN 0-300-04396-1.

Paglia, an associate professor of humanities at Philadelphia
College of the Performing Arts, burst upon the scene in 1990 with
this scholarly book and received a siege of media publicity. The
author recycles an ancient idea: Biology is destiny, or perhaps,
testosterone is destiny. Yet she presents this premise with a creative twist and a fierce intelligence. Although she does not specifically focus on sexual harassment, she does take the position that
men's sexual aggression is natural and inevitable, thus rejecting
the feminist notion that rape is about power rather than a natural
expression of sexuality.

Modern feminism's most naive formulation is its asser-
tion that rape is a crime of violence but not of sex, that
it is merely power masquerading as sex. But sex *is*
power, and all power is inherently aggressive. Rape is

male power fighting female power. It is no more to be excused than is murder or any other assault on another's civil rights. Society is woman's protection against rape, not, as some feminists absurdly maintain, the cause of rape. . . . Therefore, the rapist is a man with too little socialization rather than too much.

In this densely written, difficult, but original work, Paglia argues that society, rather than causing sex discrimination, sexual harassment, and rape, holds these natural forces in check. In general, she identifies some of the major patterns that have endured with regard to sex and sex roles in Western culture, from ancient Egypt and Greece to the present. She discusses sex and nature as brutal, demonic forces, and she criticizes feminists for exhibiting sentimentality or wishful thinking about the causes of rape, violence, and poor relations between the sexes.

Feminists, seeking to drive power relations out of sex, have set themselves against nature. Sex *is* power. Identity is power. In western culture, there are no nonexploitative relationships. Everyone has killed in order to live. . . . The sexes are eternally at war. There is an element of attack, of search-and-destroy in male sex, in which there will always be a potential for rape. There is an element of entrapment in female sex, a subliminal manipulation leading to physical and emotional infantilization of the male. . . . It is in nature's best interests to goad dominant males into indiscriminate spreading of their seed.

This is a much-discussed book, unique in the literature on sex roles and gender issues.

———. *Sex, Art, and American Culture.* New York: Vintage Books, 1992. 337p. Index. ISBN 0-697-74101-1 (paper).

In this follow-up to *Sexual Personae,* Paglia presents a series of essays on topics that range from Madonna to Anita Hill, from date rape to MTV. She continues to provide quotes for the media by denouncing feminism as Puritanism or describing a fraternity party as "Testosterone Flats" while emphasizing a woman's responsibility in instances of date rape. On the issue of Anita Hill, she applauds the idea of sexual harassment guidelines but frets that the hostile workplace category of sexual harassment claims means "women are being returned to their old status of delicate flowers who must be protected from assault by male lechers. It is anti-feminist to ask for special treatment for women." Anita Hill, Paglia argues, is "no feminist heroine. . . . If Anita Hill was thrown for a loop by sexual banter, that's her problem. If by the age of 26 and a graduate of Yale Law School she could find no convincing way to signal her displeasure and disinterest, that's her deficiency." Paglia's controversial views on date rape have raised the hackles of many feminists who believe she is simply blaming the victim by insisting that women must be more cautious in dating situations. The book is sure to fuel debate on the issues Paglia considers.

Roiphe, Katie. *The Morning After: Sex, Fear, and Feminism on Campus.* Boston: Little, Brown, 1993. 180p. ISBN 0-316-75431-5.

In this witty and well-written look at the excesses of feminism on college campuses in the late 1980s and the 1990s, Katie Roiphe joins the growing number of critics of campus speech codes and policies on date rape, pornography, and other feminist campaigns. Roiphe graduated from Harvard University in 1990 and is pursuing a Ph.D. in English at Princeton University. Roiphe was raised by feminist parents. When she arrived at Harvard in fall 1986, she found the feminism she had been taught to believe in had been radically transformed. She believes the movement that had once signaled strength and courage now seems lodged in a foundation of weakness and fear.

She found a "culture captivated by victimization," as well as a new bedroom politics that she found cloaked in outdated assumptions about the way men and women experience sex. She criticizes the "rape-crises" feminists and the growing campus concerns about sexual harassment as placing women back into the role of their grandmothers—as poor wilting violets who need the protection of the authorities. This is a controversial, engaging book.

Tannen, Deborah. *You Just Don't Understand: Women and Men in Conversation.* New York: William Morrow, 1990. 330p. Index, bibliography. ISBN 0-688-07822-2.

Dr. Tannen, a sociolinguist, professor, and author of a number of scholarly books, has written a readable and popular account, based on evidence from her own extensive studies, of why and how conversations between men and women resemble cross-cultural communication. Tannen's thesis is that from an early age, girls play with one best friend or a small group and use language to seek confirmation and reinforce intimacy, whereas boys use language to protect their independence and negotiate their status in large-group activities. Using the same conversational styles as adults, women and men hear completely different things in the same conversation. Backed by lively examples and anecdotes, this book suggests that understanding can do much to help bridge the gap between the two sexes, as well as to help men and women find a common language for communication.

Tannen, an internationally recognized scholar, has managed to translate her academic work into books and articles that are accessible to the general reading public. This best-selling book is a must for anyone who is attempting to understand how men and women may have different ideas about what is—or is not—sexual harassment and why it occurs. As Tannen concludes, "If you understand gender differences in what I call conversational style, you may not be able to prevent disagreements from arising, but you stand a better chance of preventing them from spiraling out of control."

Related Legal Issues

Friedman, Scott E. *Sex Law: A Legal Sourcebook on Critical Sexual Issues for the Non-Lawyer.* Jefferson, NC: McFarland, 1990. 167p. Index. ISBN 0-89950-540-6.

Intended to be a resource guide for lawyers and nonlawyers alike, this book steers the reader through the complicated maze of laws that govern individual sexual rights and responsibilities in the United States. As the author notes,

> This maze has grown wider and more complex over the past several decades as society grapples with the continuing sexual revolution that poses many novel and often unexpected problems for individuals and society at large. It seems to me that the legal aspects emerging from the sexual revolution are not generally understood, and many of us are often confused about our legal rights and responsibilities concerning sexually related subjects.

Friedman, a lawyer practicing in New York, clearly and concisely tackles such thorny issues as abortion, surrogate motherhood, protection of fetuses from their pregnant mothers' drug and alcohol abuse, and legal remedies for victims of AIDS and sexually transmitted diseases. Sex discrimination and sexual harassment are also addressed. The rights of gays and lesbians, paternity, and other issues are also clarified. Leading judicial precedents on these subjects are discussed, and many citations to case and statutory authority are supplied to assist readers who would like to engage in further research. A summary question-and-answer format starts each section to give readers useful, quick answers to their questions on the particular subject. Although, as the author emphasizes, no single book can substitute for conducting legal research on primary sources of state or federal laws, this book serves as a useful aid for placing the entire issue of sexual harassment into the broader context of sexual issues in the law.

Olsen, Walter. *The Litigation Explosion.* New York: Dutton, 1991. 388p. Index, biographical references. ISBN 0-525-24911-7.

Olsen, a graduate of Yale University who also studied economics at UCLA, is a senior fellow at the Manhattan Institute. In this book, he traces what happened when "America unleashed the lawsuit." He argues that in the early 1970s, Americans saw lawsuits as a last resort; today they are the world's most litigious people. In *The Litigation Explosion,* Olsen explains how this trend developed, what it means, who profits, and how it can be contained. He uses actual lawsuits to make his points. Aggressive lawyers who draw out lawsuits so that even innocent defendants are forced to settle, and expert witnesses who will say anything for a fee, are particularly responsible for the growth of costly and unnecessary litigation, Olsen believes. Although he does not mention sexual harassment cases in particular, he argues that the law should not be used as a tool to correct every perceived social ill.

Interviewed on the television show *Sally Jessy Raphael* (October 14, 1992) for a program on sexual harassment and schools, Olsen lamented the idea of bringing in lawyers to deal with this "old problem." He stated, "We have decided in the last year that we're going to bring in the lawyers and we're going to make it a matter of money, and that is slowly going to change the way kids in schools interrelate with each other, and I think it's going to change it for the worse." Such suits, he argues, will simply lead to increased expenses for schools and to an increase in taxes. Olsen's book is a good resource for those who wish to track the rise and influence of the lawsuit in the United States as a tool for resolving social problems such as sexual harassment.

The Women's Legal Defense Fund. **"Sex Discrimination in the Workplace."** 3d ed. Washington, DC: Women's Legal Defense Fund, 1988. 71p.

This handbook explains federal laws that prohibit sex discrimination in employment and the administrative procedures for enforcing those laws. Designed to provide information for employees throughout the United States, the book also includes more detailed data about Washington, D.C., Maryland, and Virginia law, as well as technical information for lawyers. Particularly useful is the section about the EEOC process, including a flowchart that details EEOC procedures in private-sector cases. Among the topics covered are sexual harassment, wage discrimination, pregnancy discrimination, and other forms of sex-based discrimination in the workplace; administrative procedures for filing a discrimination charge with the EEOC; procedures for federal employees; and an overview of state and local laws prohibiting discrimination in employment. Also included is a list of Equal Employment Opportunity Commission offices nationwide. Written in a straightforward style, this book provides a broad canvas for viewing sexual harassment claims as one species of sex discrimination in the workplace.

Loose-leaf Services

Larson, Arthur, and Lex K. Larson. *Employment Discrimination.* New York: Matthew Bender, 1992. Index. ISBN 0-8205-1626-0.

This five-volume set includes an entire volume (vol. 1) on sex discrimination in employment. Written for lawyers, the volumes are part of a loose-leaf service, so the pages can be removed and updated when necessary to keep the material current. Such services are the only way to make sure the legal material presented is accurate and timely. In these volumes, extensive detail is presented on the case law and statutes relating to employment discrimination. The layperson may find these books difficult to read, but such services are the best source of in-depth legal analysis and research. A useful pamphlet on the Civil Rights Act of 1991 is included. The volume on sex discrimination provides discussions of everything from Title VII to sexual harassment to unions and discrimination. This service is available in most large law libraries.

National Employment Lawyers' Association. *Employee Rights Litigation.* New York: Matthew Bender, 1992. ISBN 0-8205-1137-4.

This three-volume loose-leaf service is written and published by the National Employment Lawyers' Association (NELA), a group devoted to representing individual plaintiffs in employment litigation. This service is one of NELA's attempts to help bring information and knowledge of employee rights to practitioners throughout the United States. It covers the basic legal standards for the statutory and common law claims that could be raised on behalf of employees who believe they have been unjustly terminated. The service also includes sections on antidiscrimination laws plus chapters on the various emerging causes of action for wrongful discharge. Designed for lawyers, the book emphasizes pretrial advice about litigation, including extensive sample forms for use in actual lawsuits. A detailed section on sexual harassment and other forms of sex discrimination is included, as well as related subjects such as the Equal Pay Act. The extensive legal analysis of cases and statutes may be boring and confusing to the general researcher, but this service will prove highly useful for those who need to do more in-depth legal research. The looseleaf format ensures that the most current information will be included, as pages are periodically removed and replaced when new cases or information become available. Most large law libraries will have these volumes.

Periodicals

Most of the organizations described in Chapter 5 publish newsletters. Many also publish journals or other periodicals that contain articles of interest to their members. Information on these publications is often given in the discussions of the organizations in Chapter 5. *The Webb Report* is the only periodical devoted entirely to the issue of sexual harassment.

The Webb Report
Premiere Publishing, Ltd.
145 Northwest 85th Street, Suite 201
Seattle, WA 98117
(202) 782-8310 or (800) 767-3062
12 issues per year. $120/year, $180 for two years, $240 for three years.

The Webb Report is the only monthly newsletter that focuses exclusively on sexual harassment. Each report includes news items, summaries of new cases on the issue, and recent studies and commentary. Articles usually balance a feminist perspective with a recognition of the problems and needs of management.

Selected Nonprint Resources

7

Films and Videocassettes

New videos on sexual harassment are produced continually; therefore, it is impossible to write a comprehensive review of them all. This section includes a sample of the better-known and more readily available selections. The accompanying annotations are intended to evaluate the films in terms of content, as well as production value (writing, acting or presentation quality, camera work, editing, and graphics). Most of the videos were produced for use in training employees and managers and may come with training manuals. These written materials tend to be continually updated and revised and are sometimes produced for specific companies; therefore, they are not reviewed separately here. Check with the source for each video to find out if the company offers any current manuals or other material.

A Costly Proposition
Type: Videocassette
Length: 32 min.
Date: 1986
Cost: $695 (includes video and manual)
            plus $12/person participant fee
Source: BNA Communications, Inc.
            9439 Key West Avenue

Rockville, MD 20850-3396
(800) 233-6067

This video-based training program is designed to prevent sexual harassment. Five well-produced vignettes address different kinds of sexual harassment while focusing primarily on media-related companies. A hostile work environment scenario is illustrated through a camera crew on location. An example of quid pro quo sexual harassment is shown through the guise of a record company environment. In the third scenario, a secretary is harassed by a client. She complains to her boss, who avoids doing anything to stop the harassment. After the secretary leaves and files a lawsuit, the employer's liability for acts of nonemployees when the employer knew (or should have known) of the harassing conduct and failed to take appropriate action is discussed. The fourth dramatization illustrates the fact that when employment opportunities or benefits are granted because of an individual's submission to a superior's sexual advances, the employer may be liable to other persons who were qualified for but denied the opportunity. Finally, a scene entitled "Gray Areas" seeks to emphasize how subtle sexual harassment occurs, especially when workers are traveling or socializing after hours and an act of friendliness may be misconstrued as a sexual invitation. The video emphasizes hostile work environment claims because, after the 1986 Supreme Court decision in *Meritor Savings Bank v. Vinson,* this was the type of sexual harassment claimed in 70 percent of cases.

This set of stories is professionally produced, but the scenes lack resolution without the materials presented in the corresponding manuals. The current manuals are well designed and integrated with the video and contain resource information, including relevant court cases and references. The video provides employees with a clear definition of sexual harassment and its legal implications, as well as exploring sexual harassment issues as they relate to working relationships within an organization.

Flirting or Hurting? Sexual Harassment in Schools. A three-module series: (1) *What Is Sexual Harassment?* (21 min.); (2) *Stopping Sexual Harassment* (21 min.); and (3) *Teacher Guide* (15 min.).

Type:	Videocassette
Length:	See above
Date:	1996
Cost:	$69.95, plus 7 percent shipping and handling (include order number 691 and the title of the program)

Source: GPN (Great Plains National Instructional Television Library)
P.O. Box 80669
Lincoln, NE 68501-0669
(800) 228-4630

In this excellent video, jointly produced by WGBY in Springfield, Massachusetts, with the expert consultation of Nan Stein (see the biography of Stein in Chapter 3), the first two modules use reenactment and dramatized interviews to define sexual harassment, show the different effects harassment can have on students, and show students how to respond to offensive behavior—whether they are targets or bystanders. The third module is designed for teachers, with Stein leading a discussion with educators and providing background information on the subject of sexual harassment and suggestions on how to use the video effectively in the classroom. A companion written classroom guide is available from the Wellesley College Center for Research on Women, but the video can be used alone.

The video, which is narrated by a personable young African American woman, is interspersed with interviews with a diverse selection of students, who tell their individual stories of sexual harassment. Each monologue is followed by a cinema verité reenactment of the scenarios. The script, music, and graphics all have a lively feel that will keep teens engaged. The video is useful and accurate, produced in an easy style without talking down to young viewers. The video asks questions at various points and allows a break for discussion.

With its high production value and solid information, it is easy to see why this video won the American Women in Film and Television Gracie Allen Award and has been nominated for several other awards. *Flirting or Hurting?* is an excellent choice for teens, parents, and educators who want to help young people learn more about the subject of sexual harassment.

Handling the Sexual Harassment Complaint
Type: Videocassette
Length: 15 min.
Date: 1990
Cost: Purchase $595, including workbooks; rental starts at $130.
Source: American Media, Inc.
1454 30th Street West

Des Moines, IA 50265
(800) 262-2557

This video is a follow-up to "Sexual Harassment in the Workplace
. . . Identify. Stop. Prevent" (also reviewed in this section). The
objective is to provide management with specific procedures to
follow when receiving, investigating, and taking action on a sexual harassment complaint. The program offers information and
techniques for answering the question "What do I say and do
when I receive a sexual harassment complaint?"

Following the format of the previous video, this tape dramatizes a meeting between managers and a sexual harassment trainer.
The group discusses a step-by-step process to follow when investigating a complaint. The trainer also shows her own video with a
dramatization of an employee bringing a complaint to a supervisor—a secretary whose boss implies that she must accompany him
on a business trip or risk losing her job. The idea that her compan-
ionship is desired for reasons other than strictly business is never
specifically stated but is clearly implied. Thus, this scenario provides fertile ground for managers to discuss whether this implied
message should be considered sexual harassment and how to deal
with the complaint. The video vignettes include a dramatization of
how the complaint proceeds and how the supervisor investigates
it. The storyline emphasizes that those investigating a complaint
must invest a lot of time and must be prepared to use maximum
creativity to ensure that all avenues are explored, thus limiting the
company's exposure to lawsuits and low productivity. The tape
suggests that managers should consult with the supervisor's
supervisor, the human resources department, and the legal department. This is a well-produced piece that meets its stated goals.

Intent vs. Impact. A two-tape series.
Type: Videocassettes
Length: 41 min. 27 sec. (management); 26 min. (employee)
Date: 1988
Cost: $1,295 (with manual), plus $10/person participant fee
Source: BNA Communications, Inc.
            9439 Key West Avenue
            Rockville, MD 20850-3396
            (800) 233-6067

These two stand-alone videos, designed by sexual harassment
trainer Stephen Anderson, address sexual harassment from both

management and employee levels. This series was produced before *Myths vs. Facts* (also reviewed in this section), Anderson's more recent offering. The management video is intended to go beyond awareness, showing managers and supervisors how to recognize subtle sexual harassment, how to prevent it, and how to deal with sexual harassment situations if they do occur. Several dramatizations cover quid pro quo harassment and the legal and financial liabilities of managers and organizations under Title VII, Title IX, and other fair employment laws. Other vignettes address identifying a hostile work environment, distinguishing when harmless hazing becomes sexual harassment, receiving a sexual harassment complaint, talking with the alleged harasser, and dealing with thorny issues such as false charges, sexual visuals, and provocative clothing. The dramatizations include examples of retaliation when an employee refuses a supervisor's advances on a business trip and hazing that escalates to a hostile work environment.

Narrated by popular Denver television anchor Reynalda Muse, the video is particularly adept at helping participants to sort out the confusing issue of what constitutes flirtation versus what constitutes subtle sexual harassment; the scenarios illustrate a three-step process to determine the difference. Anderson's point is that subtle sexual harassment, if allowed to continue unchecked by a supervisor, can escalate into a claim of hostile work environment. The basic premise of the video is that of intent versus impact—the intent of the perpetrator is irrelevant because the law focuses on the impact on the victim. The entire effect is that of a sophisticated interweaving of actual training and dramatizations. The video comes with a trainer's manual and a participants' manual, complete with pretests and posttests, background information, legal definitions, examples of sexual harassment, and checklists to help identify subtle harassment.

The video for employees takes the position that employees are sometimes in the best position to stop sexual harassment and provides the skills and information employees need to identify and stop sexual harassment. The video covers hostile work environment and what is flirtation versus harassment, and it has a self-test for employees to show that some people may not realize that the way they have always acted in the workplace is now considered to be sexual harassment. A short assertiveness training segment is offered to help employees stop unwanted attention. The narrative answers the most frequently asked questions regarding sexual visuals, provocative clothing, no-win situations for men and women, and the changing rules in the workplace. A companion training manual for employees is also offered.

Both of these videos go beyond awareness and focus on how to resolve harassment situations. What makes these videos different from many others is that they assume that most managers and employees can now recognize blatant sexual harassment but that the boundaries are less clear when it comes to identifying subtle sexual harassment. The focus of these offerings is on changing behavior rather than just providing information.

Making Advances: What Organizations Must Do about Sexual Harassment

Type:	Videocassette
Length:	36 min. 14 sec.
Date:	1988
Cost:	$225
Source:	Phoenix Learning Group
	2349 Chaffee Drive
	St. Louis, MO 63146
	(800) 221-1274

This video is a straightforward, if somewhat dry, presentation of the cases and law on the issue of sexual harassment. Interviews with EEOC officials, who explain the law and EEOC guidelines, are interspersed with written lists of the principles of various harassment cases. The presentation emphasizes the decrease in productivity and morale caused by sexual harassment and explains how to prevent claims and how to organize complaint and training procedures within an organization. The video presents a few dramatizations of various sexual harassment scenarios and makes it clear that if someone complains of sexual harassment, the organization has a legal duty to respond. A workbook for training purposes is also offered.

Myths vs. Facts. A two-tape series: (1) *How To Recognize and Confront Subtle Sexual Harassment* and (2) *How To Manage Sexual Harassment Situations*

Type:	Videocassette
Length:	26 min. 14 sec. (each)
Date:	1992
Cost:	$1,595, plus $10/person participant fee. Packages include trainer's and participants' manuals.
Source:	BNA Communications, Inc.

9439 Key West Avenue
Rockville, MD 20850-3396
(800) 233-6067

The first video focuses on where to draw the line between subtle sexual harassment and flirtation. The production is an offering from expert Stephen Anderson, who also developed *Intent vs. Impact* (see the review earlier in this section). This production emphasizes that the rules in the workplace have changed. Through dramatizations and interviews with Anderson, conducted by Denver radio and television personality Tom Martino, the video discusses and defines sexism, sex discrimination, sexual harassment, and quid pro quo harassment and hostile work environment. This is one of the few commercial videos that uses a female narrator, who continues the discussion of the issues. Among the types of subtle sexual harassment depicted are discussing sexual material, making sexual comments, hanging around or following workers, telling sexual jokes, asking about sexual fantasies, and giving leering looks.

Anderson presents the following definition of subtle sexual harassment, which he emphasizes is not a legal definition but a practical one: "unwelcome sexual or sex-based behavior that, if allowed to continue, could create a quid pro quo or hostile work environment." He also identifies a five-step method to decide whether something is sexual harassment rather than flirting: (1) identify the people in the situation, (2) determine the relationship between them, (3) examine the behavior itself, (4) decide if the behavior is welcome or unwelcome (that is, is there equal initiation and participation), and (5) ask if the behavior is sexual or sex based. The analysis helps people to sort out an issue many find confusing, especially in the wake of the Anita Hill/Clarence Thomas hearings.

Another new issue that is discussed effectively is the reasonable woman standard. The video clarifies the sense behind the recent court decisions on this issue by emphasizing that women are still more vulnerable than men to sexual violence in U.S. society. The presentation also dramatizes same-sex, third-party, nonverbal, previous-relationship, hostile work environment, and female-to-male sexual harassment situations and shows how a supervisor can maintain a friendly work relationship when confronting a subtle sexual harasser. Finally, the video answers a question men frequently ask: "Don't women harass men by wearing sexy clothing?" Although she agrees that men have no right to harass anyone regardless of what they wear, the narrator concludes that both sexes have a responsibility to dress professionally at work. The bottom line, the narrator stresses, is that we all want to be treated with dignity in the workplace. This is a well-produced video. Comprehensive training manuals are also offered, but the video can be used alone.

The second video provides management personnel with effective techniques for interviewing alleged victims of sexual harassment, including advice on what to do if the recipient requests that no action be taken or says she wants to deal with the situation on her own. It also demonstrates the method an organization's sexual harassment resource person should use to talk with an alleged harasser and ways a supervisor can intervene when he or she observes a subtle sexual harassment situation, even though no complaint has been made. A mature, confident-sounding female narrator introduces the various dramatizations, which include examples of how a supervisor should *not* respond when an employee complains of sexual harassment. The tape emphasizes that the manager's role should be that of a supportive fact finder. The video is very specific in explaining how a supervisor should react, even providing suggested questions he or she should ask. After the dramatizations, the narrator introduces trainer Stephen Anderson, who answers questions and details management mistakes. Anderson also explains why many managers do not take the appropriate action in response to harassment complaints—usually because they are unsure of what to do and find the situation embarrassing. The presentation concludes with suggestions about how to evaluate a workplace to prevent sexual harassment and emphasizes the potential legal liability of failing to police the workplace. This is an effective presentation; corresponding training manuals are available, but the video can be used alone.

No Laughing Matter: High School Students and Sexual Harassment

Type:	Originally a filmstrip; now available on videocassette
Length:	25 min.
Date:	1982
Cost:	$45
Source:	Massachusetts Educational Television
	MET Office of Educational Technologies
	Massachusetts Department of Education
	1385 Hancock Street

Quincy, MA 02169
(800) 639-8879

Produced by the Boston Women's Teachers Collective and Media Works, Inc., this filmstrip (which has been transferred to videotape) explores sexual harassment as experienced by high school students in school and at work. Three female students, played by professional actresses, explain the harassment they received from fellow students and from an employer. Their narration is interspersed with scenes from a workshop in which student participants struggle to define harassment and to distinguish it from behavior that is acceptable, such as flirting. The leader stresses the need for a strong school policy on harassment. Students are advised to talk with someone if they experience behavior they think is harassing, to tell the harasser they are uncomfortable with the behavior, and to identify the person at their school who is responsible for helping with sex discrimination problems. The producers recommend the tape for students in grades 7 through 12, school personnel, and parents. Because it was originally produced as a filmstrip, the video is not of high visual quality, but it is one of the few tapes available for high school students on the subject of sexual harassment.

The Power Pinch
Type: Videocassette
Length: 27 min. 31 sec.
Date: 1981
Cost: $599
Source: Coronet/MTI Film and Video
108 Wilmot Road
Deerfield, IL 60015-9925
(800) 621-2131

Narrated by actor Ken Howard, this video explores what sexual harassment is and how it can be prevented. Dramatized vignettes portray three types of harassers: the power player, the office adapter, and the victim of mixed signals. Executives, attorneys, psychologists, and victims discuss the emotional, economic, and legal repercussions of harassment, and advice is given on how managers and employees can deal with the problem. The video seeks to answer the question of why sexual harassment exists, but overall it suffers somewhat from a lack of focus and of orderly progress. The video emphasizes that sexual harassment can be costly for business in terms of lost productivity, morale, and legal fees and awards. Overhead transparencies, a manager's handbook, and employee guides are also available as part of the training. The video is somewhat out-of-date, as it was produced before many of the important sexual harassment cases had been brought before the courts.

Preventing Sexual Harassment: A Management Responsibility
(*Part I—The Risk*, *Part II—Minimizing the Risk* [for management], and *Part III—Preventing Sexual Harassment: A Shared Responsibility* [for employees])

Type:	Videocassette
Length:	Part I: 27 min.; Part II: 24 min.; Part III: 13 min.
Date:	Parts I and II: 1991; Part III: 1992
Cost:	(three-tape series) $595 (includes manual), plus $10/person participant fee
Source:	BNA Communications, Inc.
	9439 Key West Avenue
	Rockville, MD 20850-3396
	(800) 233-6067

This three-tape series, complete with a comprehensive trainer's manual and participants' manual, is an integrated video-based training system designed to help organizations educate management and employees about sexual harassment. The goals of the series are to prevent sexual harassment complaints and lawsuits; resolve complaints internally should harassment occur; limit the organization's legal liability for harassment; demonstrate the organization's efforts to prevent harassment; highlight internal resolution procedures for employees and support disciplinary action should employees engage in harassment; show managers how they can be held personally liable for harassment; prevent other types of harassment based on race, age, national origin, or disability; and inform all employees harassment will not be tolerated.

The first video opens with a dramatic courtroom scene at the point at which the jury brings a million-dollar verdict for a sexual harassment claim. The three videos then intersperse scenes of the trial with discussion and background dramatizations. These methods illustrate both the right and the wrong way to handle a sexual harassment claim.

The problem with this technique is that the scenario becomes a bit old after one watches all three videos. The creators have purposely picked an ambiguous situation to illustrate a number of points. An employee has a brief affair with a supervisor. During the affair she is promoted, to the consternation of other employees who feel they were better qualified for the position. After the affair has ended (it is never clear at whose initiation), the employee feels she is treated unfairly by her former lover and eventually resigns and sues the company for harassment. It is never clear whether the initial affair was consensual, which allows the presentation to emphasize that office romances can be tricky no matter how innocently they begin. In this office, the supervisor also flirted with other workers, told sexual jokes, and made other sexual comments—behavior that was used against him at the trial. Part I of the management video shows the wrong way to handle this situation from a management point of view, part II shows the right way to handle the situation, and the employee tapes illustrate how to handle the situation from an employee's perspective.

Preventing Sexual Harassment was produced following the confirmation hearings of Clarence Thomas and includes a discussion of the Civil Rights Act of 1991, which had passed right before the video was produced, along with an explanation of the reasonable woman standard. The program emphasizes that actions can be interpreted very differently in a courtroom setting and makes supervisors aware that they can be held personally liable. Three real-life experts—a human resource manager and two attorneys—comment periodically on the storyline. The videos also cover the standard definitions of sexual harassment as they show how to handle complaints. In all, the series provides accurate information in a well-produced manner.

Sex and Justice: Highlights of the Anita Hill/Clarence Thomas Hearings

Type:	Videocassette
Length:	60 min.
Date:	1993
Cost:	$24.95
Source:	First Run Features
	153 Waverly Place
	New York, NY 10014
	(800) 488-6652

Narrated and written by Gloria Steinem, this video highlights the Senate hearings on Clarence Thomas's confirmations in fall 1991. Steinem does not pretend to be unbiased; she introduces the tape with the statement that "this story began with a lie," referring to video footage of President George Bush nominating Thomas and declaring him to be the best man for the job. Instead, Steinem asserts, Thomas was that "rare thing," a black conservative.

Anita Hill, Thomas's former employee who accused him of sexual harassment, arrived at the hearings with—in the words of her attorney—"nothing but the truth on her side and the Bible in her purse." The video footage of the hearings begins with short clips of first Hill and then Thomas telling their side of the story; the juxtaposition of the two accounts is especially effective. Other highlights include questioning by the all-male white senators, the statements of witnesses for both sides, and the confirmation debate.

The video stands as an engrossing historical document of hearings that, as Steinem asserts, "made history and changed history." For the first time in history, she states, "women and men looked at the world as if women mattered."

Sexual Harassment in the Workplace . . . Identify. Stop. Prevent.
Type: Videocassette
Length: 21 min.
Date: 1990
Cost: $695, includes written materials
Source: American Media, Inc.
                1454 30th Street West
                Des Moines, IA 50265
                (800) 262-2557

This video is meant to be a training device for managers and employees on the issue of sexual harassment. In a series of dramatizations, the video introduces the fictional Mr. Wright, who has recently heard that a company similar to his lost a sexual harassment lawsuit. Not only was the publicity embarrassing, but the settlement was sizable. To avoid this problem in his own company, Mr. Wright decides to provide management and employees with the latest information on the subject and instill in them the attitude that sexual harassment will not be tolerated. To do so, Mr. Wright hires a consultant, Ms. Hanson, and schedules a meeting with top management.

The video proceeds with a dramatization of this realistic meeting. Actors who portray top management are diverse in terms of race, sex, and points of view. The trainer shows her own video within this video, which dramatizes various sexual harassment scenarios; she then stops the tape and asks the assembled managers to discuss the implications of each vignette. A variety of scenes are presented, including scenes that illustrate how sexual relationships at the office can spur third-party complaints of preference and same-sex harassment. The trainer's explanation of the law is woven into her discussions of each scenario in a natural, realistic way. Some of the managers do not hesitate to express their disbelief about some of the rules regarding sexual harassment, as when one manager explains that he has a problem when women dress in a way he believes attracts this kind of attention. A depiction of workers looking at a magazine with pinups and making remarks to another worker spurs a discussion of the theory of a hostile work environment. The trainer also presents parts of her video to illustrate how workers can stand up to sexual harassment and explains that harassers do not respect any kind of boundaries of type or class.

The acting and production values are fairly high in this video, and the presentation offers the basic information in an engaging format. The trainer's style is natural and pleasant, and she emphasizes that the underlying reason for sensitizing managers and workers to sexual harassment is to make certain each worker has an opportunity to be valued for his or her work, not for sex. The trainer emphasizes that sexual harassment is a misuse of power rather than an expression of sexual desire. Workers are also shown how to prevent sexual harassment by dressing appropriately and acting professionally, as well as what to do if they must confront a harasser and ultimately complain about harassment.

Sexual Harassment Is Bad Business

Type:	Videocassette
Length:	22 min.
Date:	1987
Cost:	$495 purchase; $45 preview (full credit if purchased); $175 three-day rental
Source:	J. M. Glass, Inc.
	P.O. Box 90999
	Spokane, WA 99209
	(Widely available in libraries; company may no longer be in business)

This video and its companion training guide emphasize the cost of sexual harassment to business, including the loss of employee morale and the costs of litigation. The video, which has won six national and international awards, was designed primarily for managers and supervisors and examines the issue of sexual harassment through the experiences of its victims. Based on dramatizations of actual cases, it allows the audience to become personally involved with the problem of harassment. The production does a thorough job of defining sexual harassment from a legal perspective, but the definition is so detailed that this part sometimes drags. The video emphasizes the employer's responsibility regarding harassment and the fact that "you can't afford to be confused about this issue." The script includes a clear explanation of the paramour preference type of case, which was new at the time the video was produced. This is a thoroughly professional presentation, although it is somewhat out-of-date.

Sexual Harassment: Issues and Answers
Type: Videocassette
Length: 19 min. 40 sec.
Date: 1991
Cost: $60
Source: Widely available in libraries

This video, narrated by a pleasant female broadcast professional, focuses on sexual harassment on college campuses. The narration begins with a comparison of myths versus facts in the area of sexual harassment and includes a review of the surveys that show the prevalence of sexual harassment. The script goes on to examine the definitions of sexual harassment and to look at examples. The video outlines what supervisors and employees should do if sexual harassment occurs and makes it clear that educational institutions have a responsibility to protect faculty, staff, and students. One dramatization is of a rather blatant—and perhaps outdated—quid pro quo situation between an administrator and his staff. There is also a dramatization of a student and a dean discussing a consensual relationship in which the student had been seeing a professor but then broke it off. The student feels the professor is retaliating. Another scenario shows a female graduate student harassing other students. The video emphasizes that professional ethics must be addressed when power and authority clash and that universities are responsible for student-to-student harassment. There is a brief discussion of how to investigate both formal and informal complaints. The video takes the position that power, rather than male-female relationships, is the issue in sexual harassment.

Although this production is not as high in quality as some of the videos produced for the corporate workplace, it is one of the few to focus exclusively on college campuses and therefore will be particularly useful for those who deal with that environment. A corresponding booklet, "Issues and Answers," contains legal definitions and sample policies.

Sexual Harassment: Issues and Answers, Volumes I, II, and III:
(1) *Clearing up the Confusion;* (2) *How To Handle Harassment;* and (3) *Your Responsibilities as a Manager/Supervisor*

Type:	Videocassette
Length:	50–60 min. (each volume)
Date:	1993
Cost:	$399.95 (video); $299.95 (facilitator's guide with one workbook); $695.00 (video, 20 workbooks, facilitator's guide); $7.50 for each workbook; discounts available for quantities of 10 (20 percent discount), 50 (30 percent discount), and 100 (40 percent discount).
Source:	CareerTrack Publications 3085 Center Green Drive Boulder, CO 80301 (303) 440-7440

This three-volume set, produced by the prolific training company CareerTrack, covers the basics on the issue of sexual harassment. Volume I covers the legal definition of sexual harassment, the history of the issue, and some basic tests on the viewer's knowledge of sexual harassment issues. The video is designed to be used with an accompanying workbook that is filled with tests, definitions, and step-by-step guidelines. Volume II tackles the issue of what to do if one is involved in a sexual harassment incident, and Volume III covers the issue from an organizational perspective, including tips on how to receive a complaint and conduct investigations.

Narrated and written by Maria Arapakis, best-known for her 1990 book *Soft Power,* a course on assertive communication, rather than as an expert on sexual harassment, the video consists mainly of "talking heads" in a studio, with only a few dramatizations of sexual harassment scenarios. An attorney, a counselor, and the human resources director at CareerTrack provide some expert commentary. Although this series covers the basics on the issue of sexual harassment, the style and the script are not particularly engaging. The series is unlikely to appeal to sophisticated workplaces but may serve as an economical alternative to more expensively produced training videos on the subject of harassment. Without the corresponding training manual, however, the videos constitute an awkward presentation.

Sexual Harassment: It's No Game

Type: Videocassette
Length: 30 min.
Date: 1988 (curriculum revised in 1992)
Cost: $250 (includes 50-page curriculum in binder); $60 for one-week package preview/rental
Source: Center for Women in Government
University of Albany
Draper Hall 310
Albany, NY 12222
(518) 442-3900

This video-based training program was developed especially for the public sector. It includes segments from the popular former TV program *Cagney and Lacey,* repeating parts of an award-winning episode that dramatized the issue of sexual harassment in the show's fictional police department. The engaging format opens with a sexual harassment training session attended by a diverse group of public employees. The trainees are watching *Cagney and Lacey* to examine the behaviors and issues involved. The situation is powerful—and objectionable—enough to make the employees uncomfortable. In the ensuing lunchroom scenes, the workshop participants share their reactions to the television episodes. Some of the participants have experienced sexual harassment, and even the "nice guys" have been its perpetrators. Personal anecdotes are shared, thus illustrating the range of sexual harassment behaviors for the viewer. The training scenes are packed with information and answers to frequent questions, but it is the lunchtime interactions that defy stereotypes and illustrate how subtle and complex the issue of sexual harassment can be. The video also outlines the legal rights of employees and the legal responsibilities of employers and suggests procedures for addressing complaints and problems.

The video does a good job of illustrating both the professional damage and the personal anguish sexual harassment causes its victims. The leader of the training session takes the feminist position that sexual harassment is not about sex but is about power. Although the men in the group issue the standard complaint that there are no set rules regarding harassment, the trainer emphasizes that after ten years of court cases it is clear that the victim has the right to define unwanted sexual harassment. The video also makes the subtle but important point that any woman—young or old, pretty or plain—can be a victim of sexual harassment. The companion curriculum provides questions to stimulate group discussion, expands on the issues raised in the video, and addresses common viewer questions and concerns.

Sexual Harassment: Minimize the Risk. A six-volume series: (1) *Pay Attention: What Is Sexual Harassment;* (2) *Pay Attention: Don't Be a Victim;* (3) *Avoid Harm and Liability;* (4) *Investigation: Template and Techniques;* (5) *Vital Dos and Don'ts;* and (6) *In Our Schools*

Type:	Videocassette
Length:	16–24 min. (each volume)
Cost:	Volume 1, $295; Volume 2, $195; Volume 3, $295; Volume 4, $295; Volume 5, $295; Volume 6, $195; $1,175 for all six. Each volume may be purchased separately except for Volume 2, which must be purchased with Volume 1.
Source:	McGrath Systems, Inc.
	211 East Victoria Street, Suite B
	Santa Barbara, CA 93101-9835
	(905) 882-1212

This series of videos, produced by school law attorney Mary Jo McGrath, is designed to be used by schools and educators. The series has six volumes. The first two are aimed at students; the next three, which discuss liability and investigations, are aimed at teachers and administrators; and the final one is designed to help the public understand what schools are doing and why.

Each video is well produced and informative. The two designed for students, *Pay Attention: What Is Sexual Harassment?* and *Pay Attention: Don't Be a Victim,* are produced in an "MTV" style and are aimed at students ages 12–19. The videos use dramatizations and student narrators to make their points. Reproducible booklets and lesson plans for teachers to use while showing the videos are included. The videos for teachers and administrators are also high quality, although more restrained. McGrath also provides accompanying books and a complete investigation manual.

This series represents the most recent analysis currently available and is the most comprehensive program available at present for schools that want to take a total approach to preventing sexual harassment and avoiding liability.

Shades of Gray. A five-tape series: (1) *What Are We Doing Here?* (2) *What Is Sexual Harassment?* (3) *Why Should I Worry about It?* (4) *What Does the Law Say?* and (5) *What Am I Supposed To Do?*

Type: Videocassette
Length: 15 min. (each tape)
Date: 1989
Cost: $995 for five tapes
Source: Premiere Publishing, Ltd.
145 Northwest 85th Street, Suite 201
Seattle, WA 98117
(206) 782-8310
(800) 767-3062

This five-tape training series, developed by Seattle sexual harassment trainer Susan Webb, uses dramatizations of real problems from real stories to make its point. The video is one of the few that deals realistically with the concerns of workers (usually men) who feel threatened by the imposition of workplace standards they do not understand. Serving as the narrator, Webb emphasizes that harassment is not a new concern. Webb takes the position that the "trainees" often become defensive and resistant to the subject; in spite of, or perhaps because of, people's resistance, the problem of harassment is as great today as it has ever been. Because of this, Webb takes care to ensure that the information she gives is complete and accurate yet is presented in such a way that people will pay attention and learn—breaking through their initial defensiveness or resistance.

Video 1, *What Are We Doing Here?* reviews all five tapes and is an introduction to and overview of the problem of sexual harassment in the workplace. Video 2, *What Is Sexual Harassment?* defines sexual harassment in behavioral terms with a common-sense definition that uses a continuum from light-gray to dark-gray harassment. It also discusses why certain behaviors must be repeated before they constitute harassment and emphasizes the responsibility of the recipient to speak up about unwelcome behavior. Video 3, *Why Should I Worry about It?* details and emphasizes the costs of harassment to employers, victims, co-workers, and harassers. Included are consequences of harassment, such as lower productivity, absenteeism, turnover, lawsuits, and court awards and settlements. The tape also emphasizes the personal and professional liability of each employee. Video 4, *What Does the Law Say?* covers the *Meritor Savings Bank v. Vinson* U.S. Supreme Court case (477 U.S. 57 [1986]) and then examines the EEOC guidelines to explain the responsibilities of individuals in the workplace and to show how recent court decisions have supported those guidelines. Video 5, *What Am I Supposed To Do?* outlines the responsibilities of employees at all levels.

These comprehensive videos present accurate information in a nonthreatening way. This is one of the most detailed and complete packages available; resource manuals, training manuals, a leader's guide, and participants' handbooks come with the videos. Because the tapes were produced in 1989, however, more recent cases are not covered.

So Like You

Type: Videocassette
Length: 22 min.
Date: 1990
Cost: Purchase $350; rental $85
Source: Phoenix Learning Group
            2349 Chaffee Drive
            St. Louis, MO 63146
            (800) 221-1274

This comprehensive program, set in a fictional company, explores the issue of sexual harassment and shows what happens when an accusation of harassment has been made. Individuals who are experiencing sexual harassment and managers who are investigating harassment are shown steps they can take to achieve resolution. The program examines the same situation from two different points of view, those of the man and the women involved. The program is meant to provoke discussion, and it allows managers and employees to explore sexual harassment issues that may be unspoken or misunderstood. Each program includes leader's guides and participants' workbooks that provide exercises, role plays, guidelines, materials for discussion, and details of actual sexual harassment cases. Unlike some videos, this one would be incomplete and would provide inadequate information without the accompanying manuals. The video serves mainly to spark discussion of the issues raised in the written materials. In addition, because the video examines the same fact situation from both a female and a male point of view, it tends to drag in places. Still, the script is realistic and intelligent, and the dialogue and setting have a truthful ring.

The Workplace Hustle

Type: Film/videocassette
Length: 30 min.
Date: 1980
Cost: $520 16mm film; $520 videocassette

Source: Woody Clark Productions
943 Howard Street
San Francisco, CA 94103
(Widely available in libraries; company may no longer
be in business)

This documentary, which is narrated by Ed Asner and includes commentary by Lin Farley, author of *Sexual Shakedown*, the first book to use the term *sexual harassment*, won awards at both the San Francisco and New York Film Festivals. The film stresses the social and emotional dimensions of sexual harassment, especially the different ways men and women define the behavior. Dramatized vignettes and interviews with a victim and an employer underscore the personal and organizational consequences of harassment, and advice is given on steps women should take when harassed. Asner wisely acknowledges the oddity of having a male narrator but explains that those men who have been taught not to listen to women should "consider me our translator." The film does a good job of dramatizing the differences in men's and women's perceptions, with groups of both sexes discussing the issue. Farley emphasizes that much harassment occurs when women enter previously all-male professions and when men have economic incentives to "communicate power expressed sexually" but stresses that she knows "most men don't want to behave this way." Farley notes that men are trained while growing up to show their manhood through intimidation. Asner's narration adds a nice touch, as he notes that although men have used their sexuality as power, sexuality is an expression of intimacy and love, not of power, and that women want to separate sex and work to improve both. This is an effective, well-produced film, albeit somewhat out-of-date.

Would You Let Someone Do This to Your Sister?
Type: Videocassette
Length: 33 min. 38 sec.
Date: 1984
Source: Available only in libraries

This video includes interviews with female workers who have been harassed and suggests steps for victims. Focusing on the plight of office, factory, and other union workers, the presentation offers emotional and persuasive interviews with actual harassment victims. One especially effective segment shows a black factory worker describing the details of her harassment experience while her husband listens with tears in his eyes. The women describe the embarrassment and the physical and psychological effects of harassment. Male viewers may be surprised by the extent of the pain caused by sexual harassment that is revealed in this video. The speakers also emphasize that dressing unattractively did nothing to stop their harassers. Various United Auto Workers (UAW) union officials pledge to uphold the union's "no tolerance" stance on harassment. The speakers take the position that sexual harassment is not about passion but is caused by hostile aggression. The UAW president at the time, who states that sexual harassment is an insult to the worker and a barrier to equal employment for men and women, delivers a powerful message from the top to union workers. A UAW vice-president emphasizes that sexual harassment policies should be raised at the bargaining table and included in union contracts. Although the production consists mostly of talking heads, the documentary style and impassioned feelings of the presenters make this video particularly effective.

Internet Resources

Many of the organizations listed in Chapter 5 have sites on the Internet or are in the process of developing sites. What follows is a selection of the most useful Internet sites of the many that are currently available. In conducting searches on sexual harassment on the Internet, be aware that any use of the word "sex" will bring up thousands of sites, many of which may be composed of unwanted sexual material.

All Business Network
1049 Timber Vale Drive
Evergreen, CO 80439
(303) 670-9915
Internet: http://all-biz.com/articles/dating/htm and http://www.all-biz.com/harass.html

This site offers articles, case citations, and descriptions of issues relating to sexual harassment and dating in the workplace. It is part of the main site of the All Business Network, with extensive listings on various business issues. The site includes a search engine one can use to access information on sexual harassment as it relates to business from other sources on the Web.

American Association of University Women (AAUW)
1111 Sixteenth Street NW
Washington, DC 20036
(202) 785-7700
http://www.aauw.org

This is the site for the American Association of University Women. It includes a description of the organization and relevant publications, as well as a telephone number for orders. The site includes listings and descriptions of the various surveys on sexual harassment produced by the AAUW.

The Discovery Channel
Discovery Communications, Inc.
7700 Wisconsin Avenue
Bethesda, MD 20814
(800) 813-7409
http://school.discovery.com

This is the Discovery Channel's site. Under its "Teacher TV" is an extensive discussion of sexual harassment in schools, including definitions, surveys, statistics, and suggestions for further research. The channel includes discussions about how to use Discovery TV offerings in the classroom, but there were no program listings under the topic of sexual harassment.

Feminist Majority Foundation
1600 Wilson Boulevard
Arlington, VA 22209
(703) 522-2214
http://www.feminist.com

Maintained by the Feminist Majority Foundation, this site has a large variety of articles on women's issues, including a hot line resource list and an extensive list of Internet resources on sexual harassment. This site is a good place to start to find other sites on specific issues (such as sexual harassment of women in the military, state hot lines, or archive sites maintained on some sexual harassment lawsuits).

National Organization for Women (NOW)
1000 16th Street NW, Suite 700
Washington, DC 20036

(202) 331-0066
http://www.now.org/

This extensive site covers all of the issues in which NOW is currently engaged, along with links and stations to other Internet sources. Extensive resources on sexual harassment are identified. This site is updated continually to provide new information and is a good place to begin an Internet search.

9 to 5, National Association of Working Women
614 Superior Avenue NW
Cleveland, OH
(216) 566-9308
http://www/cs.utk.edu/~bartley/other/9to5htm

This is the site for 9 to 5, an advocacy organization for working women. The site includes some basic facts about sexual harassment, tips on steps to take if one has been harassed, a description of 9 to 5, and membership information.

Syracuse University
Syracuse, NY 13244
(315) 443-1870
http://web.syr.edu

This unique and highly personal site is run by a student at Syracuse University who was the victim of sexual harassment in high school. It contains an excellent list of books, articles, and other Web sites. The site is interactive, as the WebMaster writes articles and publishes comments from participants. The student includes a long article about her own experience and her personal opinion on the issue of harassment. This site represents a good support for students who may be trying to decide what to do about their own problem with sexual harassment.

Texas Association of School Boards
P.O. Box 400
Austin, TX 78767
(512) 467-0222
http://www/tasb.org/

This is the site of the Texas Association of School Boards, which includes information on sexual harassment in schools. Definitions, lists of resources, and a question-and-answer format make this site a useful basic resource. The site is not interactive and does not contain links to other sites.

Wellesley College
Center for Research on Women
828 Washington Street
Wellesley, MA 02181
(617) 283-2500
http://www/wellesley.edu

Wellesley's site includes the home page for the Center for Research on Women, which contains information on sexual harassment generally as well as in schools. The site also lists the center's current research projects and requests participation.

Women's Web
Laura Klancer, WebMaster
One Penn Plaza, 38th Floor
New York, NY 10001
(800) 542-4240
http://www/womweb.com

The Women's Web was started in reaction to the male domination of the Web and the founders' beliefs that the Web was a bastion of sexism. It is one of the oldest and most sophisticated sites on women's issues and includes a variety of information on a number of women's issues, including sexual harassment. Updated constantly with new articles and information, the site has extensive links and citations to other resources on the Web and elsewhere. The site is interactive, with e-mail provided along with many other services.

Glossary

agency The relationship in which one individual (the *agent*) acts for or on behalf of or represents another (the *principal*) under the authority granted to the actor by the principal.

assault and battery Actually two separate legal wrongs, but because they frequently occur together, they are often paired in legal complaints. To prove assault, the victim must show that the person who allegedly assaulted him or her intended to cause physical contact and that the victim feared the contact. *Battery* is actual physical contact that is harmful, offensive, or insulting. The victim must show that the person intended to touch the victim and that he or she did contact the victim physically.

common law negligence claims Negligence actions based on English common law, the foundation of the U.S. legal system. *Negligence* is failing to do what a reasonably careful person would do under the same circumstances or doing what a reasonable person in similar circumstances would not.

compensatory damages The amount of money awarded to individuals to make them whole or to place them in the position they would have been in if the situation complained of had never occurred; actual losses.

constructive discharge The theory that a resignation from employment may actually be a dismissal (and can be legally treated as such), because the employer's imposition of intolerable terms and conditions of employment gave the resigning employee no choice but to leave.

defamation An oral (*slander*) or written (*libel*) false statement that damages another's reputation.

defendant The person, employer, or entity (such as a school) charged with the complaint or wrong. Usually, an individual employee, student, or supervisor will be accused because of his or her own conduct. An employer or school may be liable through respondeat superior or agency theories.

disparate impact In discrimination cases, discriminatory effect that results unintentionally from the use of a requirement—for example, a preemployment test—that on its face is neutral.

hostile environment One of the two types of sexual harassment claims; it requires a showing of frequent, serious acts of a sexual nature that create the effect of a hostile, offensive, or intimidating work or educational atmosphere. The victim need not show monetary damages.

injunctive relief Usually, an equitable remedy ordered by the court requiring that certain activities stop, such as that an organization refrain from discrimination against women in the future. A *mandatory* injunction (*mandamus*) requires that a defendant take certain actions, such as in a sexual harassment case in which the court orders that an employer or school must implement certain policies or training.

intentional infliction of emotional distress A claim that the actor or defendant intentionally acted in a way that he, she, or it knew, or should have known, would cause nontrivial emotional pain to another. The conduct must be so shocking or extreme that a person of normal sensibilities would consider the action outrageous.

invasion of privacy A claim that the defendant intruded upon another person's solitude or into his or her private affairs; usually requires the public disclosure of embarrassing facts about the person.

negligent hiring or retention Tort action against employers that fail to protect employees from foreseeable harm by carefully checking references of new employees or that fail to terminate employees who they know have caused harm in the past.

paramour preference Term used to refer to the preference of a supervisor for the individual with whom he or she has an ongoing social or sexual relationship over others in the workplace or educational institution.

plaintiff The person bringing the lawsuit or EEOC claim; usually, the victim in a sexual harassment case.

punitive damages The money amount awarded to an individual by the jury, or specified by statute, so that the defendant is punished for its conduct and all potential defendants will be effectively deterred from acting in the same manner.

quid pro quo In Latin, literally "this for that." One of two types of sexual harassment claims; requires a showing of unwelcome activity of a sexual nature in exchange for tangible employment or educational benefits or the loss of tangible job benefits because of the rejection of such activity.

reasonable person/woman A legal standard for behavior; the judicial construct of an individual who thinks and responds the way an ordinary, logical, and careful person or woman would under the same circumstances and conditions.

respondeat superior Literally, Latin for "let the master answer." The principle that the master is responsible for the acts of the servant, usually meaning an employer is responsible for the acts of an employee, regardless of whether the employer has actual knowledge of that employee's acts.

sex discrimination The cause of action recognized by Title VII and many state statutes; the favoring of one individual or group over another on the basis of gender or stereotypes associated with gender.

sexual harassment A cause of action grounded in sex discrimination; the imposition of unwelcome sexual conduct on an employee in the workplace or a student in an educational institution that affects the student or the employee's performance.

strict liability The automatic imposition of liability, regardless of extenuating circumstances, knowledge, or intent.

tort A wrong committed by one person or institution against another, redressed by money damages; defined by state common law rather than by statute.

Index

Lynne Eisaguirre is an attorney, author, and entrepreneur who helps organizations solve employee relations problems through training, speaking, and consulting. Current topics include sexual harassment, diversity, preventing conflict and violence, helping employees acquire the skills and attitudes they will need for the Future Employment Contract, and helping CEOs and managers Lead into the Future. She can be reached at (303) 216-1020 or via e-mail at Eisaguirre@aol.com.